D1452635

Eucharistic Poetry

Eucharistic Poetry

The Search for Presence in the Writings of John Donne, Gerard Manley Hopkins, Dylan Thomas, and Geoffrey Hill

Eleanor J. McNees

Lewisburg
Bucknell University Press
London and Toronto: Associated University Presses

Associated University Presses
440 Forsgate Drive
Cranbury, NJ 08512

Associated University Presses
25 Sicilian Avenue
London WC1A 2QH, England

Associated University Presses
P.O. Box 39, Clarkson Pstl. Stn.
Mississauga, Ontario,
L5J 3X9 Canada

The paper used in this publication meets the requirements
of the American National Standard for Permanence of Paper
for Printed Library Materials Z39.48-1984.

Library of Congress-in-Publication Data

McNees, Eleanor J.
  Eucharistic poetry : the search for presence in the writings of
John Donne, Gerard Manley Hopkins, Dylan Thomas, Geoffrey Hill /
Eleanor J. McNees.
    p.   cm.
  Includes bibliographical references and index.
  ISBN 0-8387-5205-5
  1. Christian poetry, English—History and criticism.   2. Donne.
John, 1572–1631—Criticism and interpretation.   3. Hopkins, Gerard
Manley, 1844–1889—Criticism and interpretation.   4. Thomas, Dylan,
1914–1953—Criticism and interpretation.   5. Hill, Geoffrey—
Criticism and interpretation.   6. Lord's Supper in literature.
I. Title.
PR508.C65M36   1992
821.009′382—dc20   90-56215
                                                                          CIP

For Marshall Brown
and
Donald C. Baker

Rationalism takes the words of Scripture as signs of Ideas; Faith, of Things or Realities.

—J. H. Newman, "Tract 73"

Contents

Preface

In a telling personal aside in his 1950 essay, "What Dante Means to Me," T. S. Eliot speaks of Dante's influence on his life and writing: "as I still, after forty years, regard his poetry as the most persistent and deepest influence upon my own verse, I should like to establish at least some of the reasons for it." He continues a little later, "the first impulse to write about a great poet is one of gratitude; but the reasons for which one is grateful may play a very small part in a critical appreciation of that poet."[1]

In like manner, I would attest both to the gradually increasing permeation of my work by the four disparate poets in this study and also to my deepening gratitude to them for teaching me a new way of reading poetry: how to proceed from sound to sense, a backward process not easy to learn. Unlike Dante, they do not possess the universalist tendency Eliot revered in the European mind. They are, in fact, with the possible exception of John Donne, rather provincial, and extremely British. One could argue that after Donne, their scope narrows to include Hopkins, a minor because an exclusively devotional poet, according to Eliot; Thomas, today discredited or ignored by many critics; and Hill, obscure in England, virtually unknown in America.

Yet all four converge along a central line of sacramentalist poetics. Steeped in the Anglican and Roman Catholic traditions, they all strive to make their poetry reflect the religious focus of their lives, and in so doing, they exact from the reader a suspension of disbelief. They force their words to mime the fraction and communion of the eucharistic ceremony, and they attempt to make their poems elicit a real presence analogous to the Real Presence of Christ in the Eucharist. Finally, they urge one to surrender oneself to the sound and imagery as a pathway to the sense of the poem.

The sacrifice of the self to the power of language for these poets is analogous to the Anglo-Catholic eucharistic paradigm of *kenosis* and *pleroma,* or the sacrifice of the self to be filled with something greater than that self. The poets all eventually look back either to the Incarnation or forward to the Eschaton to ground their poetry in a teleology beyond the self. The eucharistic model serves as the

9

one earthly sacrament that recalls the Incarnation and heralds the Eschaton. Hence their poetry, rooted in this ritual, extends beyond their individual beliefs and agonies to capture the reader in what often seems a linguistic whirlwind. As one stumbles through Donne's paradoxes, Hopkins's and Thomas's contorted syntax and Hill's peculiar mixture of colloquial and formal idioms, one gains a new respect for the power of language to persuade one toward a new vision of the self in the world, if not toward a sacramental sense of the self's relation to that world.

My purpose throughout this book is to expose the means— mainly grammatical, tropological, and syntactical—by which these four poets continually, even obsessively, redefine their own relation to their world and God. I suggest that they inevitably place the reader in a similar position. Like Dante, they are "servant[s] of . . . language, rather than . . . master[s] of it." Their poetic statements, unlike those of the medieval and dogmatic Dante, are more suggestive than definitive, their conclusions often sorely incomplete. Nevertheless, read together, the poems of Donne, Hopkins, Thomas and Hill pave the way toward what I would term a eucharistic poetics central to the history of British poetry.

Acknowledgments

The seeds of this book were sown in discussions with one of my graduate professors, Donald C. Baker, who later became one of my two dissertation directors at the University of Colorado at Boulder. He suggested that I could not attempt to define eucharistic poetics without writing about John Donne. That made the leap from the early seventeeth century to the late nineteenth century daunting, but during the course of my research, I found the links between Donne and Hopkins indisputable even though the latter never mentions the poetry of the former in his letters or journals.

My dissertation committee, Donald C. Baker, Marshall Brown, Edward Nolan, Edward Dorn, and Nancy Hill, all deserve credit for encouraging me to develop the dissertation into a book, a process that saw fruition only after numerous conference papers and two published articles in *Texas Studies in Literature and Language* on Donne and Hopkins.

Thanks must be extended to the University of Colorado for a doctoral fellowship that allowed me a semester to complete research and to the University of Denver for granting me a quarter off from my teaching there to revise the manuscript. Special thanks go also to Frank Wallace, my first employer, who helped me finance the typing and preparation of the dissertation and to Aladeen Smith, who typed the final copy.

Among my colleagues at the University of Denver, Eric Gould and Alexandra Olsen have offered valuable insights and suggestions as has Graham Clarke from the University of Kent in Canterbury, England.

William J. Scheick, editor of *Texas Studies in Literature and Language,* gave me invaluable advice on some of the finer points of Renaissance theology and sent me back to complete more research on Donne's Anglican stance, a task well worth the effort.

Finally, I wish to extend my thanks to my husband, Mark, without whose encouragement and patience this project might never have seen fruition.

My appreciation is also due to the following publishers for grant-

The Correspondence of Gerard Manley Hopkins and R. Watson Dixon. Ed. Claude Colleer Abbott. Oxford University Press, 1935.

Further Letters of Gerard Manley Hopkins. Ed Claude Colleer Abbott. Oxford University Press, 1956.

The Letters of Gerard Manley Hopkins to Robert Bridges. Oxford University Press, 1935; rev. ed. 1955.

The Sermons and Devotional Writings of Gerard Manley Hopkins. Ed. Christopher Devlin, S.J. Oxford University Press, 1959.

The Journals and Papers of Gerard Manley Hopkins. Ed. Humphry House. Oxford University Press, 1959; rpt. 1966.

The Poems of Gerard Manley Hopkins. ed. W.H. Gardner and Norman MacKenzie. 4th ed. Oxford University Press, 1967.

The Elegies and the Songs and Sonnets of John Donne. Ed. Helen Gardner. Oxford University Press, 1965.

The Divine Poems of John Donne. Ed. Helen Gardner. 2nd ed. Oxford University Press, 1978.

John Donne. *Sermons of John Donne*. 10 vols. Ed. George R. Potter and Evelyn M. Simpson. Berkeley: University of California Press, 1953. Permission granted by the Regents of the University of California and the University of California Press.

Eucharistic Poetry

1

Eucharistic Language and the Anglo-Catholic Poet

Any attempted renewal of a claim to verbal presence would now have to be earned in the teeth of a wariness bred by the successes of two centuries of critical philosophy.[1]

Poetic language bears a long history of attempts to participate in the divine. From the Norse god Odin, who stole the poetic elixir from the gods and accidentally spilled a few drops to the poet-tasters on earth, to Milton, who proposed to "justify the ways of God to man," to Shelley, who equated the poet with a prophet, poetry has historically been allied with religion. Lest we be in too great a hurry, however, to participate in this divine art, we might pause before Ralph McInerny's warning in his *Studies in Analogy* about transferring meanings from one linguistic realm to another:

. . . if we take our words from ordinary language . . . we must respect the meanings they have there when we give them new meanings. So soon as ordinary terms are taken over by the philosopher and, by whimsy or caprice, imposed to signify what is not even remotely similar to what they ordinarily signify, we have an instrument, not of communion, but of confusion.[2]

How to speak of the divine in a commonly available language is a central problem for the religious poet. He must find a means to bridge the linguistic gap between the ordinary word and its extraordinary implications. Lacking a shared tradition of sacredness, he cannot adopt the role of the shaman and make his readers automatic participants in a divine order. Although according to Stephen Prickett, all talk about God entails a language of "disconfirmation and ambiguity," the Christian poet must discover a poetic method that will confirm and render unambiguous the central religious experiences he wishes to convey.[3] For Paul Ricoeur, "The moment of [divine] awareness can only be broken up and dispersed

17

in the predicates of the divine. These predicates are not characteristics or qualities of a being in itself; they are the multiple and
diverse expressions of a Pure Act which can only be spoken of by
being invested with these qualities."[4] In other words, language that
seeks to reveal divinity must be neither descriptive nor prescriptive
but expressive. It must somehow embody and manifest the spirit so
that the reader will be struck into belief by its authenticity.

Because, unlike Odin or Adam or the Apostles after Pentecost,
the religious poet possesses no privileged language, he must manip-
ulate the given one to make the divine manifest itself. By dislodging
theological words from their scriptural and liturgical contexts, he
substitutes a poem for a religious sacrament; he replaces a liturgical
rhythm with a poetic one. Although meter, rhyme, and syntax may
collude to create a structure analogous to the cadences of a religious service, the semantic level of the poem often purposely vio-
lates theological dogma. When this occurs, the poem subverts
liturgical language and divests it of sanctity. Alternatively, the poem
may enrich the sacrament by opening it up to new interpretations.
Meaning moves simultaneously on two levels—secular and sacred
(denotative and connotative)—and refuses to grant priority to
either. The risk of misappropriation against which McInerny cau-
tions resides in the discrepancy between the ways in which priests
and poets use the same words for different ends. The priest performs an act of *anamnesis:* he *re*calls Christ's words and actions in
the eucharistic rite. He is a medium through which sacred language
opens itself to the communicants. He does not appropriate eucharistic language to any end save its stipulated function as a
sacramental recreation of Christ's Passion and Resurrection. The
priest's goal is to disseminate Christ's actions through Christ's own
language, and thus to demonstrate the inseparability of word and
deed.

The poet, conversely, is an active wielder of words, not a medium. He is responsible for combining words, for adjusting the
tension between form and content, and for offering his particular
language to the public. The priest *inherits* a sacramental language;
the religious poet tries to *infuse* his words with sacramental power.
Even the religious poet, however, must contend with an absence of
external authority on which to ground his poetics. According to
Murray Krieger, "as poets rather than priests, they create their
justification through the internal manipulation of a language forced
to violate its own limited nature instead of relying on any external
authorization by faith."[5] Krieger sees the solution to such violation
in poetry's ability to combine *parole* and *ecriture,* speech and

writing, and thereby to avoid the Derridean fall into absence. Through the "paradoxical logic of metaphor" Krieger argues that the poem creates an illusion of presence to which the reader temporarily surrenders himself. Since the Renaissance, illusions of presence have replaced reality; consequently, any attempt by the poet to create "real" presence is suspect.

Both Anglican and Roman Catholic priests speak the Prayer of Consecration during the eucharistic celebration. This prayer recalls Christ's words of institution stipulated in three Gospels in which he equates the Passover bread and wine of the Last Supper with his body and blood, and commands the disciples to eat his flesh and to drink his blood. At this point in the Anglican service, the elements are made mysteriously to manifest Christ's body and blood under the doctrine of Real Presence. The *Oxford Dictionary of the Christian Church* rather loosely defines Real Presence as:

> In (esp. Anglican) Eucharistic theology an expression used to cover several doctrines emphasizing the actual Presence of the Body and Blood of Christ in the Sacrament, as contrasted with others that maintain that the Body and Blood are present only figuratively or symbolically.[6]

In the Roman Catholic Mass, the elements are actually transubstantiated into the body and blood of Christ. Following Aristotle's distinction between accidents and substance, the bread and wine are from this point relegated to accidents, while the true substance is that of Christ's body and blood. The doctrine, dating from the Lateran Council in 1215 and reaffirmed in 1551 by the Council of Trent, marks the cardinal difference between Anglicanism and Roman Catholicism.[7] Transubstantiation is specifically repudiated by the Twenty-eighth Article of Religion in the Anglican Book of Common Prayer and has been a key point of dissent between the churches for centuries.[8] Nevertheless, the two churches are united against the Protestant sects in their belief in the Real Presence of Christ in the elements after the eucharistic Prayer of Consecration.

The priest, acting as a mediator between Christ's words and the congregation, neither invents the words nor their combinations in the church liturgy, whereas the poet tries to consecrate his own words. He pushes language to its syntactical and semantic limits to create a sense of real linguistic presence. Like the priest, he aspires to make words perform a miracle; like Adam he tries to make names reveal the essence of the object named. The poet's real presence is necessarily less specific than that of Anglican or Roman

Catholic doctrine: It announces the corporeality of language with or without Christ as its foundation.[9]

The doctrine of Real Presence in the Eucharist is the primary sacrament in which ordinary language meets extraordinary language, where human and divine intersect. As an extension of the Incarnation, it marks the point at which the temporal touches the eternal. It allows the communicant momentarily to participate in the process of the Incarnation.[10] By swallowing the wafer, the communicant swallows the divine Word translated into human flesh. For the Anglican and the Roman Catholic, the process is not metaphorical, but mystical, mysterious, and actual. Christ's words, spoken by the priest during the Prayer of Consecration, act as the agency by which the elements are changed in use. For the Catholic, this change is transubstantial:

> . . . whereas the change which the elements in the other sacraments undergo is an accidental, the change of the elements in the Eucharist is an essential or substantial one. The substance of bread and wine ceases to be, for it is changed into Christ's body and blood. In one respect, however, this substantial change differs from all other substantial changes. In other cases, when one substance changes into another, the accidents also change. Here the accidents of bread and wine remain unaltered; and so long as they remain, the body and blood of Christ also remain concealed beneath them.[11]

For the Anglican this change is figural or typological. The bread and wine are not relegated to accidents, nor do they dwindle as in the strictly Protestant view to mere symbols. Instead they are amplified by a new presence. According to Dom Gregory Dix, "The church is in the sight of God the Body of Christ; at the eucharist and by the eucharist for a moment it truly fulfills this, its eternal being: it becomes what it is."[12]

Both Roman Catholic and Anglican doctrines of Real Presence oppose the Protestant emphasis on the Eucharist as a merely symbolic commemoration of Christ's Passion. As Dix notes, the Protestant follows a " 'religion of the spirit,' " the Catholic and Anglican a " 'religion of incarnation.' "[13] Consequently, the Anglo-Catholic poet, unlike his secular or Protestant counterparts, views liturgical language as both human and divine. This belief, rooted in the eucharistic sacrament, provides him with his sacramental approach to poetry. For such a poet, language does not aspire to name and in naming to transcend. Presence does not dwell outside of words or the temporal world; it inheres in the sacramental interaction between words and world. The poet strives to uncover presence by expressing this interaction. Unlike the priest (who has his words given him), the poet must find some activating principle with which to break open his language to presence. The words must themselves, like the *anamnesis* of the Prayer of Consecration, call up an immediate physical presence. They must operate both as containers and referents. In this sense, they often struggle against themselves, as they simultaneously seek to embody their subjects and to point beyond them. Just as the Prayer of Consecration presents a voice behind a voice (that of Christ behind the priest) that compresses eschatological and historical time into the present moment, the poet strives to compress multiple voices and chronologies into the specific moment of the poem. Behind such an effort lies the poet's belief in sacramentalism—the conviction that world and words are charged with divinity, that they are, like the sacraments themselves, outward signs of invisible grace.

Such sacramental poems must employ syntactically disruptive tropes to jolt the reader out of a typically linear and referential way of reading. In Paul Ricoeur's words, the poets must discover a "limit-language" that will evoke the "limit-experience" of incarnation or indwelling spiritual presence.[14] This "limit-language" consists of devices that puncture linear thought and syntax. Ricoeur offers hyperbole and paradox as two specific conveyors of limit-expressions (though metaphor and pun prove equally powerful). He cites Christ's proverbs, parables, and eschatological sayings as examples of an otherworldly language that forces the listener to abandon secular ideas of chronology. These sayings all exaggerate and contradict ordinary conceptions of sequence and space. They assert the impossible. Yet Christ's instigation of the Eucharist at the Last Supper specifically insists on such a physical impossibility. Bread and wine are made by words to assume the new living properties of body and blood. Christ's sayings destroy the reliance on purely referential language in order to strike one with the immediacy of revelation. Otherwise, presence is always postponed, only striven for and never achieved.

Like Christ, the sacramental poet tries to thrust words beyond their traditional semantic and syntactic confines to reveal a spiritual presence embedded in their substance. Presupposing an Adamic link between name and thing, he tries to resurrect this lost connection. He attempts to fuse past and future in the present moment of the poem. He uses disruptive poetic devices to break apart fixed secular denotations and to open the poem to sacramental connotations. This breaking finds its analogy in the fraction of the

Eucharist where the bread is literally broken and sacrificed in order to be blessed and fulfilled. The process, as J. F. Cotter notes, is one of *kenosis* and *pleroma,* where Christ empties himself on the altar to be received by the communicants.[15] A sacramental poem emulates this *kenotic-pleromic* tension by surrendering its linear syntax and secular denotations to a new unparaphrasable order of discourse. Yet like the accidents of bread and wine, the abandoned secular order survives in the reader's mind as an echo alongside the new revelatory discourse.

Any poet who aspires to activate language to produce presence faces a twofold dilemma. First he must sacrifice himself to the power of language instead of manipulating language to represent a coherent reality. In other words, he must allow himself to be struck by the revelatory quality of words as they burst their traditionally representational boundaries. Yet, paradoxically, he must still maneuver within these boundaries. In Ricoeur's terms, he must "let go" of empirically based assumptions, and testify to the erratic and often infrequent signs of divinity within the world. Such testimony demands a new language, one that severs words from inherited patterns and recombines them to create a new awareness of language's capacity to reveal hidden presence.[16]

Widely separated chronologically, yet strangely contemporaneous in their sacramental approach toward language, John Donne, Gerard Manley Hopkins, Dylan Thomas, and Geoffrey Hill use syntactically disruptive tropes in their poetry to revive a lost sacramental presence. These devices in Donne, Hopkins, and Thomas act as tropes of amplification, simultaneously reinforcing and interrogating traditional poetic rhythms. Geoffrey Hill inverts this process and employs tropes of diminution to emphasize the violation of traditional rhythms. Hill calls this violation on a semantic level the voice of the heckler who constantly questions the established order.[17] For Donne and Hopkins the heckler is internalized: It is the human will split off from God's will. It is the parenthetical "(my God!) my God" of Hopkins' "Carrion Comfort," the vocative "Looke Lord" of Donne's "Hymne to God my God, in my sickness," the "Myselves" of Dylan Thomas's "Ceremony After a Fire Raid."

All four poets introduce what Ricoeur calls "transgressions" to call attention to their struggle with a personal language of faith and a secular public language.[18] Although such Anglican poets as George Herbert and T. S. Eliot seek to balance (even to mute) personal voice and public ritual, these four force voice and ritual to clash and usually grant priority to the personal voice. Traditional

Anglican poets from Herbert to Wordsworth and Eliot focus more on devotional obedience to orthodox ritual than on the individual communicant's struggle to conform his will to God's.[19] There is in these more traditional Anglican poets a pervasive note of resignation. Eliot's plea from "Ash Wednesday" is a good example: "Teach us to care and not to care. / Teach us to sit still. / Even among these rocks, / Our peace in His Will. . . ."[20] In his poem, "Holy Communion," Herbert resigns himself to the Eucharist as only marginally effective without grace. In "Ash Wednesday" Eliot submits to the necessity of progressive ritual over individual temptation to depart from that ritual. In Donne, Hopkins, Thomas, and Hill, ritual is not enough to sustain the individual will for self-expression. Although superficially they appear to adhere to it, they simultaneously fight against the constraints it imposes. They seek to flesh it out, to fill it with presence. They press beyond ritual to its manifestation as sacrament, a process perhaps best evinced by Thomas's "Ceremony After a Fire Raid" or Hill's "Funeral Music" in which liturgical ritual is both underpinning and antagonist.

The poems of Donne, Hopkins, Thomas, and Hill act like eucharistic ceremonies, embodying *kenotic* sacrifice and *pleromic* communion through words that break down linear logic, then erect a personal logic of faith. Acutely aware of but lacking a logic of faith, Hill employs the same devices toward a different goal. Instead of trying to reinstate sacramental presence, he exposes both secular logic and religious ritual as suspicious and fraudulent. His poems reverse traditional typology; they divest the ceremony of real presence to expose absence and loss. Hill looks to the Anglo-Catholic liturgy for much of his language, yet he twists that language against itself. He illustrates the plight of the faithful agnostic, passionately attached to the efficacy of faith, yet unable to assent to its reality. He remains caught in what Newman calls notional as opposed to real assent.[21] He also marks the danger of a "limit-language" that threatens to collapse in on itself for want of a sustaining structure. Although the other three poets realize the risk of such a collapse, they retain the Christological base that guards against it. If language emanates from and is reabsorbed by Christ, the poet ultimately acts in concert with Christ while appearing to struggle against him. The struggle is necessary to provoke the poet into a sacrificial stance. If Christ is absent, the poet has no guarantee for developing an incarnational language or a language of real presence. At best, he can create a language where density replaces referentiality, where words have texture and rhythm, but where the surface becomes a replacement for figural depth.

As Mark Searle notes in an essay on the connection between liturgy and metaphor, the poet must be able to hold both parts of a metaphor in a tensive relationship:

> . . . metaphor calls for the hearer or reader to yield his ground, to part with his usual descriptions of reality, to move over onto the ground of the image, to live inside it, to look around and get the feel of it. It calls for a suspension of disbelief, a closure of critical distance, a commitment of trust to this way of seeing.[22]

By dislocating (through metaphor, paradox, pun, hyperbole) ordinary syntax and reinfusing the poetic line with a new rhythm, the poet can hope to reinfuse words with the life of actual experience. If language is to embody experience, the word must evoke the event. In a sense the poet's task is more difficult than that of the priest because he must actively break language apart. In the Eucharist the priest's words and actions have been validated and performed by Christ. In the poem, the words themselves must become the elements of communion. They must be equally bread and wine, and body and blood. The reader must be able to retain the familiarly literal while perceiving the sacramental.

Although contemporary linguists and critics dispute the values of hermetic versus referential language, they agree that loss of a sacramental relation between the world and words forces the poet into one camp or the other. Speaking of the problem of creating presence in poetry, Gerald Bruns finds a link between purely referential language and hermetic language in the concept of "energia" or a word force that both disrupts and fuses. Like Ricoeur and Karsten Harries,[23] Bruns tries to identify a process by which language and meaning can reinforce instead of negate each other:

> The poetic act may seek to disrupt the processes of signification, thus to make language itself its subject by isolating the word in a purely synchronic and wordless order, but at the same time it has the power to make signification possible by bringing both the world and man to language within a diachronic order or an order of presence.[24]

Ricoeur clarifies this order of presence by explaining the relation between metaphor and symbol. A metaphor is the semantic surface of a two-dimensional symbol. It articulates the symbol by disrupting ordinary logic and thus makes room for the manifestation of a deeper logic of faith.[25] In this sense, it is analogous to the relation between the bread and wine, and body and blood of the Eucharist.

The bread and wine are the surface metaphors that open to expose the symbols of the body and blood beneath.

Michel Foucault traces the disintegration of figural language in *The Order of Things,* arguing that people have become captives of their own words. They no longer move by analogy from the world to the Word; instead they see reality as a construct of systems. Words have lost their connection to the Logos.[26]

Such religious critics as Nathan Scott, Karlfried Froehlich, and Malcolm Ross lament the process of disincarnation in which the "grammatical surface sense" assumes priority over the spiritual subsurface.[27] As Nathan Scott remarks, the result of this process is the opposite of real presence:

> . . . once the world is "defiguralized"—once it is detached from that occult reality of which it was presumed by the archaic imagination to be a kind of veil—must it not then become an affair of taciturn blankness and inert facticity, something lusterless and distant, from the body of whose death the soul can only escape into its own inwardness?[28]

Such a movement toward *disincarnation* in poetic language partially accounts for the increasing emphasis on immanence as opposed to transcendence in several modern religious poets, beginning with the romantics and culminating in such figures as Wallace Stevens and William Carlos Williams who finally reject the spiritual dimension of words and universe.

Phenomenological in his approach and thus antithetical to the metaphysical position, Stevens recognizes the desire for transcendence or recognition of a spiritual dimension as a necessary but fraudulent illusion. He equates the deceiving and transforming imagination with God: "We say God and the imagination are one,"[29] and although he realizes in his late poem, "The Rock," that the poetic imagination is compelled to adorn the rock with leaves, "The fiction of the leaves is the icon / Of the poem, the figuration of blessedness" (*CP,* 526, ll.39–40), he appears unable to make the leap of faith that would transform the fiction into true assent.[30] Likewise, in the earlier poem, "Sunday Morning," he opposes the abstraction of the spiritual to the concreteness of the phenomenal world:

> What is divinity if it can come
> Only in silent shadows and in dreams?
> Shall she not find in comforts of the sun
> In pungent fruit and bright, green wings, or else

In any balm or beauty of the earth,
Things to be cherished like the thought of heaven?
Divinity must live within herself. . . .

(*CP*, 67, ll.17–23)

Like Stevens, William Carlos Williams shuns the metaphysical realm. He relies solely on the validly visible world and refuses to invest objects with any quality that is not immediately apparent to rational perception. Yet, again like Stevens, Williams realizes the significance of the poetic imagination as it confronts real objects:

The instant
trivial as it is
is all we have
unless-unless
things the imagination feeds upon,
the scent of the rose,
startle us anew.[31]

In his version of the Magi, "The Gift," Williams subordinates the adoration of the wise men into wonder at the common miracle of birth and nurturance. Faith, like imagination, must be rooted in the daily processes of life, not in theory, dogma, or metaphysical speculation:

But as they kneeled
the child was fed.
They saw it
and
gave praise!
A miracle
had taken place,
hard gold to love,
a mother's milk!
before
their wondering eyes.

(*SP*, 172, ll.27–37)

Giving preference to the tangible and the real, Stevens and Williams ground spiritual revelation exclusively in the perceiver's mind. The outside world is neither allegorical nor sacramental, it simply is. The poet must honestly recognize this fact before he uses faith or imagination to transform his view of that world.

Other modern poets, lacking Donne's dogmatic faith in eschatology and the promise of resurrection, look to language and nature to embody spirit. For them the world is not simply composed of indifferent phenomena. Because they believe in a spirituality outside themselves, yet not necessarily outside the world, they must find a poetic method that will allow them to detect and expose that spirit. The violent motion of their verse coupled with the scrambled syntax seeks both to embed and expose the incarnate Christ. This paradoxical effort creates a tension between the desire to incarnate and the desire to resurrect or transcend.

Hopkins and Thomas best illustrate this tension between incarnation and resurrection. They try to make words themselves revelatory; Donne, less worried about the gap between words and world, is more concerned with achieving colloquy with God than maintaining a dialectic between immanence and transcendence. Presuming the Incarnation fact, he is able to look toward the Resurrection as an extension of the Incarnation. He chooses the "limit-experiences" of conversion and death to produce a "limit-language" through which he can convey revelation. Personal conversion becomes proof of Christ's Incarnation; one's own imminent death becomes hope of the Resurrection. Less eschatologically inclined, Hopkins and Thomas are more concerned with the power of words to produce revelation. Because ordinary language no longer seems to embody spirit, they push their language to its syntactical and semantic extremes to reveal the "limit-experiences" of conversion and death. Their words seek to *manifest* the experience instead of to *tell* it. Surrendering themselves to the power of language and experience, they act like priests who use Christ's language to recreate Christ's experience in the congregation.

For contemporary poets like Geoffrey Hill, however, language and experience have colluded to produce hypocrisy and historical atrocity, not to praise God. Together they have killed the spirit—the possibility of redemption through incarnation and resurrection. Consequently, the only way language can exonerate itself is to expose its own guilt, to turn itself inside out. Unlike Stevens and Williams who seek to restore the equation between word and thing in as spare a language as possible, Hill must indict language for its excesses, its bad faith. The punishment for such bad faith is to deny language real presence and to accept death without hope of transcendence. Hill is caught in the dilemma of which Foucault speaks:

From within language experienced and traversed as language, in the play of its possibilities extended to their furthest point, what emerges is that man has "come to an end," and that by reaching the summit of all possible speech, he arrives not at the very heart of himself but at the brink of that which limits him; in that region where death prowls, where thought is extinguished, where the promise of the origin interminably recedes.[32]

Hill has arrived at the paradox of "limit-language." Language either imprisons one or opens one up to presence. The key which would unlock language to presence is a sacramental one, however. Believing in the reality of the Incarnation and its extension in the Eucharist, the poet can risk emptying words of their traditional meanings and refilling them with both palpable and spiritual presence without falling into chaos or solipsistic romanticism. The poet who cannot assent to such a sacramental belief thrusts himself up against the wall but cannot break through it. As Hill says in "The Mystery of the Charity of Charles Peguy," itself a long lament for the disjunction between language and experience, "Landscape is like revelation; it is both / singular crystal and the remotest things."[33] The crystal tempts with its brightness, but it is finally impenetrable. Hill is caught in a paradox. He must struggle with words as with an enemy. Yet his vocation as poet demands that he make some kind of peace with his language to write the poem.

Yet even Hill concedes that language is the only route to the realization of grace or presence.[34] Though it may be full of obstacles, even impassible, it is the only tool at the poet's disposal. If possible, it assumes an even greater importance to the modern poet than to the metaphysical one because it is its own foundation and ground of being. It no longer *mediates* between the poet and his world; it has become an independent force to be reckoned with, perhaps tamed. Although Donne can use paradox to shock the reader into a new kind of logic, he knows that the paradox is ultimately superficial because all language is grounded in the Word. Trusting in this security of language, he can use paradox as a device to uncover similarity, not to pit two opposites irrevocably against each other.

In tracing the devices by which poets seek to create real presence, one observes an increasing emphasis on language and rhythm over thematic reference. As the guarantee of Christ's Real Presence in the Eucharist grows more tenuous, the poet tries to substitute the physicality of language to mask spiritual absence. Donne and his contemporaries still move in an analogical and referential world. His apparent paradoxes in his Divine Poems are resolved by his acceptance of Christ's presence in both the eucharistic sacrament and in human death. In "Goodfriday, 1613. Riding Westward,"

Christ still dwells within man's memory, and memory is able to revive that presence. Yet Donne's world is no longer so safely analogical that the paradoxes are easily resolved. They jolt the reader and pit physical against spiritual presence, body against soul. The poems seek to heal that split and restore presence as the Eucharist mends one to God and prefigures the Resurrection. For Donne, realization of presence is a constant effort, aided by contrition and participation in the sacraments. Christ's presence is not continuously revealed. The constant dialectic between the speaker's will and God's will, the violent verbs and abrupted rhyme schemes, illustrate Donne's uneasiness with the more complacent *via media* Anglicanism that balances individual prayer with public ritual. In Done's poems, the individual voice cries out for God's response, asking for a grace that would ensure a permanent presence. Reciprocity is absent, however. There is no colloquy, only hope for one. Donne does not seek refuge like Hopkins in a sacramental landscape. His solace is the church liturgy and private prayer.

Although Hopkins's Victorian period is less religiously secure than Donne's, Hopkins is heir to the Catholic revival of the Oxford Movement. Converting from Anglicanism to Roman Catholicism, he directly opposes Donne's move from Roman Catholicism to Anglicanism. Yet he seeks presence and reconciliation with God with the same insistence as Donne. He moves beyond Donne's semantic paradoxes to syntactical paradox—ellipses, hyperbaton, anthimeria, compound wording—as if to force the reader first into the physicality of his language, then on to its sense. The sensuous quality of Hopkins's language demands that the reader participate in language as experience and so narrows the gap between words and the world to which they refer. Hopkins testifies to the sacramental world in language. His early journals evince his belief in the collusion between the word and its object. Studying cloudscapes, waves, sunsets, he tries to force the object to surrender its essence so that he may find the words to inscape that essence. For Hopkins language is grounded in Christ who guarantees man's ability to word his sacramental perceptions accurately. The connection between individual language and the external world is a matter of recognizing the sparks of instress that an object gives off. The poet must first empty himself of preconceived impressions and denotative words—Ricoeur's "letting go" of empirical assumptions—to be filled with this instress.

Hopkins's tropes are those of amplification; they suggest plenitude, not antithesis. He uses sound—sprung rhythm, rhyme, alliteration, assonance—to lure the reader into the dogmatically incarnational themes of his poems. In so doing, he enacts a poetics of real presence. The combination of words and rhythm stresses the communion between sound and sense, and illustrates the poet's ability to consecrate language to a sacramental use. Sense grows out of sound as body and blood emerge from bread and wine. Hopkins's theory of instress and inscape creates a reciprocity between sound and sense that is founded on a reciprocity between man and nature. The ultimate assurance of this relation is Christ who engenders language and nature. It is as if the instress of God's finger touches a responsive chord in Hopkins and allows him to open language to sacramental presence. Instress and inscape are methods of uncovering presence, not of inventing it.

Analogous on a less doctrinal plane to Hopkins's instress and inscape is Dylan Thomas's life fuse or spark, that runs through his flowing rhythms and broken syntax. Instead of easing the reader through sound into orthodoxically theological dogma like Hopkins, however, Thomas pulls the reader into semantic confusion. In fact, Thomas may indeed be guilty of McInerny's charge—of improper borrowing of theological language for secular purposes. Yet in his later poems, Thomas moves toward a recognition of sacrifice that carefully adjusts sound to sense. The words no longer fight against one another nor against the rhythm as in "Altarwise by Owl-light"; instead, sound links with sense in a sacramental recreation similar to that of Hopkins. Linear thought is disrupted and finally reintegrated. Thomas's synesthesia and anthimeria amplify both the syntactic and semantic presence of his poems. One is forced to read sensuously, to substitute sound and image for linear logic. Like Hopkins, Thomas makes the reader participate in the texture of the poem. Such immediate participation does not initially allow for intellectual detachment or logical analysis.

As he relinquishes his rivalry with God and Adam, Thomas's syntax grows less contradictory. The poetry gains sacramental presence as rhythm pushes forth the meaning. Like Donne and Hopkins, Thomas strives to sacrifice his individual will to that of God. He moves beyond an early pantheism to an eschatological vision that recalls Donne's insistence on death as a prerequisite for permanent presence. By "Poem on His Birthday," he has actually discovered what he had only asserted in the earlier "Altarwise by Owl-light": "Death is all metaphors." Death's intimate connection with life forces Thomas to acknowledge a presence that breaks the boundary between life and death. That presence depends on the model of Christ whose sacrifice links life with death and thus opens life to sacramental depth. Hopkins focuses principally in his poetry before the Terrible Sonnets on the Incarnation as the guarantee of Real Presence, whereas Donne and Thomas insist on Christ's Passion and subsequent Resurrection as grounds for belief in Real Presence. Nevertheless, all three demand personal ascesis, or self-restraint, as a prerequisite to any realization of presence—poetic or personal.

Only Geoffrey Hill recoils from this affirmation of presence. Instead Hill struggles with the emptiness of religious language devoid of a sacramental dimension. He contrasts the formality of hollow ritual with sensuous and crudely violent imagery to expose the inadequacies of both ritual and violence. His tropes are not, like those of the other three poets, ones of amplification but of antithesis *(kenosis)*. His formal poetic structures—themselves almost ritualistic—often mock the sensual, bloody content of the words. Like religious ritual, form has become a euphemism that disguises the grotesqueness of ordinary reality. Hill cannot assent to a religion that countenances slaughter. Far more politically conscious than either Hopkins or Thomas, he cannot retreat into a private world of sacramental presence in which the primary aim is communion between himself and God. Thus he is alternately suspicious of the seductive "menace" of poetic language and eager to make language "atone" for man's sins.[35] His poems simultaneously seek and deny fulfillment. Their paradoxes are truly dialectical; there is no figural relation between form and content nor between faith and skepticism. The sacramental fuse is gone. Ritual masks experience instead of enacting it.

Yet on a peculiar level Hill's poems offer an absence that continually suggests and longs for presence. They illustrate the *kenosis* without the *pleroma,* the sacrifice that is usually preparatory to fulfillment. One is tempted to push beyond the sacrificial self-abnegation toward the fullness that infuses much of Donne, Hopkins, and Thomas. At the same time, one questions the possibility of such fulfillment. Like Wallace Stevens, Hill shows in *Mercian Hymns* how it is possible to resurrect a presence without belief in a spiritual resurrection. Offa is synonymous with any corrupt twentieth-century ruler. Archaic language contrasts with colloquial words, at first creating a hiatus between the two, then exposing the same facts beneath different surfaces. Language can either hide or embellish; Hill forces it to expose its own tricks, to empty itself of pretension. Such emptying, as we see in the earlier poets, is a prerequisite to reception of real presence.

For some, the central idea of this study—the effort of the Anglo-

Catholic poet to achieve a poetic presence analogous to that of the eucharistic Real Presence—is founded on a myth or a waning belief. Linear logic and contemporary speech theory argue against such presence as miraculous and alchemical. These rationalist approaches do not allow for another order of discourse that would undermine their authority. They cannot recognize a language that defies systematization and relies on mystery.[36] Although deconstructionist critics like Foucault are willing to admit that language controls humans, they cannot assent to a supernatural or mysterious cause for such control. In this failure to assent, they are in direct contradiction to the Anglican or Roman Catholic poets whose belief in eucharistic Real Presence makes the achievement of an analogous presence in their poetry possible. To this end the poets employ discordant, seemingly incompatible poetic devices. They believe they can, like priests, make words figure forth presence. I am not as concerned with these poets' successes or failures as with their attempts and the devices they employ to evoke presence. Above all, I admire their belief in the power of words to consecrate, expose, and perhaps even to revive a figural link between person and world. The link may be illusory, as are the leaves that adorn Stevens's rock, but for Donne, Hopkins, Thomas, and even Hill, the truly felt relation between self, world, and God makes a poetry of presence their ultimate goal.

2
The Eschatology of Real Presence:
Donne's Struggle Toward Conformity
with Christ

O be thou nail'd unto my heart,
And crucified againe,
Part not from it, though it from thee would part,
But let it be, by applying so thy paine,
Drown'd in thy blood, and in thy passion slaine.
—"The Litanie" (ll.14–18)

The Anglican stance toward the Eucharist with its denial of transubstantiation but its assertion of Real Presence lends John Donne a model for the poetic paradoxes in both his secular and sacred lyrics. In the Eucharist human and divine intersect to create a sacramental presence. As the elements of bread and wine are not transubstantiated into body and blood but coexist with them, so the spirit does not deny flesh. Instead, the flesh is purged by penitential prayer, and the elements are changed in *use* after the Prayer of Consecration.[1] The Anglican compromise in the early to midseventeenth century emphasized three elemental points to which Donne (after his ordination as an Anglican priest in 1615) adhered: (1) the eucharistic elements were not (as in transubstantiation or consubstantiation) changed in *substance* but rather in *use;* (2) the sacrament operated on the faithful as a *seal* of grace, not merely as a representational *sign*; (3) the celebration of Holy Communion was fundamentally a *sacrifice* recalling Christ's Passion and exacting contrition in the communicant.

The first of these points, the shift in *use* of the eucharistic bread and wine provided Donne with an analogy for his poetic mixture of sacred and secular images in the divine poems. The coexistence of flesh and spirit, however, precedes the divine poems; it runs throughout Donne's writing from his secular songs and sonnets to his divine poems and sermons. In the secular writings the equation of sacred and profane results in true paradox; in the divine writings

33

paradox is undermined by a doctrinal belief in the sacramental connection between superficially disparate images.

One of Donne's most persistent themes, the ostensible paradox of death and resurrection, is grounded in the eucharistic ceremony with its recreation of Christ's Passion and the celebration of his resurrection in the act of communion. Donne's divine poems, however, rarely focus on the *act* of communion; rather, they are preoccupied with the repentance and confession of sins *before* participation in the act of Holy Communion. Conversely, Donne's secular lyrics frequently assert both transubstantiation and communion of body and soul with another human being. Donne freely uses Roman Catholic iconography throughout the secular lyrics partly to mock and partly to justify human love.

In his divine poems, particularly, Donne is concerned with confession and purification prior to death. His language is eschatological; it looks toward what he terms the "third resurrection" but only as a goal to be achieved after death. Throughout his sermons he spells out his doctrine of threefold resurrection: "There is a Resurrection from worldly calamities, a resurrection from sin, and a resurrection from the grave."[2] Holy Communion embodies the second resurrection while pointing toward the third. It recalls the death and resurrection of Christ and symbolically dramatizes the death of sin in the communicant, a prerequisite for the final resurrection of the body and soul from the grave. Donne attempts to make his poems enact an analogous process. Following the method of Ignatian meditation, he conjures up a vivid picture of Christ's Passion, then tries to identify himself with Christ as victim. The poem is asked to function as a vehicle of conversion that will prepare the poet for colloquy with God.[3] Death of sin can only be achieved by repentance and self-sacrifice, an emptying out of bodily evil.

In making the poem analogous to the eucharistic ceremony, Donne calls attention to the real presence of poetic language. While the poem appeals through words for the manifestation of Christ's presence, that appeal must necessarily fall short of realization because, for Donne, Christ's presence is something reserved for the moment of communion in the sacrament. Although the divine poems manifest a sacramental impulse, they are only by analogy eucharistic sacraments themselves. Only when prayer is an actual *anamnesis* of Christ's words and actions is there a possibility for Real Presence. In the poems the *anamnesis* is human memory or conjured picture. Although the priest is a medium through which the sacred words are articulated, the religious poet acts as a medium between secular and sacred language. He tries to transform mundane words into revelatory instruments of grace. To perform such a task, he must relinquish his own desire to appropriate language. He must become a servant of right words—words that work toward one goal—praising God. Yet praise falls short of realization of Real Presence. Somehow the poet must make his words *enact* a transformation, not beg for one. Like the eucharistic ceremony, the language of the poem must try to expose God to man. The divine poem's task then is not to incarnate a God already present but rather to rip away the secular obscurity of language that has prevented people from realizing that presence.

In both the *Songs and Sonnets* and the *Divine Poems* Donne attempts to describe "limit-experiences" in a "limit-language." In a series of essays Paul Ricoeur constructs a paradigm for poetic sacramental language based on Christ's parables, eschatological proclamations, and proverbs. He divides Christ's "limit-expressions" into these three categories, all of which operate by exploding logical conventions of language: "Parables, paradoxes, hyperbole, and extreme commandments, all *dis*orient in order to *re*-orient us."[4] Both parables and proverbs present the "extraordinary in the ordinary": "The parable signifies the kingdom, precisely by means of this trait of extravagance that causes it to burst out of its framework."[5] By pointing to the moment of this explosion, Ricoeur tries to prove that language can become an instrument of revelation: "an ordinary 'logic' collapses and the 'logic' of God—which is not the logic of identity, but the logic of the 'something more'—blows up."[6]

The disruption is both syntactical and semantic: It shocks the reader into a new way of hearing and seeing. Ricoeur erects an incarnation-resurrection schema to describe the steps of this revelatory process: (1) substantiation of the spirit in a concrete other, (2) death of the substance, and (3) birth of the spirit.[7] Here Ricoeur offers a truce between the battles of representational and self-referential language. Merging with its referent, the word as sign dies or kenotically empties itself to be filled with a new presence "where the manifestation of the Spirit and the death of its representation may be seen."[8] Paradox, metaphor, and hyperbole are the primary tropes that enable both poet and theologian to rupture ordinary logic. All three push words past their denotative boundaries and in so doing create a tension between denotation and the "extra meaning" suggested by the poetic device.

In paradox, two words with opposite "substances" *appear* to oppose each other semantically while being linked syntactically.

Their linkage forces the "death" of the separate substances and the "birth" of a spirit (or a new connotation) that transcends the separate substances. Similarly, in the eucharistic ceremony the communicant purges himself through confession to receive the sacrament. On reception he is physically and spiritually united with Christ. The Prayers of Confession and Consecration, and the actual communion illustrate the *kenotic-pleromic* process of presence on earth.

Applying Ricoeur's "limit-language" specifically to the Eucharist, David Klemm notes that the latter embodies a shift in discourse from bread and wine as simple elements to bread and wine as potential divinity. The words of the Prayer of Consecration are an example of "limit-language":

> The shift in discourse opens the being of the bread to the essence which it expresses: Where bread always expresses sacrifice, simplicity, and belonging to the earth, in the rite it now also expresses the body of Christ. . . . The bread changes ontologically from objective being to essential being or Christological being.[9]

Contrary to Roman Catholic doctrine, this ontological change is not a substantial one. The bread and wine remain but assume a sacramental character. This shift is effected through a special language that *re*calls Christ's words. Klemm emphasizes the importance of eucharistic language as the only means of embodying God on earth:

> God is manifest as other than God in the event of language: and the eucharist . . . is the place where the event of language is opened to its depth. The eucharist is the place in language where the referent— Christ, the *logos* or word—presents itself in and through language itself.[10]

How to open poetic language to a similar depth is Donne's task and his impossible struggle. As creator of the poem, he is its ultimate referent, shifting the focus from Christ to himself and back to Christ. In the divine poems one encounters a constant tension, even rivalry, between the poet and Christ. In seeking Christ, the poet exposes and humbles himself in words similar to the precommunion Prayer of Confession. The divine poems hinge on the validity of confession as a route to communion. Not until he has purged himself can the speaker attempt (both metaphorically and actually) to summon Christ to his lips. The twenty-ninth article of the published Anglican Articles of Religion (1571), omitted in Cranmer's early formulation of Forty-two Articles in 1553, warns against taking Communion in bad faith:

> The wicked, and suche as be voyde of a liuelye fayth, although they do carnally and visibly presse with their teeth (as Saint Augustine sayth) the Sacrament of the body and blood of Christ: yet in no wyse are the partakers of Christe, but rather to their condemnation do eate and drinke the signe or Sacrament of so great a thing.[11]

The recent addition of this article into the canon may account in part for Donne's constant emphasis on the importance of preparation before partaking of the Sacrament.

In his sermons Donne tries to expose the spirit through exegesis of a biblical text. His language is interpretive and discursive. His poems operate in an opposite manner. They contract narrative to a point where (as in Christ's parables and proverbs) the logic explodes, revealing a sudden insight into the speaker's relationship with God. This new logic is released when the old logic is pressured to the point of collapse. The syntax mimes the visceral process of confession; the weight of sin presses both penitent and language downward. The language of the poems is not so much dialectical (as in the sermons) as multilayered, volcanic. Revelation demands eruption. The old logic of sin explodes, revealing a new logic of faith. What differentiates Donne here from such *via media* Anglicans as George Herbert is this explosive approach to revelation. Instead of gradually unveiling new relations between himself and God, Donne makes his words detonate in what Karsten Harries terms "metaphors of collision."[12]

Although several critics have tried to demonstrate Donne's allegiance either to Calvinism or Roman Catholicism, Donne's poetry actually defies such labeling.[13] Raised as a Roman Catholic, strongly influenced by Calvinist doctrine, and finally an Anglican priest, Donne advances toward Anglicanism as the most catholic of all religions. More recently critics have sought a synthesis between these two extremes, although few address Donne's particular breed of Anglicanism.[14] In fact, the Anglican compromise between Roman Catholicism and Puritan Protestantism probably tempted Donne because of its ability (like paradox) to balance two extremes and renounce neither. Following article twenty-eight, "Of the Lordes Supper," Donne rejected the Roman Catholic belief in transubstantiation, which he thought bordered dangerously on the adoration of miracles. He frequently criticized the Roman church for its emphasis on visible spectacle over invisible faith.[15] He chose instead to view the eucharistic ceremony as an unfolding of Christ's presence in a typological or hermeneutical sense, and thereby to avoid controversies over the nature of the Real Presence. Christ unveiled himself in the consecrated elements; one substance was not alchemically transmuted into another. Yet the sacrament with its specific ritual and liturgical language was a mandatory condition for such unveiling.

Donne's divine poems attempt to emulate the language and ritual of the sacraments, specifically of the Passion and its extension in the Eucharist. The poem's language offers the sacramental link between divine action and personal internalization of that action. One must devour the words—their rhythm, synatax, and secular and spiritual connotations—to realize presence. This presence fuses the poet with Christ and, by extension, the reader with the Christ-poet persona. Reading the poem is an exercise in figural fulfillment. The poet conjures up a picture of both Christ and his own struggling soul and through words links himself to that picture. The reader works back through the individual voice of the poet to the picture and thus to a personal identification with the picture.

In his Christmas sermon of 1626, Donne argues for a "Manifestation of Christs birth in your soules, by the Sacrament," and, consequently, "to an unremoveable possession of heaven itself in this world" (*Sermons,* 7:289). Devout participation in the sacrament of Holy Communion represented for Donne the second of the three resurrections: "In the first, God made us; in the second, God mends us; in the third God shall perfect us" (*Sermons,* 4:93). If the communicant has repented his sins and partakes faithfully, he is typologically renewed: "If thou have truly given thy self to him in the Sacrament, God hath given thee thy selfe back, so much mended, as that thou hast received thy self and him too." (*Sermons,* 7:283).

In a figural sense, the communicant is enlarged and purified by the sacrament. He symbolically sacrifices himself and is reborn, an action that prefigures his actual death and resurrection on Judgment Day. Consequently, the eucharistic action, in Dom Gregory Dix's words, is a symbol that "*manifests* the secret reality" or the Real Presence of Christ.[16] The process entails a typological thrusting forward in which the elements of bread and wine stand as types of their antitypes of body and blood. Likewise, the communicant by participating in the corporate acts of offertory and communion moves from sinful type to Christian antitype. The dichotomy between bread-wine and body-blood, or between sinner and restored man is a prerequisite for their sacramental synthesis.

Most important, according to Donne, the eucharistic sacrament serves as a "conduit of Grace" or a route whereby the sinner may seek renewal (*Sermons*, 7:267). Donne lambasts both the Roman Catholics who focus superstitiously on the substantive elements of the bread and wine, and the Puritans who deny the Real Presence:

> As they [Puritans] that deny the body of Christ to be in the Sacrament, lose their footing in departing from their ground, the expresse Scriptures; so they that will assign a particular manner, how that body is there, have no footing, no ground at all, no Scripture to Anchor upon: And so: diving in a bottomlesse sea, they poppe sometimes above water to take breath, to appeare to say something, and then snatch at a loose preposition, that swims upon the face of the waters; and so the Roman Church hath catched a *Trans*, and others a *Con*, and a *Sub*, and an *In*, and varied their poetry into a Transubstantiation, and a Consubstantiation, and the rest, and rhymed themselves beyond reason, into absurdities, and heresies, and fallen alike into error, though the errors that they are fallen into, be not of a like nature, nor danger. (*Sermons*, 7:296)[17]

In this passage Donne exposes the veneer of false logic that obscures the mystery of the Real Presence.[18] He opposes mystery to paradox and argues that the latter is the product of a mind too bound by rationality. The Anglican must rely on the

> light of faith to see, that the Body and Bloud of Christ, is applied to thee, in that action; But for the manner, how the Body and Bloud of Christ is there, wait his leisure, if he have not yet manifested that to thee: Grieve not at that, wonder not at that, presse not for that; for hee hath not manifested that, not the way, not the manner of his presence in the Sacrament, to the Church. (*Sermons*, 7:290–91)

In a more explicit passage in the same sermon, Donne contrasts transubstantiation with transformation and presses for the latter:

> That Bread which thou seest after the Consecration, is not the same Bread, which was presented before, not that it is Transubstantiated to another substance, for it is bread still . . . but that it is severed, and appropriated by God, *in that Ordinance to another use;* it is to other Bread, so, as a Judge is another man, upon the bench, then he is at home, in his owne house. (*Sermons*, 7:295)

Through the Prayer of Consecration the elements assume a new role, a deeper identity. The prayer makes divine language work on ordinary elements. The touching of divine with natural creates the sacramental quality of the ceremony. By analogy, the imposition of poetic figures on ordinary language, disrupts that language so that the ordinary is suddenly invested with a new linguistic presence. The disruption, however, is not a contradiction or a negation of the ordinary; rather it is an addition, a replenishment of meaning.

For Donne, the doctrine of transubstantiation entails a contradiction, a displacement. Far from replenishing the natural elements, it depletes them. He faults the Roman Catholics for making God contradictory and therefore impotent: ". . . neither doth any one thing so overcharge God with contradictions, as the Transubstantiation of the Roman Church. There must be a Body there, and yet no where; In no place and yet in every place, where there is a consecration" (*Sermons,* 7:294–95).

In a final passage from the same sermon, Donne lays the groundwork for his own poetics of real presence. Emphasis on external change is specious; hence, the elaborate self-mocking conceits of the secular lyrics. Rather, the change comes from within after pious self-sacrifice through contrition:

> . . . transforming, cannot be intended of the outward form and fashion, for that is not changed: but be it of that internall form, which is the very essence and nature of the bread, so it is transformed, so the bread hath received a new form, a new essence, a new nature, because whereas the nature of bread is but to nourish the body, the nature of this bread now, is to nourish the soule. (*Sermons,* 7:295)

The unconsecrated bread is to the human body as Christ's body is to the human soul. By uniting Christ's flesh with that of the communicant, the Eucharist forces body and soul to intersect. Christ's touching of the communicant makes him in Dom Gregory Dix's words "become what he is." The divine poems work toward this internal transformation. The secular lyrics, conversely, emphasize visible transubstantiation without proper penitence. In them body and soul are only superficially joined. The secular poems bypass the sacrifical struggle toward purgation and thus can only depict a false resurrection.

As an enactment of "Holy Communion" between two human souls, "The Exstasie" stands midway between Donne's secular and divine poems. Like the eucharistic ceremony, the poem moves from an emphasis on the physical presence of the elements—the two bodies—to the spiritual union of the souls. Although this latter union is contingent on the connection of bodies (the engrafted hands and twisted eye-beams), it demands their temporary relinquishment at the moment of the souls' union: "And whil'st our soules negotiate there, / Wee like sepulchrall statues lay. . . ."[19] On earth, the physical senses of sight and touch are preconditions for the mysterious union of the souls. Like the bread and wine of Catholic transubstantiation, the bodies become mere accidents during the communion of the souls. Body and soul do not coexist.

In recounting the ecstasy of two earthly lovers, the poem uses the analogy of eucharistic communion to reinforce human union. Here, however, Donne subverts the divine process, making it serve human ends instead of vice versa. He thus mocks both human and divine love and reverses the hierarchical ascent of the human to the divine. The process the lovers go through closely resembles the position of the Roman Catholic communicant. The visible elements—bodies—become "sepulchrall statues" as they surrender their lives to a newly transubstantiated soul. Their bodies are like the eucharistic accidents of bread and wine. The transubstantiating agent is love that effects a permanent change:

> When love, with one another so
>   Interinanimates two soules,
> That abler soule, which thence doth flow,
>   Defects of lonelinesse controules.
>
> Wee then, who are this new soule, know,
>   Of what we are compos'd, and made,
> For, th'Atomies of which we grow,
>   Are soules, whom no change can invade.
>
> (SS ll.41–48)

Yet only through tangible connection and visible communion can the lovers advance to a more spiritual state. At this point Donne is unwilling to grant much weight to the bodies. The body is the book that reveals the sacramental and mysterious union of the souls. It is a precondition that instigates the spiritual union, then retires.

Like the eucharistic service, the poem turns narrative description to dramatic participation with "the device of the hypothetical listener."[20] If the listener (prospective communicant?) were adequately prepared by "good love," he "Might thence a new concoction take, / And part farre purer than he came" (SS ll.27–28). Here Donne seems to imply the figural definition of "concoction" as digestion and "ripening, maturing, or bringing to a state of perfection" (Oxford English Dictionary). Similarly, the eucharistic concoction transforms the devout communicant from a sinful state to a state of grace. The poem demands a sacrifice of body to soul, whereas the eucharistic ceremony requires a sacrifice of *both:* "ourselves, our souls and bodies, to be a reasonable, holy, and lively sacrifice unto thee."[21] The poem highlights the division between body and soul at the moment of the spiritual communion, whereas the Eucharist holds the two together. Donne seems here purposely to deny the conjunction of body and soul between human beings. That particular union he reserves for man with God.

Speaking of the eucharistic analogy in "The Extasie," Robert Ellrodt emphasizes Donne's "frontier" between the body and the soul:

> Cette conception du sacrement suppose entre l'esprit et la chair un parallelisme qui rappelle curieusement la conception de l'amour exposé dans "The Exstasie." Donne et Herbert maintiennent entre l'âme et le corps une frontière que ne franchissent pas ces esprits, engendrés par le sang, qui s'efforcent de se faire sembables à des âmes et n'y parviennent point.[22]

Nevertheless, Ellrodt admits that "un lien indissoluble" exists between body and soul. This tie recalls Donne's conception of the Eucharist as a "conduit of grace." The eucharistic action provides the temporary meeting place for body and soul. Donne allows for spiritual transubstantiation of two souls but does not permit two bodies to be similarly transubstantiated. "The Exstasie" does not effect the coexistence of body and soul on a spiritual plane. It allows bodies, then souls, then bodies to unite in a deviation from either Anglican or Roman Catholic Eucharist:

> Transposé dans la doctrine eucharistique, ce mode de pensée supposerait plutôt que la grace divine se communique à l'âme du croyant par l'entremise et le detour des espèces sensibles.[23]

The poem refuses to depict the lovers' union as exclusively spiritual or as literally transubstantial. Their communion is only partial, however, because bodies and souls are held apart throughout the poem. The end of the poem justifies the return from ecstatic union to separate bodies:

> To'our bodies turne wee then, that so
> 　　Weake men on love reveal'd may looke;
> Loves mysteries in soules doe grow,
> 　　But yet the body is his booke.
> And if some lover, such as wee,
> 　　Have heard this dialoque of one,

> Let him still marke us, he shall see
> Small change, when we'are to bodies gone.
>
> (SS, ll.69–76)

One must see and hear God through the visible sacrament and audible scripture. Roman Catholic emphasis on sacrament and sight must be balanced with Protestant stress on scripture. The body, like a book, is needed to narrate the drama of the *mysterious* union of the souls. The "weake" men need physical proof to anchor their belief. The actual mystery of the souls, like the eucharistic mystery, cannot be explained. "The Exstasie" presents a problematic view of eucharistic communion. It shows Donne playing with both Roman Catholic and Protestant doctrine but ultimately refusing to make either transubstantiation or consubstantiation support the real presence of the lover's union.

Throughout his sermons, Donne emphasizes the importance of both scripture and sacrament as aids to faith:

> Preaching is the thunder, that clears the air, disperses all clouds of ignorance; and then the Sacrament is the lightning, the glorious light, and presence of Christ Jesus himself. And in the having and loving of these, the *Word* and *Sacraments,* the outward means of salvation, ordained by God in his Church, consists this Irradiation, this Coruscation, this shining. (*Sermons,* 4:105)

In *Eucharistic Theology* Joseph Powers stresses that "man's interior reality must be incarnated in bodily signs, speech and gesture."[24] Donne seeks to body forth this "interior reality" in a manner similar to that of the priest performing the eucharistic ceremony. The lovers of "The Exstasie" enact a *kenotic-pleromic* pattern of physical self-sacrifice and spiritual fulfillment. The product of this process—the changeless abler soul—then incarnates itself in the bodies. Here bodiless communion precedes incarnation and reverses the notion of the Eucharist as an extension of the Incarnation. There is little suggestion of the struggle toward union that pervades the divine poems. Human love is elevated, not to praise God, but to make the lovers' love more lofty. The poem uses an unorthodox combination of Protestant and Roman Catholic elements to chide lovers who would make their love for each other equivalent to love of God.

Donne's depiction of the union of souls in both his secular and divine poems leads some critics to explore the influence of mysticism on his work. The eucharistic action exemplifies the communicants' membership in the "mystical body" of Christ after receiving the "holy mysteries" of the sacrament.[25] Akin to mystical union with God is the third stage of Ignatian meditation or colloquy, described by Louis Martz. Martz traces the three-part Ignatian method of composition, analysis, and colloquy throughout Donne's poetry. Although Donne freely employs the first two steps, his secular poems often conclude in a parody of colloquy (a "dialogue of one"?), and his divine poems fall short of this final goal. Martz notes that Donne's poems end "in a whip-lash of self-control and conformity with God's will."[26]

Among critics who point toward this conflict between controlled surface and latent emotion, Josephine Miles sees a corresponding opposition between reason and faith in Donne's syntax. Miles states that a poem by Donne "proposes an excess . . . then negates the excess."[27] Miles calls Donne's poetry one of "predication" in which surface logic often contradicts the underlying theme. Such a disjunction recalls Ricoeur's description of Christ's explosive logic in the parables and proclamatory sayings. The reader is jolted into the language of hyperbole, then thrust back into ordinary syntax. At such junctures faith shatters reason while appearing to subordinate itself to reason. Likewise the conceits of the secular lyrics thrust the reader beyond rational perception toward suprarational images. One is drawn logically into an irrational assertion.

Miles and other textual critics are anxious to discover in the structure of Donne's poetic language a key to the tension inhering in his paradoxes and conceits. Seizing on the disruption of the medieval analogical world view, they look to language to embody this shift. No longer do sound and sense chime; rather, like body and soul, they struggle against each other. The more disjointed the syntax or what Miles terms the "surface design" from the underlying context, the more multilayered and complex the poetry is. Paradox assumes a new dimension as the poet uses conventional meter, like conventional logic, to undercut itself. Miles herself likens this "surface design" to "bondage enforcing the limitations of the flesh."[28] John Stachniewski goes beyond Miles in asserting that "the argument of Donne's poems is often so strained that it alerts us to its opposite, the emotion or mental state in defiance of which the argumentative process was set to work."[29] In Freudian terms, the argument acts as an elaborate defense masking its opposite drive. Consequently, the poems set up a dialectic between presence and absence. The assertive presence of the argument is exploded by extravagant paradox and hyperbole. These two devices expose the flaws or the vacancy of an argument that must strain too hard to persuade. The jarring of linear logic by such tropes of amplification illustrates the process of "limit-expressions" of which Ricoeur speaks.

Essentially both Miles and Stachniewski concur with William Halewood's thesis in *The Poetry of Grace* that Donne superficially opposes a language of reason to a language of faith and thereby creates a "dialectical illusion."[30] Although reason *appears* to reinforce faith, it is actually undermined by faith: "the will, in its restricted human function, is constructed to collapse."[31] Man has invented human logic to explain divine actions; hence that logic must finally prove inadequate to the task.

In reverse order in the secular poems Donne applies divine logic to justify secular actions. The result is an ironic gap between the limitless quality of divine language and severely limited (because temporal) mortal actions. In the secular lyrics too Donne plays more freely with the Roman Catholic doctrines of transubstantiation, sainthood, and visible ceremony. His conceits are more expansive than those of the divine poems, his logic often purposely subversive.

"The Canonization," "Twicknam Garden," and "The Relique" exaggerate specific eucharistic elements and reinforce Donne's complaint that Roman Catholics emphasize miracles over faith. These poems focus on the debate between "accidents" and "substance" instead of on the figural relationship between the two. In so doing, they deny the full presence of figural fulfillment. These secular lyrics are more dialectical than typological. They introduce transubstantiation to resolve the tension, but the transubstantiation appears to be too facile a reconciliation. One is left unconvinced by the announced union.

In "The Canonization" Donne employs the revelatory device to which Ricoeur refers (substantiation-death-birth of spirit) to expose the artificial quality of secular love. Stanza 3 describes the union of the lovers in the form of the neutral phoenix that rises from its ashes. Here the lovers have been transubstantiated into a fictitious substance that claims to be immortal. The choice of the phoenix with its miraculous overtones actually undermines the religious imagery of the poem. The stanza parodies both communion and canonization ceremonies. As in "The Exstasie," liturgical language glorifies profane reality with such words as "tapers" (candles carried in the processional behind the cross by Taperers), the "phoenix" as a type of Christ able to die and be resurrected, and the "mysterious" quality that results from the union. Among the definitions of "mystery" in the *OED* is that of a "religious truth known only from divine revelation." Here the word strongly echoes the mystery of the Eucharist that symbolically reenacts Christ's death and resurrection. Beneath its liturgical veneer, the profane quality of the lovers' physical love forces the reader to see their transformation as miraculous rather than mysterious. Donne parodies Roman Catholic reverence for miracles by exaggerating the lovers' transformation.

Stanza 4 further undercuts the "mysterious" union of the previous stanza in its recourse to transubstantiation. The lovers dedicate themselves to immortality in the "pretty roomes" of sonnets instead of saints' chronicles. The sonnets are transmuted into hymns where "all shall approve / Us *Canoniz'd* for Love" (*SS* ll.35–36). The slight on the Roman Catholic tendency to multiply and revere saints is unmistakable. Also the effort to locate the *place* of immortality is a thinly disguised criticism of the Catholic focus on the how and the where of transubstantiation.

The punning on the word "love" that ends both first and last lines of each stanza reinforces Donne's distinction between visible secular love and divine love. The poem moves from the specificity of the lovers' love to a generalized quasi-religious love and finally to other earthly lovers' love. Divine love is actually obscured by secular love, although the latter purports to lead to the former. Through another exaggeration—repetition—the poem questions the efficacy of earthly love.

The last stanza further criticizes the earthly lovers' attempts to make their love holy. The canonized lovers are invoked by their earthly counterparts to "Beg from above / A patterne of your love!" (*SS*, ll.44–45)—in other words, to implore the saints for a spiritual model. Donne is repeatedly adamant throughout his divine writings about the uselessness of saints as mediators. Thus, although the poem mimes a liturgical ceremony, it criticizes both Roman Catholic practices of transubstantiation and saint worship. In undermining these processes, it also satirizes the supernatural quality of the earthly lovers' love. What allegedly elevates the lovers actually makes them appear foolish. Canonization is not a route toward the achievement of Real Presence.

On a syntactical level, the monosyllabic rhymes—"wit," "it," "fit," in stanza 3—as well as the levity of tone further undercut the supposedly eschatological thrust of the poem. Donne's "limit-language" here involves parable transmuted to parody. He employs sacred language in the service of secular narrative. Although seeming to add spiritual authority to the secular lovers, he actually emphasizes the gulf between spiritual and secular. By making religious language praise mortal actions, Donne exposes the diminution of the spiritual to the secular. The words, particularly the constantly repeated "Love," ring hollow.

Throughout "The Canonization," Donne pokes fun at the ease with which the Roman Catholics perform transubstantiation—"Call us what you will, wee'are made such by love" (l.19)—and canonization—"And by these hymnes, all shall approve / Us *Canoniz'd* for Love" (*SS*, ll.35–36). There is no hint of the precommunion penitence that pervades the divine poems. Instead of sacrificing themselves to spiritual love, the lovers have absorbed the world's soul into themselves and have abandoned others. They have proven inadequate models or mediators for other earthly lovers. The poem succeeds in wielding Roman Catholic imagery to criticize earthly or visible love.

"Twicknam Garden," like "The Canonization," parodies the double meaning of secular and sacred love. Here, too, Donne employs eucharistic language to elevate a secular theme. In "Twicknam Garden," however, love has already turned to rage and enacted a reverse transubstantiation:

> Blasted with sighs, and surrounded with tears,
>   Hither I come to seeke the spring,
> And at mine eyes, and at mine eares,
>   Receive such balmes, as else cure every thing;
>   But O, selfe traytor, I do bring
>   The spider love, which transubstantiates all,
>   And can convert Manna to gall,
>   And that this place may thoroughly be thought
>   True Paradise, I have the serpent brought.
>   (*SS*, ll.1–9)

As he will do in the later divine poems, Donne reactivates and personalizes a biblical narrative. Here, however, the drama of the Garden of Eden is denigrated to the agony of a lovesick individual who offers a sad communion to other lovers:

> Hither with christall vyals, lovers come,
>   And take my teares, which are loves wine,
> And try your mistresse Teares at home,
>   For all are false, that tast not just like mine;
>   Alas, hearts do not in eyes shine,
>   Nor can you more judge womans thoughts by teares,
>   Then by her shadow, what she weares.
> O perverse sexe, where none is true but shee,
> Who's therefore true, because her truth kills mee.
>   (*SS*, ll.19–27)

Here Donne reverses the upward movement of Christian typology from type to antitype to fulfillment in the Eschaton. By reversing this eschatological direction, he again emphasizes the gap between secular and spiritual worlds. The final couplet offers a paradoxical conceit ostensibly in the courtly love tradition. If viewed within the Christian narrative framework, however, the couplet may allude to Christ's Passion and the church's reenactment of that Passion in the Eucharist. Again Donne's theme of death as a prerequisite for eternal life surfaces. The poem ends with worldly death, completing the biblical cycle from creation to Christ's crucifixion. It is more pessimistic than either "The Canonization" or "The Relique," both of which play with eschatological themes to emphasize human foibles. In "Twicknam Garden" Donne's persona is locked into an earthly hell by earthly love. Unlike Adam, he is doomed to remain in the garden transfigured into a mandrake or a fountain, robbed of his humanity.

The poem's eucharistic imagery—transubstantiation, manna, wine—provides an analogy with which to contrast the process of unhappy and unfulfilled love. That the "spider love" can transubstantiate manna into gall stresses Donne's tendency as in "The Canonization" both to support and to undercut human fallible love with Roman Catholic imagery. The seriousness of the imagery contrasts with the levity of the theme; it simultaneously undermines the religious allusions and elevates the earthly lovers' plight.[32] Unlike the merging of the two souls in "The Extasie," the act of transubstantiation here converts one substance into another and abolishes the first. The transforming agent—love—assumes a satanic quality in direct contrast to the divine love of the eucharistic Prayer of Consecration. Donne opposes human love to divine love in this poem. He employs the Eucharist as an authoritative model for the process of disintegration, not reintegration.

In the most eschatologically oriented of his secular lyrics, "The Relique," Donne again personalizes a divine drama. Like "Twicknam Garden," the movement reverses the typological process, focusing on the tangible quality of the lovers instead of their spiritual union on Judgment Day. As in "The Canonization," Donne mocks the Roman Catholic focus on ceremony and the iconolatry of spiritual concepts. The "bracelet of bright haire about the bone" is construed by a gravedigger (one still alive, therefore not privy to the soul's whereabouts after death) as a lure to the dead lovers' souls to meet at the grave site on Judgment Day. Donne believed in the resurrection of the body and in the union of body and soul on that day. In "The Relique" he requests, however, a spiritual union *based* on a physical one (as in "The Exstasie"), not the reverse. Making a spiritual union contingent on (instead of coincident with) a physical one disrupts the eschatological thrust of Donne's sermons and divine poems. Here he seems to parody not so much the lovers' anticipated union of body and soul as the unorthodox speculations of the gravedigger who discovers the bracelet of hair.

In stanza 2, Donne overtly criticizes the Catholic reverence for relics and miracles by calling the craving for relics and miracles a time of "mis-devotion." In stanza 3, he parodies both secular love and miracle. After equating the lovers' love with miracles, he stipulates the precise nature of those miracles and thus robs them of any miraculous quality. He also implicitly criticizes the Catholic tendency to discover miracles outside of the Scriptures. If the lovers can proliferate miracles, anyone can:

> First, we lov'd well and faithfully,
> Yet knew not what wee lov'd, nor why,
> Difference of sex no more wee knew,
> Then our Guardian Angells doe.
>
> (*SS*, ll.23–26)

Again, Donne uses a Catholic allusion as a satirical defense of the lovers' position. The lame comparison to the androgynous Guardian Angels promptly pokes fun at the Catholic emphasis on intermediaries—saints and angels—between man and God. These lines echo Donne's warning in his sermons to the communicants not to question the why and how of Real Presence in the Eucharist, but simply to believe in it. The final two lines, as in "Twicknam Garden," undercut the superficial religious apparatus of the last stanza. They both reduce the definition of miracle to a synonym for the female lover and amplify it to suggest a definition beyond linguistic capacity: "All measure, and all language, I should passe, / Should I tell what a miracle shee was" (*SS*, ll.32–33). A miracle defies language; like a mystery, it cannot be codified or explained. In this poem miracle is the secular counterpart of mystery, the latter a word much used by Donne to describe the unknowable union of· Christ's body and spirit in the Eucharist.

In "The Relique" Donne seeks, in Ricoeur's words, to describe a "limit-experience"—the existence of the lovers after death. Because he chooses to focus on earthly love throughout the poem, he opts for concrete Roman Catholic imagery—"such advancers of Images, as would throw down Christ rather than his Image" (*Sermons*, 8:433)—instead of the "limit-expressions" of parable or paradox. The poem criticizes Roman Catholic reverence for saints, relics, extrascriptural miracles and angels while at the same time it uses those images to reinforce earthly love. Emphasis falls on visible signs rather than on invisible faith.

Although some commentators have argued for either chronological or typological links between Donne's secular and divine lyrics, the reverse typology of the secular lyrics appears to refute any such figural relation. As in the eucharistic elements, the difference seems to be one of the *use* to which the words are put. The secular lyrics play with both spiritual and secular connotations, often using spiritual (particularly Roman Catholic dogma) to praise secular. The two are never in harmony; they form an unresolvable paradox. The divine lyrics, conversely, allow flesh and spirit to intersect and reinforce each other in a more traditional typological movement. On cursory perusal, the secular lyrics seem more Catholic in character, the divine poems more Protestant in their attention to spiritual union as an ultimate goal. Undermining this hypothesis, however, is the overtly sensual language of the divine poems and their emphasis on both body and soul. They illustrate Donne's effort to realize the second of his three resurrections on earth—the purification and purgation of the body through penitence and prayer. The divine poems still insist, however, on a balance between body and soul that is absent in Donne's conceptions of Catholic and Puritan faiths. In this sense, they are specifically Anglican in their refusal to indulge in Roman Catholic transubstantiation or to retreat to the abstract symbolism of Protestantism. The poems are neither transformed into icons nor made into scriptural signifiers. Liturgical ritual and Scripture mix with meditation to create a presence both personal and immediate. Often, it is true, that presence seems to be that of the persona instead of Christ or God. Always, however, it is the persona trying to realize Christ in words.

Throughout his discussion of Donne and Herbert in *Les Poètes Metaphysiques Anglais,* Robert Ellrodt keeps his eye on the specifically Anglican character of both poets' divine verse. Ellrodt does not argue for a typological link between secular and divine, flesh and spirit. Instead, he proposes through the peculiarly Anglican doctrine of Real Presence without transubstantiation a "concomitance, conjonction, distinction."[33] Ellrodt insists on the doubleness of Donne's poetry rather than on the assimilation of one thing into another. Spirit and flesh touch at the point of the eucharistic communion as they do in the Incarnation and the Resurrection. One is not subsumed by the other. Speaking of both Donne and Herbert, Ellrodt writes:

Chez l'un et l'autre, le centre même de l'inspiration poétique est à la fois la double nature de l'Homme-Dieu, gagé de la conjonction du temps et de l'éternité, et la double nature de l'homme, ce composé de chair et d'esprit.[34]

Christ has provided the basis for the intersection of temporal and eternal, for the human body with the human soul. Instead of seeing the union of the souls in "The Extasie" figurally, Ellrodt views Donne as maintaining a contiguity without perfect unity:

L'originalité de la poésie religieuse de Donne est précisément de toujours maintenir présente à notre ésprit les 'doubles natures' et leur signification profonde; de toujours unir *l'idée* de la Redemption au *fait* de l'Incarnation.[35]

The "idée de la Redemption" is an example of eschatological "limit-language" in its prophetic and unrealized character. Donne's divine poems all point toward this end while relying on incarnational themes and language to describe the possibility of resurrection. The significance of the Eucharist as the only point of intersection of divine and temporal thus becomes a cornerstone of the divine lyrics. The Eucharist manifests the *fact* of the Incarnation in its doctrine of Real Presence. It signifies the *idea* of the Resurrection in its promise of redemption from sins through communion. One might allege that Donne is poised between the Catholic reliance on Incarnation and the Protestant focus on Eschatology. The Anglican Eucharist allows both to meet and absolves Donne from membership in either Catholic or Calvinist camps.[36]

In his longer divine poems, Donne is almost exclusively absorbed with the mystery of the Incarnation and Resurrection. His Holy Sonnets compact the persona's struggle toward death and resurrection into pleas to God to punish him so that he will be worthy of salvation, whereas the longer hymns and monologues protract that struggle. In these longer poems, Donne attempts to speak about the kingdom of God. To this end he uses the "limit-language" of paradox and parable. The speaker is less agonized, the poem less intensely personal than in the sonnets.

"The Crosse" and "Upon the Annunciation and Passion Falling Upon One Day. 1608," particularly, are miniature sermons occasioned by specific symbols or events. As he expands and explicates biblical texts in his sermons, so Donne takes the cross in "The Crosse" and pushes both thematic and linguistic capacities of the word to their limits. "The Crosse" insists on the ability of the Prayer of Consecration to put a word to another use or to make the natural sacred.

In a thickly textured criticism of the Puritan desire to remove the cross from church altars, Donne multiplies superficial paradoxes. He builds an argument that mimes the symbolic cross's bisection of time and eternity. Here the doubleness of which Ellrodt speaks becomes multiplicity: The argumentative strands intersect in the horizontal and vertical axis of the cross:

> From mee, no Pulpit, nor misgrounded law,
> Nor scandal taken, shall this Crosse withdraw,
> It shall not, for it cannot; for, the losse
> Of this Crosse, were to mee another Crosse;
> Better were worse, for, no affliction,
> No Crosse is so extreme, as to have none.
> Who can blot out the Crosse, which th'instrument
> Of God, dew'd on mee in the Sacrament?
> Who can deny mee power, and liberty
> To stretch mine armes, and mine owne Crosse to be?[37]

Here metaphorical cross (cross of burden) meets symbolic cross (cross on the altar), which, in turn, leads back through the sacrament of the Eucharist to the actual cross on Calvary. All levels of the word are valid; the play of language illustrates Donne's refusal to allow one meaning to be swallowed up by another. All three coexist, loading the word with secular and spiritual presence. Yet Donne insists on the priority of the spiritual cross: "Materiall Crosses then, good physicke bee, / And yet spirituall have chiefe dignity" (*DP*, ll.25–26). The tight compression of "dew'd on me in the Sacrament" slices through time to capture the actual moment of Christ's blood falling from the cross. This blood is immediately turned to sacramental blood and gives the speaker strength to sacrifice himself in a mimesis of Christ. The sacrament leads inward until the speaker becomes his own cross or part of Christ.[38] Acting as a seal of grace, the Eucharist guarantees the existence of the cross on these three levels. One must continually sacrifice oneself before partaking of the sacrament. Such an individual cross touches Christ's actual cross at the altar's cross in the Eucharist.

In addition to exegesis of the word "cross" on a semantic level, Donne internalizes the emblem of the cross to *re*-present it, further advancing his belief in transformation as opposed to transubstantiation. Although Christ is already implanted in men and women, they must duplicate Christ's sacrifice to stand in sacramental relation to him. Otherwise the image, as in "Goodfriday, 1613. Riding West-ward," grows tarnished and recedes. Such sacrifice involves a strip-ping away of false ceremony and imagery before Christ's presence can be realized:

> As perchance, Carvers do not faces make,
> But that away, which hid them there, do take;
> Let Christs, soe, take what hid Christ in thee,
> And be his image, or not his, but hee.
>
> (*DP*, ll.33–36)

These lines mark Donne's middle stance between Roman Catholi-cism and Protestantism. The cross is not mere icon to be adored for itself nor accidental symbol to be discarded when one reaches colloquy with God; internalized in a person, it demonstrates Real Presence, the intersection of divine and human natures. Such pres-ence is contingent on mutual sacrifice. Missing in all the divine terminology of the secular poems is this realization of sacrifice.

Midway through the poem after disclosing the meanings of the *noun* cross, Donne switches to the *verb*. He does this only after enjoining the reader to recognize the emblem of the cross in him-self. By entering into communion with Christ through imaginative participation in the crucifixion, the communicant reactivates the word. On a grammatical level this *presencing* of the noun parallels the activation of the elements of bread and wine to a different use after the consecration. In both, the focus shifts from stationary elements to active presence. The verb "cross" takes on different meanings: the first (to afflict), abstract; the second (making the sign of the cross), concrete. Crossing or afflicting oneself pushes one toward contrition where one learns forgiveness and is prepared to make the sign of the cross on his chest. Such penitential exercises must be constantly repeated as preparation for the final crucifixion of death. For Donne, the penitential offering is unending. The punning repetition of "cross" compresses sacrifice and redemption into a double image. It evinces Donne's ability to condense and explode several meanings in one major symbol.

The 1559 *Book of Common Prayer* places more emphasis on the danger of receiving the sacraments unworthily than do later revi-sions. An optional precommunion prayer warns the communicants of "the great peril of the unworthy receiving thereof" and exhorts them "so to search and examine your own consciences, as you should come holy and clean to a most godly and heavenly feast, so that in no wise you come but in the marriage garment.[39] The prayer proceeds to spell out the methods by which the communicant must purify himself through private self-examination and public restitution of wrongs done to others: "For otherwise the receiving of the Holy Communion doth nothing else but increase your damnation."[40]

As both Douglas Peterson and Patrick Grant note, Donne is specifically concerned with the Anglican distinction between attrition and contrition.[41] For Donne, attrition—fear of divine punishment—is inadequate preparation for salvation. The sinner must reach a state of contrition where he loathes his sin and loves God alone. Grant suggests that Donne follows a pattern of Franciscan conversion by conjuring up sins in his poems to increase his hatred of them. Thus the poems serve as punishments (crosses) and as steps toward the contrition preliminary to eucharistic communion. "The Crosse" offers such a study in contrition.

In "Upon the Annunciation and Passion Falling Upon One Day. 1608," Donne adopts the apparent paradox of the conception and death of Christ falling on the same day in the liturgical year. This coincidence allows him literally to equate life with death and to compress life on earth into a day. Furthermore, the paradox offers him the excuse to push language to its semantic limits to reconcile the mortal human world with God's eternal one. The poem echoes the paradoxes of the Annunciation sonnet in *La Corona*. In both, Donne is concerned with Incarnation—the point at which Christ enters human flesh and crosses his divine nature with man's human one. The simultaneous celebration of the Annunciation and Passion allows him to collapse time into a divinely charged present where Mary is "seen at once, and seen / At almost fiftie, and at scarce fifteene" (*DP*, 11.13–14), and where "Gabrielle gives Christ to her, He her to John" (*DP*, 1.16). This collapsing of time triggers one of Donne's favorite paradoxical analogies—that of west meeting east—which becomes the main consolation of "Goodfriday":

> All this, and all between, this day hath showne,
> Th'Abridgement of Christ's story, which makes one
> (As in plaine Maps, the furthest West is East)
> Of the'Angels *Ave,*' and *Consummatum est.*
>
> (*DP*, ll.19–22)

The liturgical coincidence has offered Donne an authoritative (if specious) resolution of the paradox of life and death: "This Church, by letting these daies joyne, hath shown / Death and conception in mankinde is one" (*DP*, ll.33–34). This coincidence calls forth the

eschatological connection between Incarnation and revelation, between the *idea* of the Redemption and the *fact* of the Incarnation.
Chronological time defers to eternal time. Both Annunciation and
Passion pinpoint this deference as the former enters chronological
time, and the latter leaves it. Falling on the same day, these two
events vividly exemplify the typological movement toward resurrection and revelation. Annunciation bows to Passion; the Eucharist that would ordinarily be celebrated at the Annunciation is
denied by the Passion:

> Tamely fraile body'abstaine to day; to day
> My soule eates twice, Christ hither and away.
> She sees him man, so like God made in this,
> That of them both a circle embleme is,
> Whose first and last concurre; this doubtfull day
> Of feast or fast, Christ came, and went away;
> She sees him nothing twice at once, who'is all.
>
> *(DP*, ll.1–7)

Caught in time between conception and death, the body gives way
to the soul that transcends both events. Ironically, the double
presence of the Annunciation and the Passion denies the Real
Presence of Christ or the conjunction of body and soul in the
Eucharist. Although it provides Donne with a good argument for
his doubled images and paradoxes, it prohibits mutual celebration
of body and soul, the goal of many of Donne's later divine poems.
Instead, Donne chooses the oddly physical image of the soul eating
twice, once hither for the body and once away for death, as if to
compensate for the body's abstention.
   Stressing the intersection of vertical and horizontal (sacred and
historical) time in the action of the Eucharist, Geoffrey Wainwright
states that the ceremony signifies a "tension between the 'already
now' and the 'not yet.' "[42] Similarly, in his appendix to the 1559
Book of Common Prayer Book, John Booty insists on the eschatological compression and transcendence of time in the Eucharist as a "dynamic view of time in the Holy Communion with its
remembering *(anamnesis)* of events past, in the light of things to
come (the messianic banquet), whereby Christ's presence is realized and human existence transformed in the present."[43] In "Upon
the Annunciation and Passion" Donne exposes this doubleness by
mediating on the church and its primary sacrament. The poem
looks back to the *La Corona* sequence that Helen Gardner notes
was probably written in the same year. Although both poems are

meditative and narrative, "Upon the Annunciation and Passion" thwarts narrative sequence, substituting simultaneity of events for linearity. Nevertheless, the poems have the same hermeneutical quality as the sermons in their uncovering and explaining of liturgical acts. Their "limit-language" is sanctioned by the "limit-experience" of Christ's life as celebrated in the liturgical year. The church calendar's compression authorizes a similar linguistic compression.

In his later divine poems, Donne moves from description of liturgical "limit-experiences" to personal dramatizations of them. Language begins to mime experience as the priest's words during the Prayer of Consecration parallel his action with the eucharistic elements. The language of "Goodfriday," "Hymne to God my God, in my Sicknesse," and the Holy Sonnets internalizes the public eucharistic and eschatological language of the previous poems to depict the persona's own private spiritual struggle. In a sense, as in his secular lyrics, Donne appears to convert Christ (antitype) to a type in a reversal of traditional typology.[44] This conversion, however, serves a different purpose. In the secular lyrics, the lovers absorb the whole world into themselves and make universal drama subservient to their own personal drama. In the Holy Sonnets universal biblical drama narrows to an individual struggle to realize in both words and deeds the "limit-experience" of union with God. Rarely, however, do these poems succeed in effecting this union. Instead, they are like preliminary ceremonies designed to prepare the sinner for absolution and communion.

"Goodfriday, 1613. Riding Westward" internalizes the didactic, epigrammatic language of "The Crosse" and "Upon the Annunciation" to depict the persona's private spiritual struggle to realize Christ's presence within himself. Like "The Crosse," it moves from conjured picture of the cross—Christ's crucifixion—to a plea for affliction and sacrifice before that presence can be realized. Because the internal struggle is more complex and personal, the language and logic of "Goodfriday" are also more complex. Donne abandons the repetitious pun for elaborate analogy and paradox, both of which collapse by the end of the poem.[45] There is no easy resolution of the conflict between body and soul here: The two are at odds as the body initially refuses the challenge of "The Crosse" to look at the crucifixion.

The poem begins with an analogy of man's soul to a sphere moved by misguided intelligence. Here Donne blames the contrary westward direction of his journey on an analogical argument that lacks a solid ground. As in "Upon the Annunciation" he metaphorically assigns the soul concrete properties: "Let man's Soul be a Sphere, and then, in this, / Th'intelligence that moves, devotion is" (*DP*, ll.1–2). Here Donne presents the already outdated Ptolemaic analogy as a superficial (and incorrect) rationalization of the speaker's willful action. This evidence—whether logical, pseudo-scientific, or theological—does not justify action. Instead it exposes the persona's willful tendency to snatch at visible excuses, to rely on false or inappropriate authority. In "Goodfriday" the gap between secular logic and faith is too great. One cannot be used to ratify the other.[46]

The original superficial argument against riding eastward to face Christ is abandoned for a movement inward toward rhetorical self-examination. Donne moves from faulty analogy to a series of paradoxical questions that pit his own limited humanity against the godliness of Christ. The five questions concern the persona's reluctance to see God (Christ) humbled, humanized, and tortured. They compose a kind of negative meditation or epic catalog. As he repeats his inability to view Christ's wounds, the speaker perversely recalls vivid details of the Passion, thus substituting remembered scene for actual confrontation or *anamnesis*. Although his body is still turned away for multiple *reasons*, his *faith*, through sensuous contemplation of the Passion, has begun to pull him eastward toward identity with Christ. Will bows to memory as reason gives way to faith.

Yet the persona still struggles with the problem of Christ's dual nature. He is unable or unwilling to regard him as human:

> Could I behold those hands which span the Poles,
> And tune all spheares at once, peirc'd with those holes?
> Could I behold that endlesse height which is
> Zenith to us, and to'our Antipodes,
> Humbled below us? or that blood which is
> The seat of all our Soules, if not of his,
> Make durt of dust, or that flesh which was worne
> By God, for his apparell, rag'd, and torne?
>
> (*DP*, ll.21–28)

Unsure of the relationship between Christ's blood and Christ's soul, Donne still appears reluctant to assert a eucharistic Real Presence, although he admits the presence of Christ's blood in man's soul in the sacrament. Intellectually, his questions echo the Puritan difficulty of realizing Christ simultaneously on earth and in heaven. Yet the emotional vividness with which Donne catalogs the crucified

Christ's physical traits is indeed reminiscent of the first step of the Ignatian meditational method—composition of place. The carnal imagery suggests that Donne is conjuring up Christ's physical presence (albeit in conditional language) to identify himself with Christ's sacrifice and thereby become worthy of partaking in the eucharistic meal. Yet this process is backward. To achieve true conformity with the crucified Christ, the speaker must first suffer his own internal crucifixion through penitence.[47]

The persona concludes in a tone reminiscent of the penitential sonnets for a wrathful Christ to

> . . . thinke mee worth thine anger, punish mee,
> Burne off my rusts, and my deformity,
> Restore thine Image, so much, by thy grace,
> That thou may'st know mee, and I'll turne my face.
>
> (*DP*, ll. 39–42)

The speaker's promise of future action is predicated on first action by Christ. By using memory, however, to revive a vivid sense of Christ's presence, Donne indicates his capacity to realize the physical presence of Christ within his own mind. Although communion has not occurred in the present moment of the poem, it has been both remembered and promised. The poem demonstrates Donne's belief in the necessity of corrective affliction as a prerequisite for true realization of Christ's presence.

"Hymne to God my God, in my Sicknesse," possibly Donne's last poem,[48] offers "Goodfriday" a destination. It adopts the familiar east-west debate and resolves it by planting the poles within the persona:

> I joy, that in these straits, I see my West;
>   For, though theire currents yeeld returne to none,
> What shall my West hurt me? As West and East
>   In all flatt Maps (and I am one) are one,
>   So death doth touch the Resurrection.
>
> (*DP*, ll. 11–15)

Unlike "Goodfriday," "Hymne to God my God" uses analogical reasoning to argue toward, not away from, faith. Here analogies do not offer excuses for turning away; rather, they reinforce the speaker's final sacrifice—his acceptance of his own death. The simile incorporates the parenthetical metaphor "(and I am one)" and compresses geography, speaker, and spiritual event into an elaborate analogy. Man and world are sacramentally identified through Christ. The equation of a physical surface with a spiritual event forces the reader to jump from a literal to a spiritual plane. Prostrated by physical sickness, the speaker's body is horizontal while his soul awaits ascension. The formation of a cross by body and soul stresses the sacramental identification of the speaker with Christ. In addition, the horizontal meeting points of the map—east and west—create a cross as they intersect with the vertical typology of death and resurrection. West (death) and east (resurrection) act to double presence by retaining both their directional signification and their spiritual symbolism. The initial directional paradox is resolved by the deeper spiritual symbols of death and resurrection.

Stanza 5 pushes analogy toward typology. It forces the typological movement from Adam to Christ toward eschatological fulfillment in the speaker. In death the three are typologically united. The persona steals the "limit-language" of biblical typology to apply it to his own "limit-experience" of dying:

> We thinke that *Paradise* and *Calvarie*,
>   *Christs* Cross, and *Adams* tree, stood in one place;
> Looke Lord, and finde both *Adams* met in me;
>   As the first *Adams* sweat surrounds my face,
>   May the last *Adams* blood my soule embrace.
>
> (DP, ll.21–25)

Here the speaker, on the brink of death, is about to partake of the communion previously denied him. Already a type of Adam in life, he will soon be united with Christ in death. The sweat of the sickness has afforded him the penitential affliction he requested as a prerequisite for union. Adam and Christ are equated by simile (which falls just short of metaphorical identification) to emphasize the figural relation among Adam, Christ, and the poet, and *not* their identity. As in the previous stanza, the first Adam is physical, met through sweat, whereas the second is both physical and spiritual, encountered in the meeting of Christ's blood with man's soul. The extent of the sacrifice that links the two Adams also differs. The first is sweaty from struggle and hard work, the second bloody from death. The stanza ends conditionally, resting on an ontological base and begging for an eschatological one. The eschatological promise of communion with Christ at death allows the speaker to accept self-sacrifice as a precondition for resurrection.

In his letters, Donne frequently expresses a desire for a struggle with death so that it not ambush him unaware and unrepentant.

This struggle is reminiscent of his constant hope in the poems that God will overpower him. It hints also at Donne's fear of his own inaction:

> I would not that death should take me asleep.
> I would not have him meerly seise me, and onely
> declare me to be dead, but win me, and overcome
> me. When I must shipwrack, I would do it in a
> Sea, where mine impotencie might have some excuse;
> not in a sullen weedy lake, where I could not have
> so much as exercise for my swimming.[49]

Likewise Donne writes to another friend, "I am afraid that Death will play with me so long, as he will forget to kill me; and suffer me to live in a languishing and useless age, a life, that is rather a forgetting that I am dead, than of living."[50] It is as if Donne wishes to make violent language instigate personal action. By constantly beseeching God to punish him directly and forcefully, Donne pushes language to substitute itself for action.

It is, however, in his final sermon, "Deaths Duell," that Donne explains the typology of his "Hymne to God my God." In counseling his congregation as to the necessity of preparing themselves for the sacrament of Holy Communion, Donne likens this penitential action to that of the dying man. The sacrament serves as a preliminary death where the communicant learns to mingle sweat and tears with blood. By meditating on Christ's Passion as the persona has done in "Goodfriday," and by imaginatively participating in Christ's crucifixion as he has done in "Hymne to God my God," the communicant has achieved conformity with Christ and is ready for communion or the further "limit-experience" of death:

> If that time were spent in a *holy recommendation* of thyself to *God*, and a *submission* of *thy will* to his, it was spent in a *comformity* to him. In that *time*, and in those *prayers*, was his *agony* and *bloody sweat*. I will *hope* that thou didst *pray*; but not *every ordinary* and *customary prayer*, but *prayer actually* accompanied with *shedding of tears* and *dispositively* in a readiness to *shed blood* for *his glory* in *necessary cases*, puts thee into a *conformity* with him.[51]

Prayer and tears must mix with action and blood. Passive meditation does not equal self-sacrifice. Because the speaker of "Hymne to God my God" has experienced this agony, he has earned the right to commune with God through Christ:

So, in his purple wrapp'd receive mee Lord,
     By these his thornes give me his other Crowne;
And as to others soules I preach'd thy word,
     Be this my Text, my Sermon to mine owne,
Therefore that he may raise the Lord throws down.

(DP, ll.26–30)

In his final stanza Donne the priest achieves the "limit-experience"
of death and communion by making Christ's Passion his own.
Unification with God depends first on unification with Christ at the
moment of death. The language of the last two stanzas finds its
counterpart in the end of "Deaths Duell": ". . . and as *God
breathed a soul into* the *first Adam,* so this *second Adam breathed
his soul into the hands of God.*"[52] Whereas the sermon maintains
the distinction between the meditative communicant and his biblical counterparts, the poem merges the two. As preacher, the persona has been the first Adam giving out God's word; in death, he
returns this gift. Although the sermon prescribes and depicts, the
poem dramatizes the union of man with God. The "Hymne" ends
with a declarative cause-effect statement, not a conditional one.
The last two lines survey the action of the poem—the "throwing
down" of the speaker in death—and affirm the reason for this
action: that God might raise man. Donne writes his own epitaph,
circling back from his public life as a priest to his private one as
faithful communicant. The sermon moves inward as the priest
blesses himself. In death he has gained the authority to declare
God's intention.

Like the "Hymne," the Holy Sonnets press for the necessity of
repentance and contrition as prerequisites to union with God. Also
like the "Hymne," they view identification with Christ's Passion as
a route toward that union. To this end they continually seek affliction as a means of realizing Christ's presence. They dramatize the
sinner's confrontation with his sin and his petition for grace to
receive Holy Communion. The sonnets borrow liturgical language
and rhythm to lend authority to the individual drama. The sonnet
form, like the structured liturgical prayers, encloses the drama and
imposes a familiar framework that both restrains and emphasizes
the individual voice. Although most of these sonnets discuss the
sinner striving for grace, several conclude with specifically eucharistic imagery. Blood and tears mingle in the sonnets as blood
and sweat meet in the trinity of Adam, Christ, and the persona of
the "Hymne."

"Oh my Blacke Soule," second in Gardner's 1633 sequence,

initiates the soul's quest for purity through Christ's blood. Addressed to the sinful soul, the octet describes the death-in-life fate of an unrepentant soul. The sestet turns on the word "grace." Though still addressed to the soul and not to God, it suggests a course of action the static predicament of the octet lacked:

> Oh make thy selfe with holy mourning blacke,
> And red with blushing, as thou art with sinne;
> Or wash thee in Christs blood, which hath this might
> That being red, it dyes red soules to white.
>
> (*DP*, ll.11–14)

Unlike the poems addressed to God, this sonnet charts the route toward personal self-sacrifice. It calls for individual action independent of God's command. Donne plays on the secular and sacred connotations of black and red throughout the sonnet. After the octet, these secular meanings are "consecrated" to spiritual ones; sinful black becomes the black of holy mourning; red shame washed in Christ's blood is transformed to pure white. Here, blood, part of the sacrament, is the "conduit of grace" that links man to God. On a syntactical level, the similes of the octet ("like a pilgrim," "like a thiefe") are transmuted to active metaphors in the sestet. This metaphorical action is based on the speaker's own penitentiai ability to "make" himself black with mourning and red with blushing in preparation for Christ's eucharistic offering—"dying red soules to white."

This concept of washing oneself in Christ's blood derives specifically from the Anglican liturgy of Holy Communion. The next-to-the-last prayer before actual communion runs thus:

> We do not presume to come to this thy table (O merciful Lord) trusting in our own righteousness, but in thy manifold and great mercies. We be not worthy so much as to gather the crumbs under thy table, but thou art the same Lord, whose property is always to have mercy. Grant us therefore (gracious Lord) so to eat the flesh of thy dear Son Jesus Christ, and to drink his blood, that our sinful bodies may be made clean by his body, and our souls washed through his most precious blood, and that we may evermore dwell in him, and he in us.[53]

The sonnet's sestet depicts the process of the repentant communicant. After contritely offering up his sins, he is ready to participate in the Eucharist that offers to absolve the soul with Christ's blood. Like the precommunion prayer, the Holy Sonnets attest to the sinner's unworthiness and plead for cleansing. They transform the corporate language of the communion prayer into a private demand for absolution. As in "Goodfriday," however, they fall short of realizing actual communion with God.

"At the Round Earths Imagin'd Corners" is the most explicitly eschatological of Donne's sonnets. The octet begins with a discursive description of the Last Judgment that includes both dead and living. The sestet shifts inward like that of the second sonnet, begging for the grace to begin repenting: "Teach mee how to repent; for that's as good / As if thou 'hadst seal'd my pardon, with thy blood" (*DP*, ll.13–14). The couplet echoes Donne's belief in the sacrament as a "seal of grace"; if the persona learns to repent, he will be able to participate worthily in Holy Communion and have his pardon "sealed." Yet the conditional "as if" alerts the reader to the actual absence of pardon. God has neither taught the speaker how to repent nor has He sealed his pardon with Christ's blood. Furthermore, repentance does not constitute pardon. The conditional simile does not merge repentance with pardon as metaphor would. It holds the two apart by comparing the speaker's action to God's. Although God will not directly subdue the speaker's will, His tutelage may cause the speaker to subdue his own will, an action prior to receipt of grace.

Oddly, in both sonnets penitence does not join with communion. Rather, the two seem to offer separate routes toward redemption. The second sonnet balances the alternatives with the coordinate conjunction "or" instead of a subordinate conjunction or a conditional clause. The subordinate conjunction "for" of the fourth sonnet introduces a clause that emphasizes the unaccomplished subjunctive action: "As if thou 'hadst seal'd my pardon" (*DP*, l.14). In both sonnets, the imperative voice conveys the illusion of forceful action yet lacks a response. God is present only as a passive listener. The entire drama occurs within the speaker.

As in "Goodfriday," and other Holy Sonnets, the persona here and in the second sonnet is confounded by the problem of repentance. Being washed in Christ's blood is still only an anticipated reward. The prayer before the General Confession in the Anglican liturgy requires a personal response from the communicant before his communal participation in the Confession. The priest says to the congregation:

> You that do truly and earnestly repent you of your sins, and be in love and charity with your neighbors, and intend to lead a new life, following the commandments of God, and walking from henceforth in his holy ways: Draw near, and take this holy Sacrament to your comfort; make

your humble confession to. Almighty God before this congregation here gathered together in his holy name, meekly kneeling upon your knees.[54]

The sonnets express the quandary of the communicant on the verge of confession. The prayer demands from the communicant a promise governing all his future actions. The persona of the sonnets lacks the faith in himself to make that promise. The third sonnet of the Westmoreland group describes precisely this predicament:

> Oh, to vex me, contraryes meete in one:
> Inconstancy unnaturally hath begott
> A constant habit; that when I would not
> I change in vowes, and in devotione.
> As humorous is my contritione
> As my prophane love, and as soone forgott:
> As ridlingly distempered, cold and hott,
> As praying, as mute; as infinite, as none.
> I durst not view heaven yesterday; and to day
> In prayers, and flattering speaches I court God:
> To morrow' I quake with true feare of his rod.
> So my devout fitts come and go away
> Like a fantastique Ague: save that here
> Those are my best dayes, when I shake with feare.
>
> (*DP*, ll.1–14)

It is possible that having renounced Roman Catholicism for Anglicanism and having subsequently supported the *Articles of Religion,* Donne is wary of overpromising himself. Such a fear of possible recusancy could partially account for the overwhelming self-accusation in the sonnets. More likely, however, the struggle toward active repentance involves a personal battle with the speaker's individual will. He alone must subdue that recalcitrant will.

"If poysonous mineralls" and "I am a little world made cunningly" both allude to the hope that the Eucharist will drown or wash away black sin. The former begins with what Ricoeur refers to as the harsh Old Testament logic of God. In distinguishing between the Old Testament "logic of punishment" and the New Testament "logic of superabundance," Ricoeur states, "On the side of the logic of equivalence: sin, law and death; on the side of the logic of superabundance: justification, grace and life."[55] He further notes that Christ's Passion "breaks the moral equivalence of sin and death."[56] The Passion throws the old equation into question as it opens up the possibility of a pardon through Christ's sacrifice and the sinner's repentance. The eucharistic *anamnesis* of that Passion offers the persona an earthly reprieve from sin.

The poem pits these two logics against each other and acknowledges the need for punishment as a prerequisite for redemption. The octet describes an Old Testament world—the Garden of Eden—with its nonhuman elements—the tree, the serpent which "cannot be damn'd." After comparing his own plight with the other elements' freedom from damnation, Donne asks, "And mercy being easie and glorious / To God, in his sterne wrath, why threatens hee?" (*DP*, ll.7–8). The sestet charts the New Testament logic of superabundance based on Christ's Passion. The speaker chastizes his own Job-like behavior as he realizes the need for mutual sacrifice:

> O God, Oh! of thine onely worthy blood,
> And my teares, make a heavenly Lethean flood,
> And drowne in it my sinnes blacke memorie.
>
> (*DP*, ll.10–12)

Both the tears of repentance and the blood of communion combine to drown not the sins themselves but the memory of them. Donne stops short of Christian absolution; he mixes mythological and biblical references (Heaven and Lethean Hades' river of forgetfulness) into an orymoronic conceit. The speaker still quests for blind forgetfulness over remorse and contrition. Unlike more orthodox Christians who claim their sins' debts to be forgiven, he wishes God to forget instead of forgive.

"I am a little world made cunningly" deviates from the octet-sestet divisions of the previously mentioned sonnets. Like the love lyrics, it plays on the microcosm-macrocosm connection between the seas and tears, asking God to "Powre new seas in mine eyes, that so I might / Drowne my world with my weeping earnestly, / Or wash it, if it must be drown'd no more" (*DP*, ll.7–9). Again, the persona demands the motivation to repent through alternative actions separated by the conjunction "or." These alternatives, uncoupled with Christ's blood, fail. Next, the persona negates his previous petition by stating that his sinful world "must be burnt." He retracts this solution too and finally turns to God in the couplet, asking Him to "burne me ô Lord, with a fiery zeale / Of thee' and thy house, which doth in eating heale" (*DP*, ll.13–14). Here Donne transfigures the word "burne" from its secular to sacred use by imploring God's intervention as opposed to that of the secular explorers. With this transformation he surrenders his temporal control over language to God's sacred control.[57]

Although Helen Gardner cites David's Psalm 69 as a possible source for the final couplet ("For the zeal of thine house hath eaten me up; and the reproaches of them that reproached thee are fallen upon me"), it seems again that Donne is fusing Old Testament allusions with New Testament solutions. The psalm opens with David sinking in mire "where the floods overflow me." It ends with his assurance that God will save Zion. The sonnet is entirely personal and concerned less with life on earth than with preparation for death and salvation. It seems instead that Donne is converting David's lines to a request for fulfillment through participation in the eucharistic meal. David can only pray for salvation and deliverance from his enemies while the persona of the sonnet can participate in sacramental salvation. As in "Oh My Blacke Soule," if he has received the zeal (motivating grace) to repent, he can be healed by eating.[58]

In *Devotions Upon Emergent Occasions* (1624) Donne specifies the process through which the individual must go to realize Christ's presence on earth. The passage helps to clarify the ambiguity of the poems. He moves from the corrective affliction of physical sickness to an examination of his guilty conscience to the preparation for reception of the sacrament. On the threshold of receiving the sacrament he warns against "unnecessary disputations," presumably alluding to the furor over the various definitions of eucharistic presence—transubstantiation, consubstantiation, Virtualism, Memorialism. He then proceeds to give his own definition of the realization of Christ's presence, both physical and spiritual, in the sacrament:

> . . . to know that the bread and wine is not more really assimilated to my body, and to my blood, than the body and blood of thy Son is communicated to me in that action, and participation of that bread and that wine.[59]

Although he casts this realization in negatives, he balances the physical with the spiritual. He avoids the "heresy" of consubstantiation here by the careful distinction between "assimilated" and "communicated." "Assimilated"—to absorb and incorporate—stands parallel to the less precise "communicated." The latter allows for several interpretations ranging from tangible to aural to intangible transmission. Donne also avoids the Virtualist position by speaking directly of Christ's body and blood, not the virtue or power of the body and blood within the communicant. By treading a fine line between Roman Catholic transubstantiation and Lutheran consubstantiation on the one hand and Calvinistic Virtualism on the other, Donne maintains an orthodox Anglican stance toward the doctrine of Real Presence in the Eucharist.

Although the language of the secular and divine lyrics is similar, the real difference arises in the separate goals the words serve. The divine lyrics continually transform secular denotation to sacred connotation as the eucharistic ceremony transforms secular food into the spiritual food of Christ's body and blood. Within this sacramental framework, the divine lyrics are chary of such overtly Roman Catholic practices as miracles and transubstantiation. In his love lyrics, Donne is able both to parody Roman Catholic practices and make them appear to reinforce earthly love. In the divine poems he is less indulgent. Instead of seeking visible transformation, he focuses on the sinner's struggle for union with an invisible God. This struggle tends to make the human lovers' unions appear too easy.

The peculiarly Anglican quality of eucharistic Real Presence without transubstantiation offers Donne a foretaste of the kingdom of heaven on earth. This doctrine of Real Presence acts in the divine poems like a frequently frustrating lure to the sinner who has not yet learned how to repent. It is an example of a "limit-experience" that can only be described in the "limit-language" of paradox. Because of its sacramental character, it displaces linear logic; it amplifies instead of transforms the elements. Although transubstantiation also defies linear logic, it distances the bread and wine from the body and blood by relegating the bread and wine to accidents. The Anglican Real Presence forces the natural and spiritual elements to coexist and thus provides a model for Donne's compression of diverse images into an illusory paradox.

Donne's method of realizing such a presence in his poems is to multiply the meanings of words by playing on their secular and spiritual definitions and contexts. In this way he is able to effect a type of consecration that allows for a confabulation of meanings. Because he has not yet experienced death, Donne can use "limit-language" only to approximate the eschatological language of Christ in the parables, proverbs, and proclamatory sayings. Borrowing terms (wine, tears, body, blood) from the only earthly sacrament that merges human and divine, Donne is able to make his poems partial mimeses of the Anglican Eucharist. By incorporating eucharistic symbols into his poetry, he can juxtapose secular and sacred in the love lyrics and comingle them in his divine poems.

Donne's poetry looks forward to that of Gerard Manley Hopkins in its technique of doubling language by paradox and hyperbole to create real presence. Although Hopkins pursues a more incarnational method, seeking to discover Christ in humanity and nature, Donne looks toward the Eschaton heralded by Christ's death and resurrection, and typologically previewed by his own death. Because one can only experience pleromic Real Presence through kenotic death and self-sacrifice, Donne employs paradox as his chief poetic tool. Paradox forces death and resurrection (east and west) to clash, then erupt in a revelatory vision antithetical to linear logic.

3

Real Presence through Incarnation: Hopkins's Eucharistic Poetry

> For Christ plays in ten thousand places,
> Lovely in limbs, and lovely in eyes not his
> To the father through the features of men's faces.
> —"As Kingfishers Catch Fire" (ll. 12–14)

Speaking of the lacunae of references to Donne in Hopkins's journals and letters, W. H. Gardner states:

> It is remarkable that nowhere in his writings does Hopkins mention Donne; yet it is difficult to believe that he had not read a poet who in personality, intellect, and style was so like himself. That Hopkinsian felicity of syntax which ensures the closest union between the semantic and audible rhythms is anticipated in many passages of Donne; and there is a psychological significance in this tendency of two poets, each passionately intellectual and morally earnest, to unite similar unconventional modes of rhythm and grammar.[1]

Later in the book, Gardner returns to this puzzle and hints at a solution:

> His [Hopkins's] affinity with Donne derives from the play of intellect on the problems of faith and religious endeavour—the yearning of imperfection toward perfection, the desire to know and hold God more closely—together with the play of individual sensibility upon the materials of poetry and on the conventional standards of diction and rhythm. In Donne, the clash between the "man of the world" temper and the claims of a pious and ascetic calling did not admit of a poetic reconciliation so clear and sharp as that of Hopkins; for Donne never found, as Hopkins did in Catholicism, an interpretation of life which would be so flushed with feeling as to become a complete and illuminating experience.[2]

While still an undergraduate at Oxford in 1866, Hopkins had eschewed this " 'man of the world' temper" and decided to convert to Roman Catholicism. By 1868, he had determined to become a priest, choosing the more ascetic Jesuit order over the Benedictine. Throughout his journals and letters to Robert Bridges, Canon Dixon, and others, he emphasizes self-denial, self-sacrifice, and the problem of the *arbitrium,* or self-will, as the central concerns of his life. His goal is to steer the *arbitrium* unflinchingly toward God. On such a journey, action and will are not, as in Donne's "Goodfriday," severed; rather, they cooperate in what Hopkins terms a "doing-agree," or an aspiration in return for God's inspiration.[3] This agreement of will and action specifically separates Hopkins from Donne. Donne's divine poems concern appeals for grace instead of the actual achievement of grace. Hopkins's poetry, conversely, deals largely with the "after-consent," in which the poet beseeches God to lift him

> from one cleave of being to another and to a vital act in Christ: this is truly God's finger touching the very vein of personality, which nothing else can reach and man can respond to by no play whatever, by bare acknowledgement only, the finger counterstress which God alone can feel . . . the aspiration in answer to his inspiration. (*Sermons,* 154–58)

Much more concerned with spiritual touching than Donne, Hopkins depicts an active reciprocal process that has its foundation in the achievement of Real Presence in the Eucharist. For Hopkins, presence is based on what Newman terms "real assent" or assent to something actual and not notional.[4] Donne is torn between real and notional assent; frequently his arguments focus on theological dogma instead of on religious faith.

Perhaps also Donne's struggles were too familiar, his vacillations too anguished for the young Hopkins. One is tempted to speculate that Hopkins chose to avoid Donne for the same reason he decided to shun Whitman. In a letter to Bridges he confesses, "I always knew in my heart Walt Whitman's mind to be more like my own than any other man's living. As he is a very great scoundrel this is not a pleasant confession. And this also makes me the more desirous to read him and the more determined that I will not."[5]

Aside from a potentially dangerous kinship with Donne, Hopkins may have been angered by Donne's conversion from Roman Catholicism to Anglicanism and by his oratorical and financial success as an Anglican priest. Donne's avowedly hostile reaction to the religion he had rejected (and particularly toward the Jesuit order) could only have irritated and saddened Hopkins in light of the latter's conversion.

Nevertheless, as others besides Gardner remark, Donne and Hopkins possess a surprising affinity. Specifically, David Morris and Walter Ong point toward syntactic and metrical similarities. Morris notes the use of the conceit—"expanded" in Donne, "condensed" in Hopkins—as well as the tendency toward physical transfiguration of a spiritual conflict.[6] Ong credits Hopkins with following the "sense stress" tradition of Donne over the running stress of Spenser and explains that sense stress grants priority to emotion over grammatical clarity.[7]

Apart from these similarities, however, is another, certainly the most crucial for this argument: the striving by both poets to effect a real presence in their poetry analogous to the Real Presence of the Eucharist. Although Donne stresses the ultimately eschatological power of language to manifest Christ's presence, Hopkins emphasizes the capacity of language to *inscape* or *incarnate* that presence in nature and in man. For Donne, poetic language always moves toward a constantly postponed communion. His pleas for grace are cast in the conditional or future tense. Though he envisions a human dialogue between himself and God (following traditional Ignatian colloquy), he finally recognizes the hopelessness of such reciprocity before Judgment Day.

Hopkins, conversely, portrays an immanent presence based on the Incarnation of Christ in the world. Consequently, Real Presence for Hopkins is not something that occurs in typological stages nor merely in brief moments in the Eucharist. Rather, it is a constant Christological fact. This *fact* unites persons, nature, and language in a sacramental union.

In both his journal observations and his poems, Hopkins tries to inscape or draw forth this sacramental presence. His action is analogous to the priest's office as consecrator of the eucharistic elements. The priest repeats the words of the liturgy; however, Hopkins as poet must invent his own consecratory words. In his poetry, Hopkins transmutes nature into words to demonstrate the mystery at the heart of both nature and language. This mystery, or Real Presence, as he tells his skeptical friend Bridges, is specifically Catholic. It is an "incomprehensible certainty" as opposed to a Protestant "interesting uncertainty," or a "reserve of truth beyond what the mind reaches and still feels to be behind" (*Letters to Bridges*, 187).

Although Donne's poetry reflects an ambiguous struggle both to affirm and to penetrate that mystery, Hopkins's work seeks to *express* its fullness and complexity. This theological difference leads to two divergent routes toward a poetics of real presence.

Donne travels through paradox, dialectic, and typology to an affirmation of the resurrection. His destination of life after death draws the reader steadily forward and upward.

Conversely, Hopkins often appears to entice the reader backward and downward to the manifestation of Christ on earth. Such a route entails labyrinthine syntax aided by such poetic devices as suspension or hyperbaton, compounding, anthimeria, and severe grammatical compression. More than Donne, Hopkins tries to make language itself incarnational. His goal is finally to reveal the one Word behind the "skeined strained veined variety" of life—Christ. That Word is the sole guarantee of stability and immortality; it is the God who "fathers-forth whose beauty is past change."[8] In praising Him, the poet, like the priest, offers his words as kenotic proof of his attempt to return language to God. Hence, God is both originator and receiver of the poet's speech. Hopkins's world is circular; the variety of nature and language, even of one's own selfhood, is strictly subordinate to a buried identity with Christ. Thus, too, the invalidity of metaphor for Hopkins—the initial shock produced by the equation of two disparate objects eventually dissipates, like Donne's paradoxes, to reveal their original identity. For Hopkins, metaphor is a superficial device that produces a false tension between two already united objects.

That Hopkins's poetry owes its insistent power to his belief in Real Presence is fortified by his continual allusions to Christ as the ground of being. In 1864 he tries to persuade his college friend Coleridge that "The great aid to belief . . . is the doctrine of the Real Presence in the Blessed Sacrament of the Altar. Religion without that is sombre, dangerous, illogical, with that it is—not to speak of its grand consistency and certainty—*loveable*. Hold that and you will gain all Catholic truth."[9] In 1866, in response to his father's request that he delay his conversion to Roman Catholicism, Hopkins writes:

> I shall hold as a Catholic what I have long held as an Anglican, that literal truth of our Lord's words by which I learn that the least fragment of the consecrated elements in the Blessed Sacrament of the Altar is the whole Body of Christ born of the Blessed Virgin, before which the whole host of saints and angels as it lies on the Altar trembles with adoration. This belief once got is the life of the soul and when I doubted it I should become an atheist the next day. (*Further Letters*, 92)

Here, the "literal truth" of the eucharistic sacrament provides a key to Hopkins's theory of language, specifically to his poetic language.

All language—both theological and poetic—for Hopkins literally originates in the Word of God.[10] In his retreat notes of 1882 he affirms: "God's utterance of himself in himself is God the Word, outside himself is this world. This world then is word, expression, news of God." The poet's task is to return his words to God in the form of prayer, "sign or aspiration or stirring of the spirit towards God" (*Sermons,* 155).

Donne charts a route of personal salvation through the more conventional body-soul paradox, whereas Hopkins makes syntax itself paradoxical and problematic. He forces the reader to exchange an intellectual logic of reading for a sensuous logic of sound and rhythm that eventually leads to a logic of faith. Donne *imposes* extravagant figures of speech—hyperbole and paradoxical conceits—as rhetorical devices to distort and explode ordinary logic, whereas Hopkins *embeds* these devices in his syntax to *evoke* instead of *invoke* real presence. The poem, like the Eucharist, becomes a sacrament that demands participation from the reader. The elements of the poem (words, syntax, rhythm), like the bread and wine of the Mass, no longer refer to objects; instead, they enact a ceremony and thereby gain a new spiritual presence. The poet's transubstantiation of these elements is the key to their renewed spiritual vigor.[11] The poet alone cannot consecrate words to a new use or imbue them with spirit, however. Rather it is God working through him—speaking His will in the poet that produces this doubleness. Such action Hopkins terms "instress."

Like Donne's view of the Eucharist as a "conduit of Grace," Hopkins's poems up to the Terrible Sonnets act themselves as "conduits of Grace" linking man, nature and God. They demonstrate the ability of language to merge sense and spirit in a constant *anamnesis* of the Incarnation. This *anamnesis* surfaces in the poetry as a symbolic and sacramental (not metaphoric) summoning up of Christ in nature and in man. To aid in this task, Hopkins poses the Eucharist as an analogical model for his poetics. In the Eucharist the priest inscapes Christ in the elements through the Prayer of Consecration. In the poem the poet seeks to consecrate words, to reanimate them by means of rhetorical devices that will effect a doubled presence.

At the heart of this model is the Feast of Corpus Christi, the supreme affirmation of the "literal truth" of the Real Presence. Hopkins tells Bridges,

. . . Corpus Christi is the feast of the Real Presence; therefore it is the most purely joyous of solemnities. Naturally the Blessed Sacrament is

carried in procession at it. . . . But the procession has more meaning
and mystery than this! It represents the process of the Incarnation and
the world's redemption. As Christ went forth from the bosom of the
Father as the Lamb of God and eucharistic victim to die upon the altar
of the Cross for the world's ransom; then rising returned leading the
procession of the flock redeemed / so in this ceremony his body *in statu
victimali* is carried to the Altar of Repose . . . and back to the taber-
nacle at the high altar, which will represent the bosom of the godhead.
(*Letters to Bridges*, 149)

In this passage Hopkins evinces his belief in sacrifice as a prerequisite for redemption or a renewal of presence on earth. He also
shows his reliance on the feast as an intersection of the Incarnation
and the Resurrection, a divine connection that defies chronological
time. This intersection of Incarnation and Resurrection recalls
Donne's frequent image of west meeting east. Both poets recognize
a sacramental time that transcends human temporality.

Confronted with such a sacramental reality, Hopkins must devise
a means of *eliciting*, not merely *representing*, it in his poetry. Like
modern hermeneutical attempts by such contemporary theological
scholars as Paul Ricoeur, Thomas Altizer, and Carl Raschke, he
must "deconstruct" linear syntax and semantics to reveal a presence obscured by referential language. Of *anamnesis*, Altizer notes
that voice and act must combine to announce presence. Of western
poetics, he states, "Here God is not simply the object of speech,
but the subject of speech as well, a subject which the Christian
identifies as the Word of revelation."[12] As instigator of speech, God
thrusts Himself through the subjective poet to the objective world.
On a grammatical level, He unites subject with object, the poet's
"I" with the world's "it." The object becomes a predicate nomi-
native separated from its subject by "is," a word Hopkins often
reduces to a hyphen. Altizer goes on to distinguish between the
horizontality of metaphor and allegory as opposed to the verticality
of eschatological parables. Like Ricoeur, Altizer asserts that parabolic sayings explode ordinary logic and pave the way for revelation. Although Hopkins does not imitate the semantic content of
Christ's parables, he does structure his poems in a nonlinear,
thickly textured language that defies logical paraphrase. Words and
phrases are propelled by rhythm into a state of breathlessness
where one reaches toward the limits of speech. Such breathless
boundaries signal Hopkins's attempt to mime the language of revelation where vision or sound are more immediate than signifying
words. In this breathlessness Hopkins literally seeks to *ex*pire or to

reveal Christ.[13] Donne's poems never reach this climax; Donne is intent on articulating his own relationship to God, not on emptying himself of language to reveal God. By interrupting ordinary syntactic patterns (hyperbaton) and transposing parts of speech (anthimeria), Hopkins eliminates semantic distinctions between subject and object, thereby subordinating content to sound and image. Because all subjects and objects are rooted in Christ and can be reduced to one Word, there is neither a semantic nor a grammatical hierarchy.

In seeking to reveal Christ in his poetry, Hopkins bases his belief in the tangibility of words on the original Word's translation into Christ on earth. Words are like elements that, if properly acted on, will grant grace and communion with God. Hopkins employs linguistic transubstantiation in the same way that Donne uses paradox: to reveal at bottom the similarity of the apparently opposed or separate substances. Transubstantiation (like metaphor), however, for Hopkins is finally tautological as all substance leads back to Christ. Through selving or "saking," Christ is already present in the elements of bread and wine before the Prayer of Consecration. By "marking," "catching," or "inscaping" these natural elements, Hopkins hopes to show how spiritual essence can manifest itself through its physical disguise. In a late journal entry he explains this method:

> The sensible thing so naturally and gracefully *uttering* the spiritual reason of its being . . . and the spring in place leading back the thoughts by its spring in time to its spring in eternity.[14]

Important to note in the journals and in the poetry is that physical accident (in Aristotelian terms) does not simply give way to spiritual substance. Rather, by a verbal trigger, the spiritual presence is drawn forth through its external form. The relation in the poems is not precisely transubstantial as the physical neither disappears nor wholly gives way to the spiritual. This collusion of sensible and spiritual constitutes Hopkins's definition of Real Presence. Like Donne, Hopkins was never able to deny the physical properties of nature or of his own body. He explains this emanation of things in secular terms as "saking":

> . . . the being a thing has outside itself, as a voice by its echo, a face by its reflection, a body by its shadow, a man by his name, fame, or memory, *and also* that in the thing by virtue of which especially it has this being abroad, and that is something distinctive, marked, specifically

or individually speaking, as for a voice and echo clearness. (*Letters to Bridges*, 83)

In his poetry Hopkins directs all his efforts toward inscaping Christ's presence or having Christ "sake" himself through language. This priestly ability to inscape, however, demands personal self-sacrifice. To inscape Christ, one must imitate him. This imitation involves, as J. F. Cotter notes, a process of *kenosis* and *pleroma,* an emptying of self and a filling of self. Such an action is based on the two-part eucharistic Mass where the communicant is asked to offer himself, soul and body, to be a "reasonable, holy and living sacrifice" to be filled with Christ. Cotter emphasizes the Mass as "the bridge and stem of stress between God and man, between man and his world." He later adds, "The Sacrament is not a static hiding of the godhead, but a dynamic action of self-giving, a circle and center . . . into which all contracts and which still fills all who partake of this body and blood."[15] Hopkins illustrates this dual process of self-sacrifice and self-fulfillment throughout his poetry on both semantic and syntactic levels. In his poetry up to the Terrible Sonnets of the 1880s, he emphasizes the *pleromic* or fulfilling moment of communion far more than does Donne who halts at self-sacrifice and penitence. Self-sacrifice (at least until the 1880s) typically leads to self-fulfillment in Hopkins, whereas the two are rarely united in Donne. Donne relies more heavily on the promise of communion and grace than on the achievement. This battle between his individual will and his God-turned will prevents Donne from making as thorough a self-sacrifice as Hopkins.[16]

Connecting *kenosis* and *pleroma* is stress—outstress (Christ as the "first outstress of God's power") and instress (God's finger touching man and man responding to the touch).[17] In his spiritual writings Hopkins describes this reciprocal process as evidence of the Incarnation:

For the forestall on God's part, in which the creature's correspondence is bound up, is a piece bodily taken out of the possible world, the "burl of being," of that creature and brought into this actual one, which is . . . one cleave of it; but the forestall on the creature's side, towards which of course God too plays his part, is in this actual world. (*Sermons*, 155)

Here "forestall" means a preview or a promise of something to be done. Without the fact of Christ's Incarnation as proof of the intersection of divine and human wills, one could not experience the sensual stress of one's relationship to God. Not accidentally,

Hopkins's poems are full of allusions to taste and touch, both senses demonstrating pressure or stress and both instrumental in the liturgy of the Mass.

It is possible to view *kenosis* as the outstress of Christ, man, and nature, or the "saking" that results in separation or extension. Instress as *pleroma* would then be the reception of this outstress. In turn, the reception would induce a *kenotic* impulse to return fullness to its original source. To sum up this tripartite process: First, God outstresses himself; second, one receives this outstress as a bolt of lightning or electric finger of instress; third, one says "yes" to this touch. This "yes" responds to God's pressure by effecting the surrender of the self to God. In the moment of self-giving, all senses are receptive, and one is able to inscape presence in a way previously denied him. Finally, the ability to inscape derives from a prior reception and acknowledgment of grace. Grace opens a person to further visitations of instress and triggers the ability to inscape. Viewed in this light, much of Hopkins's poetry can be seen as an attempt to disclose the one revelatory Word in the object and return it to God. Such an effort is the antithesis of the poetic tendency to name and by naming to appropriate. By depriving language of its exclusively referential properties, Hopkins seeks to revive a presence—both spiritual and material—that has been obscured by the rhetoric of traditional poetic or "Parnassian" language.[18] In effect, he opens language to presence by making it receptive to new forms and combinations. A word or phrase is like a creature or a spring "uttering" the spiritual principle of its being. By touching, instressing the Word, the poet allows it to disclose a presence that the reader must then inscape.

Consequently, Hopkins crafts a poem as a kind of Mass in which all words work to voice the one Word—Christ. The successful poem enacts the eucharistic process and encourages the reader to sacrifice logic to faith. The moment of this sacrifice is the culmination of real presence in the reader. Grace is the *pleromic* reward. The rhetorical and syntactic devices reinforce this movement instead of reducing it to an impossible linearity. The reader is dominated by the words and rhythm instead of trying to dominate them. Alliteration, onomatopoeia, and hyperbaton force the reader to suspend logical and linear thinking, and to participate directly in the sound patterns. The sound leads to an altered understanding of the words.

One can trace this process of *kenosis* and *pleroma* in the preconversion poems of 1865, "Barnfloor and Winepress," "Easter Communion," and "The Half-way House." Still, all three are more linear and referential than the later *Deutschland* or the Terrible Sonnets. The poems thematically *refer to* instead of *enact* the eucharistic sacrament. Syntax is not yet irrevocably disrupted; the sound does not encroach on the sense. Instead, a narrative operates chronologically, ending with an invitation to the reader to partake in the eucharistic meal. As in Donne's poems, the real presence is promised or stated, not evoked. In these early poems, the doubling devices of speech—compression, compounding, hyperbaton—are largely absent. The rhyme schemes are regular and confined to iambic pentameter and iambic tetrameter.

Nevertheless, in these poems Hopkins stresses the centrality of eucharistic Real Presence and charts routes toward achieving it. Although the poems rely on traditional theological metaphors, Hopkins begins to expose his belief in the tautology of metaphor. In "Barnfloor and Winepress" transubstantiation appears to be the cornerstone on which the entire poem rises. The Passion is depicted in homely harvest imagery: Christ is equated with wheat—ground, then made into bread. Here Hopkins begins to evince his dependency on nature's literal ability to body forth Christ. Here metaphor in its traditional distinction between tenor and vehicle collapses.

In the first two stanzas, the reader is led *metaphorically* through the harvest to the communion altar. At this point metaphor gives way to a doubled presence—the natural harvest and the supernatural Passion simultaneously enacted. Incorporated within the harvest imagery of the first stanza is the Passion narrative. Here Hopkins achieves real presence by using such double-edged words as "first-fruits," "sheaved," and "scourged" to elicit images of Christ's torture as well as of natural harvest. Though ostensibly couched beneath the harvest allusions, the Passion subsumes them and is revealed through them in the Eucharist. In the last two briefer stanzas, the reader is introduced to the aftereffects of grace and redemption. The "riv'n Vine" becomes a Tree connecting heaven and earth, and sheltering man with its branches. The movement, as in "Easter Communion" and "The Half-way House," is inward toward shelter, away from natural elements.

"Barnfloor and Winepress" is both a declaration of and an invitation to communion. In addition, it deals with the kenotic self-surrender of the faithful and their subsequent transformation from harvesters to seedlings, both a backward growth and a new beginning. Thematically and imagistically the poem demonstrates what Hopkins was later to perform syntactically. The human being is condensed into a seed "sheaved . . . in His sheaf, / When He has made us bear His leaf."[19] The entire poem evinces Hopkins's concept of "saking" as the natural elements reveal their spiritual core—Christ—and as the harvesting process reveals the Passion. Hopkins conveys his eucharistic theology to show how Christ selves Himself. The harvest and planting images uncover a spiritual meaning, but they never lose their physicality. The communicant is not transported to a heavenly, bodiless realm; he is fused with Christ's body, "grafted on His wood" (l.33).

This grafting image is a further extension of Real Presence for Hopkins: Not only is Christ physically present in the elements of bread and wine, but he also re-presents himself in man during communion. In this consubstantial vision, there is no distinction between the substance of Christ and the accidents of bread and wine found in the Roman Catholic version of the consecrated elements. The scourging of the wheat to make flour translates into Christ's body being first tortured, then crucified. The wine is synonymous with Christ's blood:

> For us by Calvary's distress
> The wine was racked from the press;
> Now in our altar vessels stored
> Is the sweet Vintage of our Lord.
>
> (ll.17–20)

Christ is the vine that provides wine for "dry plots" of sinful Christians; the branches of the vine are his limbs stretched on the cross. Natural and spiritual mingle in equal relation. Neither is a metaphor for the other; both are physically present.

The person acquires a new presence as well. As Hopkins explains to Bridges, "Christ is in every sense God and in every sense man, and the interest is in the locked and inseparable combination or rather it is in the person in whom the combination has its place" (*Letters to Bridges,* 188). In no sense then is Christ metaphorical, and in no sense does Hopkins's poetry, based on this inseparable combination, employ the severing device of metaphor. What seems to be metaphor is actually figural symbol; the word and its referent are literally connected by Christ.

The final stanza moves beyond this equation of natural and spiritual to grant momentary preference to the latter before returning again to the word "wood." By the last word in the last line, however, the balance has been struck again:

> The field where He has planted us
> Shall shake her fruit as Libanus,

> When He hás sheaved us in His sheaf,
> When He has made us bear His leaf.—
> We scarcely call that banquet food,
> But even our Saviour's and our blood,
> We are so grafted on His wood.

(ll.27-32)

The earthly food of bread and wine has *almost* been eclipsed by the spiritual body and blood of Christ. In the communicant's acceptance of Real Presence, Christ and communicant are united in *almost* mutual sacrifice: the communicant has been grafted by Christ onto the wood that is both the cross and Christ's body. This process is in keeping with both Anglican and Roman Catholic belief in the Eucharist as part sacrifice, part thanksgiving. The movement from Christ "sheaved in cruel bands" in the first stanza to the communicant sheaved in Christ's sheaf in the final stanza reinforces the eucharistic movement from sacrifice to thanksgiving.

The poem is far less personal than the later *Deutschland* or even than "The Half-way House." The "Thou" of the first line is invited to join in the "harvest" of the faithful group of communicants. Real Presence is seen as a communal endeavor in which all believers can participate, not as an individual meeting of one person with Christ. The pervasive confessional element in the *Deutschland* is missing here. Hopkins still belongs to the majority, to the Anglican Church.[20]

"Easter Communion" deals more orthodoxically with the theme of sacrifice or kenotic self-punishment as a prerequisite for the fulfilling grace of communion. The penance of "sackcloth and frieze / And the ever-fretting shirt of punishment" is exchanged for "myrrhy-threaded golden folds of ease" (ll.11–12). Here Hopkins begins to employ compounds and to pile up verbal adjectives to reinforce the theme of sacrifice and fulfillment. The words themselves—"rough-scored," "ever-fretting," "myrrhy-threaded," "scarce-sheathed"—enact this dual process through the strain of the hyphen that both separates and connects them.[21] Likewise, they act as doubling devices; the first word of the compound fulfills the second, and both together qualify and fulfill the following noun. In addition, the participles recall action stilled to service nouns; the nouns act as receptacles for the preceding compounds. In this syntactical and grammatical progression, Hopkins forces language toward a kind of communion that supports the semantic call to communion.

Hopkins also uses the colon in "Easter Communion" as a kenotic device. The first line—"Pure fasted faces draw unto this feast:"—receives its fulfillment in the next eleven lines. These lines promise more than a compensatory reward for penance: "God shall o'er-brim the measures you have spent / With oil of gladness" (ll.9–10). Likewise, the next-to-the-last line briefly recapitulates the pattern of the first twelve with its kenotic statement, "Your scarce-sheathed bones are weary of being bent," and its pleromic promise, "Lo, God shall strengthen all the feeble knees" (ll.13–14). Furthermore, a slight confusion between the declarative and imperative moods in the first line ("draw") makes what follows both a promise and a command, and adds an authority that promise alone would lack.

On a grammatical level, the compounds of "Easter Communion" serve to stress the nouns that follow, and each word still possesses its own stress mark. Hopkins departs from iambic pentameter, though he still confines himself to the sonnet form. Even at this level, the sonnet acts like a container whose recalcitrant meter threatens to overflow its brim. The tension between the two— container and contained—once more demonstrates not only the reciprocity of the *kenotic-pleromic* process but also serves as an apt emblem for the chalice and wine of Holy Communion. Although less vividly exuberant than "Barnfloor and Winepress," "Easter Communion" represents a subtle linguistic advance. It remains for the later poems to bring sound and sense closer together.

"The Half-way House," unlike the two preceding poems, does not experiment with much semantic or linguistic doubling to create presence. Although it personalizes the quest for Real Presence, like "Barnfloor and Winepress," it fails to effect an analogous poetic real presence. Here the principal doubling device is Hopkins's repetition of "Love" eleven times in three stanzas. The word "catch" in the first stanza indicates the goal of the final stanza—the speaker is bid to "catch" or instress Christ "ere the drop of day" (l.2). The drop of day signifies death before which the speaker must "o'ertake Thee at once and under heaven" (l.11). In other words, he must participate in Holy Communion on earth as a preparation for encountering Christ in heaven.

Stanza 2 hints at the mandatory kenotic self-surrender before communion:

> My national old Egyptian reed gave way;
> I took of vine a cross-barred rod or rood.
> Then next I hungered: Love when here, they say,
> Or once or never took Love's proper food;

But I must yield the chase, or rest and eat.—
Peace and food cheered me where four rough ways meet.

(ll.7–12)

The problem is how to "catch" Christ on earth. Images of punishment—"cross-barred rod or rood"—lead here to emptiness, hunger. The speaker realizes that, unlike Christ, he needs continual sustenance to survive, to pursue the chase or the inscaping of Christ.

The last stanza depicts the paradox of the would-be communicant. Like the persona of "Goodfriday," the speaker realizes his reliance on the visible and tangible Christ to cement his faith. Hopkins has transferred the proper noun Love or Christ to the verb "love," a technique increasingly common in his later poems. Such a transformation fuses the subject with the reciprocal action demanded by that subject. The persona learns by the end of the poem how he must respond. At first he begs Christ to "come down to me if Thy name be Love" (1.6). By the second stanza he realizes the inadequacy of this request and at the same time prepares to relinquish his "national old Egyptian reed" for a "vine . . . cross-barred rod or rood."[22] This new stick is both a support and a cross; it entails the self-sacrifice exemplified and demanded by Christ. The poem ends with what the persona calls a "paradox" but what in Roman Catholic terms would not be a paradox:

Here yet my paradox: Love, when all is given,
To see Thee I must see Thee, to love, love;
I must o'ertake Three at once and under heaven
If I shall overtake Thee at last above.
You have your wish; enter these walls, one said:
He is with you in the breaking of the bread.

(ll.13–18)

Read as the central tenet of the Roman Catholic Mass—transubstantiation—these lines call for the necessity of realizing Christ physically beneath the accidents of bread and wine—"To *see* Thee I must *see* Thee" (italics added). This realization on the poet's part is at once reinforced by someone (Newman?) already within the new faith. The adviser bids the poet enter the new church and requests him to participate in the Mass. Read eucharistically, the final line—"He is with you in the breaking of the bread"—signifies the actual presence of Christ in the consecrated elements. The poet must leave the "half-way house" of the *Via Media*—the Anglican Church—to wed himself physically and spiritually to Christ in Roman Catholicism.

In his *Apologia Pro Vita Sua* published in 1864, one year before Hopkins wrote these two poems and two years before Hopkins converted to Roman Catholicism, Newman concludes, "there are but two alternatives, the way to Rome, and the way to Atheism: Anglicism is the halfway house on the one side, and Liberalism is the halfway house on the other."[23] Although Hopkins tries to tie the two religions together through the doctrine of Real Presence, his poetry demonstrates his need for a more concrete definition of Real Presence than the Anglican religion could offer him. Accordingly, he, like Newman, found this definition in the doctrine of transubstantiation. As Newman notes in his defense of transubstantiation: "The Catholic doctrine leaves phenomena alone. It does not say that the phenomena go; on the contrary, it says that they remain; nor does it say that the same phenomena are in several places at once. It deals with what no one on earth knows any thing about, the material substances themselves."[24]

In "Barnfloor and Winepress," "The Half-way House," and "Easter Communion," Hopkins stresses the centrality of Real Presence in the Eucharist and charts routes toward achieving it. With the possible exception of "Easter Communion," however, these poems do not precisely mime the eucharistic ceremony. One has a sense of words searching for fulfillment instead of enacting it. Semantic and syntactic levels are not yet in perfect concert. Such enactment falls to *The Wreck of the Deutschland,* written expressly to praise God and to witness His actual presence in poetry.

Although most critics concur that the *Deutschland's* foundation rests firmly on Hopkins's Christology, they quibble as to the poet's means of manifesting this foundation. Central to this dispute is the problem of metaphor, variously defined by such Jesuit critics as Robert Boyle and J. F. Cotter as a sort of symbol or "existential metaphor" to be distinguished from simile or analogy. In a crucial discussion of metaphor in Hopkins, Boyle submits secular definitions to a Catholic reinterpretation:

> The Catholic view does not picture an analogy between Christ and the Christian in the same way that other views do, as a simile rather than an existential metaphor. The Catholic view does picture a literal union, so that the Christian and Christ are fused in one being . . . sharing one life. The Incarnation itself can be viewed . . . as an existential metaphor, in which the Divine Word joins with a human nature in the perfect personal union of one divine act of existence. Again, the union of Christ with His member can be viewed analogously as an existential metaphor in which the God-Man shares with a human being His divine life, so that in a true and literal sense that human being, while remaining himself,

becomes Christ. The mind of a Catholic poet, then, which is saturated with this view and most deeply motivated by it, inclines most naturally toward that metaphor which expresses the union of knowledge and love between the mind itself and some real object outside the mind. This is all the more true because for such a mind every object speaks and reflects the Word.[25]

Boyle views "existential metaphor" as the projection or *out*-stressing of the mind toward another object and the consequent fusion of mind and object in a moment of real presence. What Boyle seems to slight, however, is Hopkins's tendency to emphasize in his poems sacramental manifestation over intellectual knowledge of one substance. Knowledge is dependent (as "The Half-way House" indicates) on the external sacrament as a guide. Instead of searching for metaphors to portray such knowledge, Hopkins allows knowledge to spring from the mystical equation of two separate substances. For "existential metaphor," Boyle might have substituted *mystical metaphor* or *mysterious metaphor* in the strictly Catholic way that Hopkins defines mystery:

Christ is in every sense God and in every sense man, and the interest is in the locked and inseparable combination, or rather it is in the person in whom the combination has its place. . . . Therefore we speak of the events of Christ's life as the mystery of the nativity, the mystery of the Crucifixion and so on of a host; the mystery being always the same, that the child in the manger is God, the culprit on the gallows God, and so on. (*Letters to Bridges*, 188)

When intellect appears to reign over sacramental evidence as in the Terrible Sonnets, Hopkins does revert to metaphor that is more akin to self-projection than to fusion. In the *Deutschland*, however, as he confesses to Bridges, he is concerned with the *literal*, not the *figurative:* "what refers to myself in the poem is all strictly and literally true and did all occur; nothing is added for poetical padding" (*Letters to Bridges*, 47).

Although it departs somewhat from Boyle's definition of metaphor, Hillis Miller's earlier stance in *The Disappearance of God* (1963) also regards metaphor as an appropriation of something outside the self instead of a revelation of hidden identity:

For him [Hopkins] language originates in a kind of inner pantomime, in fundamental movements of the body and the mind by which we take possession of the world through imitating it in ourselves. Words are the dynamic internalization of the world.[26]

Although he admits that, for Hopkins, all things emanate from Christ, Miller persists in maintaining a clear separation between nature and Christ. Here he allows for the possibility of rhyming or chiming, but not for indwelling or fusion. He concedes that "He [Christ] is the ultimate guarantee for the validity of metaphor. It is proper to say that one thing is like another only because all things are like Christ."[27] *Likeness* for Hopkins is insufficient, however. Speaking of grace in his spiritual writings he notes, "It is as if a man said: That is Christ playing at me and me playing at Christ, only that is no play but truth; That is Christ *being me* and me being Christ" (*Sermons*, 154). For Hopkins, metaphor is a kind of play that *imitates* but does not *produce* real presence. It emphasizes difference, not identity, through its separation of literal and figurative levels. Hopkins denies the distinction between the two and insists on the literal as the only ground of being.[28]

Miller comes closer than many critics to urging the importance of the Christological ground of Hopkins's poetry and connecting that ground to language.[29] Still, the problem of metaphor's inability to create real presence persists. To inscape real presence in nature, the poet must mark and uncover, not assert and appropriate. Hopkins harps in his journals on the difficulty of this process. In one particular entry, his distinction between the *kenosis* of inscape and the *pleroma* of instress becomes clear: "I saw the inscape though freshly, as if my eye were still growing, though with a companion the eye and the ear are for the most part shut and instress cannot come" (*Journals*, 228). In other words, the ability to inscape presence requires an emptying of selfhood, a sort of negative capability that allows the perceiver to be touched by God. Instress is the God-given force that triggers the capacity to perceive structure and form, to find unity in discord. Without reception of instress, the mind cannot inscape the distinctive qualities that announce an object's individuality. The object remains impenetrable. In eucharistic terms, without God's instress, one would be unable to inscape Christ's presence beneath the elements of bread and wine. Real Presence would collapse to inference or "notional assent."

Also eschewing traditional metaphor in Hopkins's poetry, Jerome Bump argues for the influence of medieval vertical typology as opposed to the horizontal analogy of Renaissance philosophy. According to Bump, Hopkins's emphasis on the Incarnation lends the poetry a pattern of ascent-descent. This pattern slices through chronological wording and adds a further dimension to time. Speaking of "Rosa Mystica" but also tracing a process in the later poems, Bump states:

the operative concept of metaphor is reversed, from an allegorical trope of transference in which the unknown is described in terms of the known to a sacramental symbol of convergence modelled on the Incarnation and the Eucharist in which the unknown meets and mixes with the known.[30]

This assessment coincides with Hopkins's insistence on the literalness of the eucharistic Real Presence as well as his reverence for mystery. Unknown fuses with known in a mystical union as the communicant is fed with the mystical body of Christ. Although metaphor ultimately tries to clarify and explain, sacramental symbols evoke a presence that explanation would make implausible. As James Milroy explains, "Language, like nature, is governed by 'laws' which are not imposed by man, but are God-given and therefore inherent in the phenomena—to be 'discovered' and revealed rather than suppressed, controlled or distorted by rules imposed from outside."[31]

Although Hopkins is clearly a devotional poet before his conversion in 1866, he becomes a sacramental poet by the time he writes *The Wreck of the Deutschland* in 1877.[32] Unlike the preconversion poems, the *Deutschland* is an explicit reenactment of Hopkins's own conversion as well as a poetic Mass offered to Robert Bridges and the British public. Unlike Donne's "Goodfriday" and "Hymne to God My God," the *Deutschland* presents the acheivement of what Hopkins calls "the after use of the uplifting grace," in which God elevates man from pitch to pitch after He has instressed the affective will (*Sermons*, 149, 156). To inscape this process, Hopkins employs both semantic and syntactical doubling devices to reveal the intersection of man and God on earth. On the most general level, the ode mixes both public and private sacramental language of the Mass, punctuating linear narrative with abrupt revelations of personal communion. As Robert Boyle explains, the poem is designed to call its readers to the eucharistic sacrifice

effected on Calvary . . . [which] is extended throughout time and space in the Mass, where the Host, the same Victim, still offers Himself and His flock with Him. Hopkins joins the host on the altar in Part 1 and thereafter comprehends the mystery of which St. Paul constantly speaks, of Christ present in the universe.[33]

In a more recent eucharistic reading of the *Deutschland*, James Cowles equates Hopkins's personal conversion with eucharistic transformation and denies that either is merely metaphorical:

. . . this transformation must be understood, not metaphorically, but as it were eucharistically. According to Catholic teaching, the bread is not merely like the Body of Christ. Rather, it *is* the Body of Christ. The transformation of the bread to the Body is not a transformation merely of word, but of substance. By portraying his own union with Christ in eucharistic terms, Hopkins implies that this is the nature of his own transformation. His conversion to Catholicism was not merely an intellectual exercise.[34]

Cowles acknowledges the importance of self-sacrifice as a prerequisite for eucharistic transformation, though he stresses this sacrifice more heavily in part 2 with reference to the dying nun than in part 1.

To frame his narrative and to establish his priestly authority, Hopkins first catapults the reader into a personal experience of grace.[35] Faith precedes explanation and theological documentation. Such a method allows Hopkins first to evoke God's presence by direct private invocation ("Thou mastering me / God! giver of breath and bread" [ll.1–2]), and later to lead through narrative to public prayer. The thrust of the poem is outward toward the public's need for grace, not inward as in the earlier eucharistic poems.

Believing, like his Tractarian predecessors, that the sacrament is an extension of the Incarnation, Hopkins tries to reveal a literal incarnation—the Word made flesh—in his poem.[36] As Miller affirms, Christ is the central principle of this attempt: "The *Incarnate God,* mediator between heaven and earth, possessor of both a divine and human nature, is the model for the double nature of all created things."[37] Hopkins tries to expose this doubly physical and spiritual nature in his syntax as well as in his choice of words and images. Poetical grammar reinforces dogmatic theology.

According to the Roman Catholic Missal, the Prayer of Consecration acts as the transubstantiating agent. It is the voice of God speaking through the priest who has become a vehicle for the process. As he speaks, the priest reenacts the words and actions of Christ at the Last Supper, consecrating the bread and saying, "For this is My Body," and then consecrating the wine, saying, "For this is the chalice of My Blood, of the new and eternal covenant: the mystery of faith; which shall be shed for you and for many unto the forgiveness of sins."[38] In the *Deutschland* Hopkins must first establish his identity as a priest able to consecrate elements (here the words of the poem) to offer the poem as a sacrament to the British people.

Hopkins internalizes the external facts of the wreck of *The*

Deutschland into a revelation of his own personal conversion in
part 1. In part 2 he recounts his second conversion of "after-
gracing." In offering the poem as a sacrament to the British people,
Hopkins follows the *kenotic-pleromic* process of the Mass. Both
parts 1 and 2 stress self-sacrifice as a prerequisite for identification
with Christ. Even finding the right words to reveal the process
involves sacrifice. The poet must temporarily surrender his desire
to be single-eyed and single-voiced like the nun who

> Read the unshapeable shock night
> 　　And knew the who and the why;
> Wording it how but by him that present and past,
> Heaven and earth are word of, worded by?
>
> 　　　　　　　　　　　　　　　　　　(ll.227–30)

to communicate Christ's presence through language to the reader.
This surrender involves a central problem for the religious poet: the
tension between poetic abundance and religious asceticism.
Throughout the *Deutschland* this tension is marked by hyphens,
ellipses, exclamations, hyperbaton, and synesthesia. These ruptures evince the actual stress of the two-part eucharistic process.
Both the poet and his language must first be shipwrecked by God's
stress ("And the midriff astrain with leaning of, laced with fire of
stress" [1.16]) before they can "say yes" to Christ's presence.

Miming the eucharistic liturgy, stanza 1 announces the consecration and offering in line 2: "God! giver of breath and bread."
Breath is God's inspiration of grace and life that man answers by
aspiring to higher pitches of grace. At the same time, it is the poet's
request for inspiration that here is tantamount to a request for
grace. Bread alludes to Christ (bread of life), his Incarnation in the
world, and subsequently to his bodily presence in the Eucharist.
The Christological basis of the poem allows Hopkins rein to express
spiritual conversion in physical terms. Like Donne in "Batter my
Heart," Hopkins uses violent imagery to wrest the reader away
from mere spectatorship to active participation:

> 　　　　　I did say yes
> 　　　　O at lightning and lashed rod;
> Thou heardst me truer than tongue confess
> 　　　Thy terror, O Christ, O God;
> Thou knowest the walls, altar and hour and night:
> The swoon of a heart that the sweep and the hurl of thee
> 　　　　　　　　　　　　　　　　　　trod
> 　　Hard down with a horror of height:

And the midriff astrain with leaning of, laced with fire of
stress.

(ll.9–16)

Unlike the situation in "Batter my Heart" or "Goodfriday," grace
has already been granted; it is being reenacted, instressed this time
in words. As in the Eucharist, the process is one of *kenosis* and
pleroma: instress from God demands a corresponding sacrifice of
the individual's heart. As in "Barnfloor and Winepress," Hopkins
again fuses natural and spiritual through figural language. He describes his personal conversion in terms of stormy sea imagery,
inscaping his spiritual plight through the natural elements. Such a
double description places him in a sacramental relation to the
world. The storm of conversion is figured forth in the external
storm; poet and nature are linked with each other through their
mutual connection with Christ.

Stanza 3 depicts the poet as a bird (type of Christ) or an angel
who momentarily hesitates, then surrenders itself in communion
with Christ. The hyperbaton of the third line—"where, where was
a, where was a place?"—mimes the moment of panic and hesitation
before the convert answers God's instress with his own *kenotic*
aspiration: "I whirled out wings that spell / And fled with a fling of
the heart to the heart of the Host" (ll.20–21). The language precisely reenacts the moment of eucharistic communion as well as the
culmination of conversion. Alliteration forces the line to race toward the final long-voweled "Host." "Host" assumes a double
nature—that of God welcoming the convert and Christ's body in the
Eucharist. Repetition of "heart" illustrates the process of sacrifice
and fulfillment in which the convert-communicant must surrender
his heart to be filled with Christ's heart. After this first surrender
and reception of grace, he is ready for God's successive elevations
from "one cleave of being to another and to a vital act in Christ . . .
truly God's finger touching the very vein of personality, which
nothing else can reach and man can respond to by no play whatever,
by bare acknowledgment only, the counterstress which God alone
can feel . . . the aspiration in answer to his inspiration" (*Sermons*,
158). Stanza 3 concludes with the process of the "after use of
uplifting grace":

> My heart, but you were dovewinged, I can tell,
>   Carrier-witted, I am bold to boast,
> To flash from the flame to the flame then, tower from the
>   grace to the grace.

(ll.22–24)

Though the language appears to reduce past action to telling and boasting, the conflation of bird and heart imagery allows the poet to make an abstract event concretely present. The passage refers to the "Eucharistic Dove," a "hollow receptacle in the shape of a dove to contain the Blessed Sacrament."[39] The compound "dove-winged" compresses Hopkins's heart into the eucharistic chalice and perfectly illustrates the achievement of Real Presence.

By stanza 4, God's finger becomes Christ's presence in the poet, roping him with "a vein / Of the gospel proffer, a pressure, a principle, Christ's gift" (ll.31–32). Throughout the poem, heart and vein imagery connect human beings literally to Christ and also recall the eucharistic sacrifice in which Christ's blood is given to the communicants. For Hopkins, this vein echoes Donne's "conduit of grace"; both poets acknowledge this possibility of Real Presence in man, although Donne is less sure of its constant existence.

In stanza 5, Hopkins can finally offer thanks for the reception of grace and is able to acknowledge his role as a priest who must labor to reveal Christ to himself and to his congregation: "Since, tho' he is under the world's splendour and wonder, / His mystery must be instressed, stressed; / For I greet him the days I meet him, and bless when I understand" (ll.34–36). Even though in Hopkins's theology Christ is immanent in nature, the priest, religious poet, or sacramentalist must work to instress him (to realize his presence), then stress that presence to others. Having now received grace, Hopkins is free to direct his *arbitrium* or elective will toward God. God has become the sole object of the field of choice.

Speaking in his spiritual writings of the difference between the first grace, the "instressing of the affective will," and the second, the direction of the *arbitrium*, Hopkins states:

> The first is a change worked by God of something in man; the second an exchange of one whole for another whole, as they say in the mystery of Transubstantiation, a conversion of a whole substance into another whole substance, but here is not a question of substance; it is a lifting him from one self to another self, which is a most marvelous display of divine power. (*Sermons*, 151)

The first three stanzas of the *Deutschland* present the "instressing of the affective will"; the rest of part 1 deals with the after-gracing of the elective will. Hopkins probes the main element of this after-gracing (stress) throughout time from Christ's "dense and . . . driven Passion" (l.53) to the conversions of Paul and Augustine. Here Hopkins labors to show that the ability to discover and commune with Christ does not lie in an eschatological belief in judgment or resurrection nor in the sudden descent of "grace to repent." Rather "it rides time like riding a river / (And here the faithful waver, the faithless fable and miss)" (ll.47–48). In other words, the entire earth is sacramental—filled with Real Presence— if, as Hopkins frequently laments, people only had eyes to perceive it.

Stanzas 7 and 8, separated only by a comma, condense the stress of Christ's Passion and its instressing in the Eucharist to reinforce the timelessness of grace and Real Presence. For Hopkins, Real Presence is not confined to the moment after consecration. It is figural, extending throughout the ceremony and embedded in man. He allows stanza 7 to act as a conduit to stanza 8, by equating the discharge of Christ's Passion with a river that flows throughout history:

> Thence the discharge of it, there its swelling to be,
>   Though felt before, though in high flood yet—
> What none would have known of it, only the heart, being hard at bay,
>
> 8
>   Is out with it! Oh,
>   We lash with the best or worst
>   Word last! How a lush-kept plush-capped sloe
>   Will, mouthed to flesh-bursh,
> Gush!—flush the man, the being with it, sour or sweet,
>   Brim, in a flash, full!—Hither then, last or first,
>   To hero of Calvary, Christ's feet—
> Never ask if meaning it, wanting it, warned of it—men go.
>
> (ll. 54–64)

The river suddenly gives way to a "plush-capped sloe" to depict the moment of communion, "flesh-burst." Then, after flushing the communicant, it moves outward again toward Christ's Passion in a constant reminder of the sacrifice implicit in Holy Communion. Hopkins accurately portrays his belief in spiritual penetration (Incarnation) and its emanation throughout human history. The run-on lines, the alliteration and assonance, add momentum to the swelling of grace. Choice of the word "sloe," literally fruit of the blackthorn, cleverly acts as a doubling or tripling device that unites nature, Christ's Passion (crown of thorns), and the person who eats the consecrated fruit. It collapses the crucifixion into communion and resurrection and thus reinforces the twofold nature of the Mass as sacrifice and thanksgiving.

These two stanzas evince nearly all of the doubling devices—
condensation, compounding, hyperbaton, anthimeria—Hopkins
employs to create a poetic real presence that will reveal the Real
Presence of Christ. The two compounds used to describe the sloe—
"lush-kept plush-capped"—assert through assonance and
onomatopoeia the richness of the fruit that, like the eucharistic
bread and wine, purges or "flushes" the communicant. The ambiguous compound "flesh-burst" suggests both the burst body of the
Host and also the verb "burst." Specifically, the compound enacts
the moment of Holy Communion when the wafer, dipped in wine,
touches the tongue, then moves to realize Christ's presence in the
recipient. It also recalls the Crucifixion in which Christ's flesh was
stretched and finally burst on the cross. Literally, Christ's flesh
must burst or be broken for his spiritual presence to burst in on the
communicant. In addition, "flesh-burst" momentarily hyphenates
the communicant and Christ as one flesh merges with another. The
hyperbaton, "Brim, in a flash, full," by separating "brim" and
"full," emphasizes the rapidity with which the communicant receives and is recharged by Christ's body and blood. Secondarily, it
alludes to the chalice of Holy Communion, the brim of which
touches the lips. Logical distinctions—"best or worst," "sour or
sweet," "last or first"—are also leveled or condensed into one
central action. Hopkins makes the process of communion inevitable. Unlike Donne, he focuses much less on precommunion penitence; he chooses instead to emphasize the actual moment of
communion.

The two stanzas combine public and private modes, changing
from third-person singular—Christ—to the general negative *none*
to the personal plural *we*. At the moment of communion Hopkins
reverts to man, then later shifts to men. Such a movement reinforces the changes in viewpoint in the actual eucharistic ceremony
from a narrative recalling Christ's words and actions at the Last
Supper to a collective address to the congregation, then inward to a
singular moment of communion, and outward to a collective
thanksgiving. Finally, stanza 8 is packed with various types of
sentences—interjection, exclamation, command, declarative statement. Such sentence variety speeds up the pace and also breaks
normally linear narrative. Particularly the hyperbaton and zeugma
of the last line with its switch to imperative voice ("Never ask if
meaning it, wanting it, warned of it—men go") and the parallel
constructions lend a kind of urgency and presence to the end of the
stanza that culminates in the active "go," the "doing agree" of
man's acceptance of grace. Here Hopkins has made linguistic com-

munion perfectly congruous with eucharistic communion. He has attempted to prove his theory of language—that it is ultimately incarnational and therefore shot through with divine presence.

This insistent linguistic presence has been noted by several critics, the most extreme among them Sprinker and Korg, both of whom adopt a Saussurean distinction between *langue* and *parole*. They see Hopkins's poetry and specifically the *Deutschland* as an effort to detach words from their referents, in effect, to debunk Aristotle's mimetic theory of art.[40] Although the *Deutschland* does wrench words from their traditional order, it actually reinforces the reference to a sacramental world. What Sprinker's and Korg's analyses ignore is Hopkins's incarnational theory of language. They see the language of the poem recreating a texture or presence wholly apart from its semantic value. In this, they deny any possibility of real presence in Hopkins's terms—a real presence created not by the gap between semantic and syntactical realms, but by the collusion of syntax and semantics to form something extraordinary, revelatory.[41]

What gives the lie to these postmodernist theses regarding Hopkins is their denial of any ground of being, specifically that of Christ as the promulgator of language. Granted, Hopkins's thickly textured, often agrammatical poetry intentionally ruptures traditional views of language, but for opposite reasons. Like Donne, Hopkins views language as embodying and revealing, not referring to, spirit. Instead of resorting to purely nonreferential language in reaction to increasingly relative meanings in Victorian England, Hopkins tries to rejoin words and spirit, and return them to the original sanctity of the Word. Poetry reaches back to the Logos as its origin while instancing the referential variety of language on earth.

More compromising in their discussions of Hopkins's language are Hillis Miller and Paul Mariani. Although they tend to see Hopkins's efforts at creating real presence in terms of a dialectic instead of an emanation or fusion, they nevertheless try to pinpoint connections between language and meaning. They base their opinions on an anti-incarnational theory, however. Miller sees an irrevocable tension between the all-encompassing unity of the Logos and the hopeless multiplicity of language. He argues, "There is no masterword for the Word, only metaphors of it, for all words are metaphors, displaced from their proper reference by a primal bifurcation."[42] Mariani views the poem as a battle between "lexical plenitude" and "lexical spareness" that "reflects Hopkins'[s] consciously failing attempts to utter what can, finally, only be imperfectly uttered no matter how rich the verbal lode one has at one's command."[43]

Critics have borrowed a final dialectical interpretation from Hopkins's terms "overthought" and "underthought" coined in a letter to his friend Baillie. Speaking of Greek tragic poets Hopkins says:

> there are . . . two strains of thought running together and like counter-pointed; the overthrought that which everybody, editors, see . . . and which might for instance be abridged or paraphrased . . . the other, the underthought, conveyed chiefly in the choice of metaphors . . . used and often only half realized by the poet himself, not necessarily having any connection with the subject in hand but usually having a connection and suggested by some circumstance of the scene or of the story. (*Further Letters*, 106)

Trying to adapt these terms to his discussion of the *Deutschland*, Miller states:

> If the overthought of "The Wreck of the Deutschland" is the story of the tall nun's salvation and its musical echo both before and after by the poet's parallel experience of grace, the underthought of the poem is a constant covert attention to the problems of language. This linguistic theme is in a subversive relation of counterpoint to the theological overthought.[44]

Insisting on the subversive relationship between poetic language and theological dogma, Miller does not observe that the struggle is rather one of the poet's imperfect pitch, his search for perfect conformity to Christ. Such conformity would reduce language to one Word and thus preclude the poetic struggle to discover and speak that one Word. In fact, Hopkins's definition of counterpoint refutes Miller's contention of linguistic subversion. Hopkins introduces a counterpointed rhythm over an expected (and therefore heard) rhythm to *double* presence, not to see it in conflict with itself. In his author's preface to his later poems, he defines counterpoint as "the *mounting* of a new rhythm upon the old . . . two rhythms . . . in some manner running at once . . . something answerable to counterpoint in music, which is two or more strains of tune going on together" (*Poems*, 46). Overthought and underthought intertwine and complement each other; they do not destroy each other.[45]

What deconstructionist critics abjure is Hopkins's central concern: the intimate relation between theology and language. Far from illustrating that his "linguistic underthought undoes his Christian overthought,"[46] Hopkins's poetry accomplishes the reverse. The primal bifurcation between language and God caused by the Fall is according to Hopkins redeemed by Christ's sacrifice. That sacrifice offers one the opportunity to imitate the *kenotic* example of Christ and to receive grace and redemption through the Eucharist. On this sacrament, then, depends Hopkins's faith in his own ability to consecrate language. As he notes of Christ, "The Eucharistic Sacrifice was the great purpose of his life and his own chosen redemption" (*Sermons,* 162). The doctrine of redemption gives language a second chance to redeem itself. It heals the split between the word and its referent and restores both to a single presence. Believing in this healing, the poet must try to show how the meaning or spiritual essence "sakes itself" outward toward the external world. Stanzas 7 and 8 of the *Deutschland* illustrate the process of the incarnation and resurrection that language embodies. Consequently, the eucharistic moment in stanza 8 assumes a primary linguistic importance as does the second communion of the nun in stanza 28. In the former, Hopkins makes words mime the process of communion. Description becomes process; language creates linguistic presence through anthimeria, compounding, assonance, and rhyme.

After the narrative account of the *Deutschland* from stanzas 12 to 17, Hopkins interjects a stanza in which personal exclamations and questions express his attempt to enter into colloquy with his own heart and with the nun. Such colloquy would teach him how to word faith and make language create presence. The stanza moves from third person to second as it ambiguously addresses both the nun and the poet's own heart, of which the nun is now a part. She has become the authoress of the poet's language:

> Ah, touched in your bower of bone,
>   Are you! turned for an exquisite smart,
> Have you! make words break from me here all alone,
>   Do you!—mother of being in me, heart.
> O unteachably after evil, but uttering truth,
>   Why, tears! is it? tears; such a melting, a madrigal start!
>   Never-eldering revel and river of youth,
> What can it be, this glee? the good you have there of your own?
>
>   (ll.137–44)

Recreating the nun's experience and spurred on by her cry of " 'O Christ, Christ, come quickly,' " Hopkins realizes once again in her

the process of grace from the instress of God's touch to the "corrective, turning the will from one direction or pitting into another" to
the "elevating, which lifts the receiver from one cleave of being to
another and to a vital act in Christ" (*Sermons,* 158). Through the
simultaneity of grace he is united both with the nun and with his
own heart—"mother of being in me, heart"—and receives a doubled presence. Still, however, he cannot reach the meaning of her
cry. In stanza 25 he asks God to reinspire him, to "Breathe, arch
and original Breath" that he, the poet, may inscape precisely the
same vision as the nun.

After a difficult linguistic struggle in stanza 28, in which language
threatens to prove insufficient to vision, Hopkins recovers his ability to inscape grace. The fragments of the first four lines—"But how
shall I . . . make me room there: / Reach me a . . . Fancy, come
faster— / Strike you the sight of it? look at it loom there / Thing that
she . . . There then! The Master" (ll.217–20)—express the poet's
near-despair at his inability to inscape grace in words. Interrogative
and imperative fragments clash in the first four lines as if at once to
beg and to command language to ascend to vision. Here vision and
action momentarily overpower language. In stanza 28, the linguistic
debility expresses a temporary failure to depict a "limit-experience" in "limit-language." Because he still lacks the nun's "limit-
experience" of death, Hopkins is at odds with her vision until he
grasps its significance: "*Ipse,* the only one, Christ, King, Head
(1.221). Gradually Hopkins receives the words adequate to the
vision. In realizing Christ through words, he demonstrates the
interdependence of language and vision and their collaboration to
elicit Real Presence.[47] For the Roman Catholic poet recognition of
Christ's presence is not a literal theophany, but a revelation of how
the sacramental landscape unfolds Christ as its first principle.[48]

The nun is returning her word to Christ at her death: "Wording it
how but by him that present and past, / Heaven and earth are word
of, worded by?" (ll.229–30). Having received God's instress, having
emptied herself of all other words, the nun rises to respond to that
instress. In that moment Hopkins sees her as the Virgin Mary who,
having held the Word (Christ) inside herself, now gives it back in a
"heart-throe, birth of a brain, / Word, that heard and kept thee and
uttered thee outright" (ll.239–40).

Here Hopkins strikes at the foundation and process of his poetics
of real presence. If words are generated through the one Word of
Christ, all language that people speak links them literally to Christ.
The equation of Christ with the Word refutes the idea of language as
metaphor and upholds Hopkins's theory that separate words and

objects are internally linked to each other through their origin in Christ, the Logos. Most of all, it sanctions his belief in poetry's ability to evoke real presence. Language is charged with a sacramental reality that finds its most significant symbol in the Eucharist where the communicant actually digests the Word.

On the brink of death, the nun is about to enter the "limit-experience" that will link her permanently with Christ. She will have more than a "vein of the gospel proffer"; tuned to the highest pitch, she is proof of language's ability to compress itself back to the one Word from which it originated. Seen in this light, Hopkins's faltering in stanza 28, as well as his prolonged string of possessives to describe Christ in the final stanza, indicates his inability to utter the one Word alone, a Word that might be reserved for the soul at the extreme stress of death. In addition, the listing of epithets suggests the straining toward a higher pitch or cleave of being. Hopkins struggles through the nun's persona to voice the "yes" that transcends human speech. He pushes language to its breaking point, and in that ellipsis the revelatory language that expresses the poet's certain knowledge of God emerges.

For Hopkins, knowledge is inextricably linked to presence, or in Scotian terms, to being—*haecceitas*. Words extend this presence not just by *what* they say but by *how* they say it. Poetry, like the sacraments, is to be performed, not read silently. Throughout the *Deutschland*, Hopkins strives to activate language to express the actual process of instressing grace. This instressing reaches its highest pitch in both the eucharistic sacrament and in a human being's final "limit-experience" of death. Both events coerce the communicant to empty himself of all words, ideas, aspirations, save one: the striving toward God. How to develop a reciprocal language that can stress man's meeting with Christ is the supreme task of the poem.

The last three stanzas of the *Deutschland* deal with Christ's resurrection and the ability of the faithful (in this case, the nun) to "fetch" him "in the storm of his strides" (1.264). "Fetch," used previously to describe the nun with one "fetch" in her, is a keen example of Hopkins's condensation of many meanings into one word. Here, among the numerous definitions of "fetch" in the OED, the two that stand out are "to derive etymologically" and "to draw breath."[49] The nun's call reaches back to the origin of the incarnated Word. Stanza 25 asks for inspiration (breath) from God and from the "body of lovely Death"—Christ. Not only is Christ brought to the ship, but he is actually drawn into the body as a breath by "The-last-breath-penitent spirits" (1.262). As early as

"Easter Communion," Hopkins had used the word "breathe" to describe the method of instressing the resurrection: ". . . you whom the East / With draught of thin and pursuant cold so nips / Breathe Easter now" (ll.5–7).

Stanza 34 uses further doubling devices as Hopkins rises to a final crescendo in which he employs multiple compounds and possessives. If unable to return words to the one Word, he will link them by stress marks that both connect and separate one word from another. Stanza 34 is based on a tripartite scheme in which the phrasal groupings imitate the trinity:

> Now burn, new born to the world,
> Double-natured name,
> The heaven-flung, heart-fleshed, maiden-furled
> Miracle-in-Mary-of-flame,
> Mid-numbered he in three of the thunder-throne!
> Not a dooms-day dazzle in his coming nor dark as he came;
> Kind, but royally reclaiming his own;
> A released shower, let flash to the shire, not a lightning of
> fire hard-hurled.

(ll.265–72)

This stanza, more even than stanzas 7 and 8 in part 1, recapitulates the theme of the poem and employs syntactic devices that enact the events of the Incarnation-Resurrection and grace-communion. Particularly, the strong-stressed, heavily alliterated, and hyphenated two lines, "The heaven-flung, heart-fleshed, maiden furled / Miracle-in-Mary-of-flame," illustrate the process of Christ's first outstressing from God, his fleshly Incarnation on earth and his Resurrection. "Heart-fleshed" echoes the earlier heart flushing of grace in stanza 6. Likewise, "not a lightning of fire / hard-hurled" recalls the strain of stanza 6 where Hopkins says yes "O at lightning and lashed rod" as God hurls "Hard down with a horror of height." Here, the ecstasy of Christ's Resurrection answers the pain of God's instressing grace in part 1. Furthermore, Hopkins seems to contrast the wrathful Old Testament God with His forgiving New Testament counterpart. The nature imagery—lightning bolt followed by purgative shower—evokes both the conflict between the two as well as the necessary connection: destructive lightning heralding rain. The antithetical sentence structure—not-but—completes this contrast.

Finally, after offering his own personal conversion and the nun's death as sacramental celebrations, Hopkins beseeches the nun to

"Remember us in the roads, the heaven-haven of the reward" (1.275). He wishes for a similar conversion-communion for England. Here he transforms the noun "Easter" into a verb: "Let him easter in us, be a dayspring to the dimness of us, be a crimson-cresseted east" (1.277). In these two lines, Christ, human beings, and nature are sacramentally linked through the ascendency of the son-sun images, syntactically connected through the repetition of "east" and rhythmically joined by the stressed first syllables of the alliterated words. All three levels operate simultaneously to intensify the climactic invocation for Christ's presence in man. The eastward direction echoes the sought-for direction of Donne's "Goodfriday." Yet here the "let" is more hopeful and supplicatory than the command and conditional response of "Goodfriday."

Crucial to Hopkins's understanding of Real Presence is the possibility of experiencing Christ on earth through sacramental grace. In a sermon of 1879, he warns his congregation that Judgment Day will catch them by surprise if they have not converted:

And this night is not of so many hours, a number known beforehand; it is of quite uncertain length; and there is no dawn, no dayspring, to tell of the day coming, no morning twilight, the sunrise will be sudden, will be lightning . . . will overtake us without warning, will entrap us, will come as a snare upon all that are on the face of the earth. (*Sermons,* 110)

In both the sermon and in the *Deutschland,* "dayspring," the dawning of grace in human beings, will only be achieved through a *kenotic* self-sacrifice of the *arbitrium.* Such sacrifice is rewarded by eucharistic communion, a *pleromic* fulfillment or "fetching" of Christ. The series of possessives in the heavily alliterated last line ascends to modify the two nouns, "fire" and "lord." The poet, dead nun, and England are reunited through the fire and dawn imagery of the Resurrection. Hopkins has defeated his difficulty of stanza 28 where he could not at first name Christ. He reverts finally to multiplying epithets—"Pride, rose, prince, hero of us, high-priest"—pushing them toward fulfillment and containment in the final "Lord" as part 1 had thrust repetition of the same phrase—"but be adored"—toward culmination in "King."

The Wreck of the Deutschland fuses Incarnation and Resurrection by miming the process of the Eucharist. In viewing both his personal conversion and the wreck of *The Deutschland* as types of Christ's Passion and Resurrection, Hopkins offers the entire poem as a eucharistic sacrament to the English people. The poem "fathers-forth" this "limit-experience" from its source in the

Word—Christ. The personal convert (poet), the tall nun, and the English souls are all types of Christ. The scheme is not, however, as in Donne's "Hymne to God My God," typological, moving from Adam to Christ to the Christ of a second coming. Rather, for Hopkins, types are coterminous, connected by the Real Presence of Christ on earth as "Ground of being, and granite of it" (l.254). Resurrection depends on Incarnation, and both are embodied in the Eucharist.

Although Miller argues in *The Disappearance of God* that this belief in an immanent God had given way to a detached or transcendent God by the Victorian period, Hopkins resisted this movement. The God Hopkins searches for in his last five bleak years in Ireland, though no longer clearly visible in Hopkins's surroundings, has not receded from the world. Sadly, his Terrible Sonnets instead lament the absence of Christ who, far from being transcendent, seems to be hiding from the poet. "Carrion Comfort" and "I Wake and Feel the Fell of Dark" both seem to reverse the instressing of grace in the *Deutschland*. They lament the poet's lost ability to inscape Christ's presence in the visible world. Without God's sensible instress the sacramental relation between man and God collapses as does that between body and soul. Consequently, Christ seems to absent himself from the poet's perceptions. Left alone, without visible evidence of Christ's presence, the persona of these late sonnets resorts to instressing himself in terms reminiscent of Hopkins's 1883 meditation on the fallen angels in hell. These angels, Hopkins (in astutely modern psychological terms) asserts, were trapped by their own repressed energy and alienated from God:

> This throwing back or confinement of their energy is a dreadful constraint or imprisonment and, as intellectual action is spoken of under the figure of sight, it will in this case be an imprisonment in darkness, a being in the dark; for darkness is the phenomenon of foiled action in the sense of sight. But this constraint and this blindness or darkness will be most painful when it is the main stress or energy of the whole being that is thus balked. This is its strain or tendency towards being, towards good, towards God . . . not to speak of grace. (*Sermons*, 137)

In his Retreat notes of 1888, Hopkins records in himself an analogous state:

> This morning I made the meditation on the Three Sins, with nothing to enter but loathing of my life and a barren submission to God's will. The body cannot rest when it is in pain nor the mind be at peace as long as something bitter distills in it and it aches. This may be at any time and is

at many: how then can it be pretended there is for those who feel this anything worth calling happiness in this world? There is a happiness, hope, the anticipation of happiness hereafter: it is better than happiness, but it is not happiness now. (*Sermons*, 262)

Although Hopkins acknowledges to Robert Bridges that he is frequently depressed and even sometimes fears madness, he retains his belief in Ignatian meditation with its opposing concepts of consolation and desolation.[50] This doctrinal discipline allows him to express his own inner anguish at Christ's apparent absence in the personal Terrible Sonnets but nevertheless to continue his university teaching and priestly offices.

It is possible to read the sonnets, specifically "Carrion Comfort" and "I Wake and Feel the Fell of Dark," as expressions of spiritual desolation and requests for consolation.[51] Hopkins notes that there are three causes of desolation:

The first is because we are tepid, slothful or negligent in our spiritual exercises; and thus through our faults spiritual consolation is removed from us. The second is that God may try how much we are worth, and how much we progress in His service and praise, without such bountiful play of consolation and special graces. The third is that He may give us a true knowledge and understanding whereby we may intimately feel that it is not in our own power to acquire or retain great devotion, ardent love, tears, or any other spiritual consolation, but that all is a gift and grace of God our Lord; and to teach us not to build our nest in another's house, by allowing our intellect to be lifted up to any kind of pride or vainglory, by attributing to ourselves the devotion, or other kinds of spiritual consolation. (*Sermons*, 204–5)

As his sonnet "Patience, Hard Thing" documents, the only solution for one in desolation is to "strive to remain in patience, which is the virtue contrary to the troubles which harass him." (*Sermons*, 204).

Yet the earlier two sonnets express the reverse of patience. Defiant, angry, "inspirations unbidden" (*Letters to Bridges*, 221), they rail at the self for failing to rescue Christ's presence. The poet can no longer inscape Christ because he does not receive God's instress or the pressure of grace. Here, the eucharistic imagery focuses on the natural elements, not on their spiritual substances. Without consecration, neither transformation nor "saking" can occur. Consequently, the poems, as Daniel Harris notes, fall in on themselves.[52] In a late journal entry Hopkins foreshadows this process, which is the reverse of instress. There is no reciprocity, no corresponding strain between God's instress and man's inscape:

The feeling is terrible: the body no longer swayed as a piece by the nervous and muscular instress seems to fall in and hang like a dead weight on the chest. I cried on the holy name and by degrees recovered myself as I thought to do. It made me think that this was how the souls in hell would be imprisoned in their bodies as in prisons. (*Journals*, 237)

In his meditation notes of 1884 and 1885, Hopkins turns to Christ's Passion as a model for his own misery. By sacrificing himself and imitating Christ, he may yet reach the joy of the conclusion of the *Deutschland*. The meditation, like the journal entry, introduces the themes and imagery of the two late sonnets:

Calvary after Christ's death; grace devotion to the Passion. Seeing Christ's body nailed consider the attachment of his will to God's will. Wish to be as bound to God's will in all things, in the attachment of your mind and attention to prayer and the duty in hand; the attachment of your affections to Christ our Lord and his wounds instead of any earthly object. (*Sermons*, 255)

The nailing of the individual will to God's will (reminiscent of Donne's violent appeals for punishment) offers the only release from despair. Yet the sonnets, like Donne's Holy Sonnets, struggle with such total subordination. Here wrestling with one's soul is not rewarded by grace or communion. In fact, "Carrion Comfort" and "I Wake" fail to achieve even the first step in Ignatian meditation— composition of place. Hopkins's vision has failed; without instress, he cannot even inscape the visual image of Christ. Consequently, Real Presence is reduced to real absence; the Eucharist degenerates to a ceremony in which the believer is tempted to feed on himself. Perhaps more than in his other poems, however, Hopkins does exude a kind of insistent presence, this time a personal one. He himself becomes the elements that fail to undergo transubstantiation because he has forgotten how to consecrate or inscape them. He cannot make what is dead come back to life if he can no longer feel the instress of God's finger.

Speaking of the failure of this reciprocity and the consequent inability to inscape the "Invisible within the visible," Daniel Harris remarks, "When Christ's immanental presence fades out of ken, the mind . . . incorporates the world in a parody of Incarnation."[53] Lacking Donne's refuge in typological or eschatological certainty, Hopkins can no longer summon his connection with Adam and Christ. Instead he focuses on his own isolation. With Christ living away, nature too loses its ability to manifest Christ's presence. In these late sonnets, Hopkins transforms external nature into mental topography. The poems seem to contract; the imagery and feelings retreat inward in contrast to the outward expansion of the *Deutschland*. This retreat is the opposite of the nun's linguistic reduction to one word. In fact, Hopkins does not name Christ here. It is as if naming truly depended on inscaping presence. Without that presence, Hopkins can only call on a remote God who has withdrawn His Son from the poet's senses.

Writing of Hopkins's Dublin years, David Downes identifies three different critical reactions to the Terrible Sonnets and late spiritual writings:

> One group reads these writings as the sufferings of a saint in the making; another reads them as religious calamity stressing the darkness and doubt; a third group takes a position between these two critical polarities, emphasizing the isolation, misery, and abandonment without finally arranging them as spiritual descent or assent. The matter will never be settled.[54]

Downes himself opts for a fourth position, terming the sonnets "part of the visionary literature of the religious imagination" or "prophetic poetry" in which "personal apocalypse prefigure[s] the general Apocalypse."[55]

Father Devlin, Geoffrey Loomis, and Peter Milward stand squarely in this first optimistic camp. They all argue that Hopkins moves from visible or incarnational presence to eschatological presence or invisible grace.[56] Loomis takes this argument furthest when he suggests in complete contradiction to Harris that the late sonnets are actually more sacramentally potent than the earlier poems. He sees "Carrion Comfort," for instance, as a poem of spiritual impregnation and "inner gestation," not as a travesty of transubstantiation but as its deepest embodiment.[57] Although Downes interprets Hopkins's confession to Bridges that the late sonnets were "written in blood" as "poems that should not have been written,"[58] Loomis views these words as signifying "born into the blood of Christ."[59] Harris and Loomis, then, represent the extreme opposites of which Downes speaks, the former arguing for Hopkins's religious breakdown, the latter for a religious break-through to an intensified sacramental vision.

Between Harris and Loomis, Philip Endean and David Jasper view the Terrible Sonnets as irreconcilable with Hopkins's dogmatic faith and therefore poetic failures. In an attempt to rescue Hopkins's spirituality in the late writings, Endean and Jasper both pit these late poems against Hopkins's vocation as priest. Endean argues that the Terrible Sonnets evince a true sacramentalism or an increasing realization of the necessity of self-abandonment to God. Such a realization entails the Ignantian concept of desolation—"a deeper abandonment to the gratuitousness of God's action."[60] In this view, the sonnets are lessons to the poet that self-reliance emphasized by the solipsistic task of writing poetry is wrong.

Jasper sees Hopkins's late poetry haunted by the emphasis on selfhood and fixity: "Instead of glorying in the one voice of all creation in Christ, Hopkins lives increasingly within the self, bound by his own poetry of fixity and finitude, and unable to escape to an ever more transcendent God."[61] Jasper argues that Hopkins must finally leave his poetry behind him.

Although I find myself in closer agreement with Harris, I would strenuously argue against any loss of faith on Hopkins's part in the Terrible Sonnets. Rather, they seem to me to be anguished calls for a lost sense of Christic presence, both in the natural world and in the poet's self. If indeed Hopkins's elective will overruled his affective love of God's natural beauty, as Devlin, Loomis, and others contend, it seems an unfortunate and heartbreaking bifurcation, and a willed exile from Real Presence. One is reminded of Hopkins's early tendency toward self-denial, for instance, his refusal to inscape the budding spring flowers because he had been doing a half-year's self-imposd penance (*Journals*, 190). The Terrible Sonnets in this sense serve as penance poems in which Hopkins actively withdraws himself from the comfort that the doctrine of Real Presence previously afforded him.

"Carrion Comfort," especially, wrestles with the poet's temptation to enter into a blasphemous self-communion and thereby banish Christ from his soul. This process would be the opposite of God's stressing finger in the *Deutschland*. In fact, Hopkins does finally refuse to unstress "these last strands of man / In me" (ll.2–3). The first line—"Not, I'll not, carrion comfort, Despair, not feast on thee;"—juxtaposes comfort and Despair to reveal their similarity. Both false comfort (taking communion without prior confession) and despairing are Catholic sins that Hopkins abjures. Furthermore, the line is interesting in its ambiguous use of parts of speech. In one reading, Hopkins transforms carrion—dead flesh—into a verb that takes "comfort" as its direct object and thereby denigrates comfort to the opposite of solace. Read as a poetic inversion with "comfort" as the verb, however, Hopkins appears to suggest that he will not comfort or commune with elements that have not undergone consecration; to do so would be to feast on "Despair," or, as Hillis Miller explains:

> To feast on Despair would be to yield to the lure of a kind of self-cannibalism, to eat the dead body of one's loss of hope, to succumb to the diabolical pleasure of luxuriating in one's own bad selfhood. In place of this a man must endure the agony of being remade by God, and only then feast, but on Christ rather than on the carrion comfort.[62]

Miller reads "carrion" as a verb, "comfort" as a noun, and chooses to personify carrion as loss of hope. Though this is certainly the obvious meaning, is not the notion that Hopkins may be operating here by inversion equally possible? To comfort carrion would be, as the Jesuit-trained Sephen Dedalus fears in Joyce's *Stephen Hero*, to participate in cannibalism of Christ's body. Similarly to despair would be to feast on carrion or unconsecrated flesh, a Catholic sin.

Another possibility is to see the phrase "carrion comfort" in apposition to the personified "Despair." Despair then signals the death and putrefaction of comfort, possibly the comfort that the doctrine of the Real Presence has provided Hopkins. Despair is the opposite of Real Presence, a hollow and sinful state that Hopkins rejects with difficulty. In this reading, "Despair" becomes a sort of dead comfort, the last resort of the "wretch" of "No Worst, There Is None" who would "creep / . . . under a comfort serves in a whirlwind: all / Life death does end and each day dies with sleep" (ll.12–14).

In stanza 2 Hopkins questions the logic of an Old Testament God who, like the God of Job, refuses to answer his cries. The finger of the gracing God in the *Deutschland* has become a "Lion-limb." The speaker must supply his own answers: "Why? That my chaff might fly; my grain lie, sheer and clear" (l.9). The sestet introduces Christ (but not by name) and directly echoes and subverts stanzas 5 and 34 of the *Deutschland*. The poet has kissed the rod and made a *kenotic* self-sacrifice to a priestly life based on the Passion. In the next line, however, he offers a correction—"Hand rather"—that harks back to the poet's ability in stanza 5 of the *Deutschland* to kiss his hand to the stars and to waft Christ out of the heavens—in other words, to instress Christ's presence.

Here one is confronted with the central problem of instress in the Terrible Sonnets. Hopkins harps on the distinction (not the identity) between himself and Christ: "Cheer whom though? The hero whose heaven-handling flung me, foot trod / Me? or me that fought him? O which one? is it each one" (ll.12–13). By cheering himself, instressing his own will, he realizes that he is wrestling with "(my God!) my God" (l.14). The "hero whose heaven-handling flung me" ironically echoes the risen Christ of the *Deutschland:* "The heaven-flung, heart-fleshed, maiden-furled / Miracle-in-Mary-of-flame" (ll.267–68) who has also been trodden by God. The confusion of identities in the sestet (poet-Christ) reinforces the implied linguistic confusion of the first line. Christ, heaven-handled by God and flung earthward in the Incarnation, exacts this same process from the poet. The latter, however, must deal with a heretical realization that Christ escapes. Unlike Christ's, his will is not in perfect accord with God's; hence, the realization and exclamation of the poet's audacity. Here the parenthetical "My God!" interrupts the syntactical flow by announcing a sudden revelation that thwarts the linear chronology of the line. The revelation of presence is that of two separate and conflicting identities, not the figural fulfillment of God in man.[63]

These abrupt revelations (like Donne's conditional and imperative moods), often introduced by the exclamatory "O," break Hopkins's attempts at positive declarative statements throughout the poem. On a grammatical level, the poem sets up a dialectic between determined declarative statements and direct address questions and interjections. This syntactical dialectic closely parallels the semantic conflict between the poet's orthodox acceptance of God's will and his own questioning *arbitrium*. James Milroy terms such a close relationship between syntax and semantics "semantic counterpoint."[64] Mind and ear strive to follow the sequential progress of the lines but are continually halted by a kind of vertical insistence on the "O" of lines 5, 8, and 13. It is as if the previous two "O's" added up to reinforce the desperation of the thirteenth: "O Which one?" Such counterpoint compresses the doubling method of the *Deutschland* where narrative and revelation are juxtaposed mainly by stanzas. Here, in "Carrion Comfort," the mind and ear must work more rapidly in concert to assimilate syntax and semantics.

"I Wake and Feel the Fell of Dark" fights with the same mood of despair as "Carrion Comfort," yet it minimizes both syntactic and semantic dialectic. Instead, the poem introverts colloquy and communion. Hopkins here realizes a eunuch-like self-presence but no dialogue with God. Again, taste, a primary sense in both Holy Communion and Ignatian meditation, is dominant. The octet splits the persona in two as the head addresses the heart. "Cries like dead letters" (l.7) no longer serve to "fetch" the presence of "dearest him [Christ] that lives alas! away" (l.8). The hyperbaton of "alas" weakly echoes the parenthetical "my God!" of the previous sonnet. Like the "O's" of "Carrion Comfort," "alas" acts as a parenthetical sign, activating the personal exhalation of despair. The tone, now, however, is resigned. The single interjectory "O" of line 2 serves merely to draw out repetition of "black hours," not to direct questions to God.

The sestet employs specific eucharistic imagery to show the futility of self-communion in the absence of grace and Real Presence:

> I am gall, I am heartburn. God's most deep decree
> Bitter would have me taste: my taste was me;
> Bones built in me, flesh filled, blood brimmed the curse.
> Selfyeast of spirit a dull dough sours. I see
> The lost are like this, and their scourge to be
> As I am mine, their sweating selves; but worse.
>
> (ll.9–14)

The bitterest punishment is to be denied Christ's presence and to be aware only of one's self-taste. Reduced to the unconsecrated elements, the poet is passive, a victim awaiting grace and consecration. Yet here as opposed to the struggle in "Carrion Comfort," he appears to have bent his will to accept such a curse. "Heartburn" diminishes the spiritual heart to a state of physical indigestion and self-repugnance. God's active instressing of the body in the *Deutschland*—binding of bones, fastening of flesh—is now limited to a "deep decree" in which apart from any agency of self or God, bones build, flesh fills, and unredeemed blood reinforces Adam's original sin.

Like the "heart" of the octet, the spirit also assumes a purely carnal role. In a reversal of transubstantiation, the spirit, turned in on itself instead of outward to God, "sours," an allusion not only to the physical "selfyeast" but also to the souring of hope for grace. Seeing further eucharistic significance to this line, Daniel Harris states that the yeast image "inflates into a distorted Communion wafer the self that God has commanded to remain unleavened."[65] Yet here, no rising occurs. Having no other elements but itself to act on, the self merely putrefies like the carrion of the earlier sonnet. Sweat does not, as in Donne's "Hymne to God My God," mingle with blood and tears to make Adam prefigure Christ. Instead it conjures up the lost souls, "the Comfortless unconfessed" ones of the *Deutschland* with whom the persona empathizes. Hopkins likens himself to the unredeemed, the "sweating" Adams," before he realizes that their scourge is worse: Christ is permanently absent from their lives.

Instead, however, of denying God's immanence and thus blaming Him, the poem expresses the poet-priest's failure to receive God's instress and the correspondent failure to inscape the spirit in natural elements. Hopkins has not moved toward a transcendent or apocalyptic God. Consequently, his solution does not lie in the false comfort of death nor, like that of Donne, in an eschatological redemption. This is underscored by his late retreat notes of 1888:

> but what is life without aim, without spur, without help? / All my undertakings miscarry: I am like a straining eunuch. I wish then for death: yet if I died now I should die imperfect, no master of myself, and that is the worst failure of all. (*Sermons*, 262)

For Hopkins, failure of instress—the touch of God's finger upon the human self—means failure to achieve Real Presence. This late entry differs markedly from Donne's fear of impenitence in his divine poems. In fact, here Hopkins seems to fear the loss of self, a loss or an exchange usually demanded before the receipt of grace. Yet in Hopkins's theology one's stature, his self-worth, is a sign of God's presence within him; his weakness signals God's withholding of instress. The relationship between God's instressing of a person and that person's reciprocal ability to inscape Christ's presence in nature structures the *Deutschland*. The loss of this ability reduces the Terrible Sonnets to a real presence of self, not of the self's identity in Christ. Far from becoming transcendent, the poet's world has become purely physical, the incarnational link to the transcendent God obscured or hidden. In a journal entry of 1871, Hopkins predicts the ill that later befalls him:

> I thought how sadly beauty of inscape was unknown and buried away from simple people and yet how near at hand it was if they had eyes to see it and it could be called out everywhere again. (*Journals*, 221)

By 1888, a year before he died, he realized that eyes and faith were not enough to elicit such presence: "It is as if one were dazzled by a spark or star in the dark, seeing it but not seeing by it: we want a light shed on our way and a happiness spread over our life" (*Sermons*, 262). The lack of such a light pervades both "Carrion Comfort" and "I Wake and Feel the Fell of Dark." On a structural level, the compression of the expansive ode into the tight sonnet form stresses the withdrawal of this light. The *Deutschland* is flooded with the light of dawn and resurrection, whereas the Terrible Sonnets depict a midnight world.

This focus on the self in the Terrible Sonnets, however, as Hopkins finally realizes, is a necessary step toward directing one's faulty *arbitrium* toward God. As he concedes in his sonnet "Patience":

> We hear our hearts grate on themselves: it kills
> To bruise them dearer. Yet the rebellious wills
> Of us we do bid God bend to him even so.
>
> (ll.9–11)

Desolation, the withdrawal of Christ's presence, can finally be borne only with patience and not with the frantic cries of "Carrion Comfort" nor "I Wake and Feel the Fell of Dark." Neither can consolation, the renewal of Christ's presence, be won by feeding on oneself and on one's sorrows. Nevertheless, the Terrible Sonnets of 1885 present us with the dark side of Hopkins's spiritual life, and in doing so they show even more strenuously than the nature poems the crucial role the doctrine of Real Presence played in Hopkins's life.

Hopkins looks back to Donne in his insistence on the instressing of grace as a prelude to realization of Real Presence. Unlike Donne, however, he does not rely on an eschatological sense of redemption; rather he tries to achieve redemption through Christ's Incarnation on earth. In this sense, he looks forward to Dylan Thomas who posits a thoroughly immanent view of God in both the world and the self. As this emphasis on immanence increases, poetic language becomes weightier and more visceral as if to contain the spirit and prevent its escape. It also grows more material and less referential. In Dylan Thomas it ceases almost entirely to point toward objects and tries instead to embody these objects within its scrambled syntax. Thomas follows Hopkins's lead in his experimentation with incarnational language. Yet what united Hopkins and Donne—a deeply held dogmatic belief—is absent in Thomas. One is finally tempted to ask if poetic language can really achieve any kind of real presence without a grounded metaphysical belief.

4

Wounding Presence: The Sacrificial Poetry of Dylan Thomas

> . . . the story of the New Testament is part of my life.
>
> —"Poetic Manifesto"

Aligned with Donne or Hopkins, Dylan Thomas is at best a religious renegade, a Welsh nonconformist with neither a strictly Anglican nor Roman Catholic affiliation. Though familiar with the Bible and with the Protestant Welsh Chapel, he was not raised with a reverence for the Eucharist nor with the Anglo-Catholic's belief in the Real Presence of Christ in the sacrament.[1] He cannot be said finally to ground his poetics on an explicitly Christian faith. Yet, his poetry, like that of Donne and Hopkins, is riddled with religious imagery and frequently assumes a sacramental view of mankind and nature, and their link to God. Like his two predecessors, he employs similar tropes of amplification to heighten the immediacy of his poetry and to explode ordinary logic. The result of this revelatory mode is a surprisingly sacramental vision. Searching for the source of this vision, however, is fruitless, for Thomas's eclecticism defies any attempt to pigeonhole his poems into neat categories. Donne and Hopkins root their work in an overtly Christian ontology, whereas Thomas has no steadfast dogma on which to lean. That he is attracted to Roman Catholicism and equates it with the inner world he longs to express in his poetry is evident in an early (Feb. 1933) letter to his friend Trevor Hughes:

> You may think this philosophy—only, in fact, a very slight adaptation of the Roman Catholic religion—strange for me to believe in. I have always believed in it. My poems rarely contain any of it. That is why they are not satisfactory to me. Most of them are the outer poems.[2]

In fact, reading Thomas's poems, one is left largely with the outer world and the way it comes to absorb the inner world so that the two are often indistinguishable. The self, always carefully preserved in Donne and Hopkins, loses its boundaries in Thomas, and this amorphousness generates confused clusters of images and rhythms. At their best, the rhythm and imagery recall Donne's paradoxes and Hopkins's compression. At their worst, they collapse, like the body, into a morass of dense and disconnected images.

In a later letter to Hughes, Thomas admits that his goal is to draw the external in, "to bring those wonders into myself, to prove beyond doubt to myself that the flesh that covers me is the flesh that covers the sun, that the blood in my lungs is the blood that goes up and down in a tree. It is the simplicity of religion" (*CL,* 89–90). Yet this religion and its attendant poetic expression are far from simple. The mixture of religious, sexual, and bestial allusions thwarts the critic who wishes to argue for a thoroughgoing Christian interpretation of the poetry.

Nevertheless, an effort to discover a common ground from which the poems spring reveals the dilemma in which many modern poets find themselves. Bereft of the traditional Christian trinity of Incarnation, Crucifixion, and Resurrection, yet still saturated with the vocabulary of that structure, they wrench the religious images out of their orthodox context. The effect of such dislocation is at first shock, then a puzzling sense of doubleness as sacred images are subordinated to or merged with secular ones. Consequently, the traditional upward typological movement toward increasingly spiritual types collapses.

This doubleness of sacred and secular yields a presence akin to that in Donne's and Hopkins's poetry where the reader is made to view sacramental and secular worlds simultaneously. Thomas does not, like Donne, parallel the two, nor, like Hopkins, devise a method of reciprocity based on a *kenotic/pleromic* process of instress and inscape; rather, he randomly intertwines natural, biological, and religious realms, and announces that all three are equally sacramental. He bases this conclusion on his own body, substituting himself for God and Christ and thereby assuming a prophetic authority.[3] For Thomas, Christ is not the ground of being unfolding himself in man and nature. Instead, man and nature seem, especially in the earlier poetry, to usurp Christ's place. As protean prophet, Thomas can variously be Adam, Noah, Christ, even God, as well as an unborn baby speaking from within its mother's womb. To what extent the body can stand as a replacement for a universal faith or how successful the body as ground of being is in generating presence are two questions Dylan Thomas's "religious" poetry poses.[4]

Acknowledging the lack of a common spiritual climate in the twentieth century for poetic metaphor, Karsten Harries identifies a descent to the body characteristic of poets like Thomas. Harries pinpoints Thomas's quasi-sacramental stance when he refers to the modern poet's effort to erect a private ontology where he can satisfy his "desire to reincarnate the dislocated spirit, the longing for words that will let us rediscover where we belong and thus defeat that sense of contingency and arbitrariness."[5] The danger of such a stance, as Harries warns, is a solipsism in which the poet's language is sealed off from the audience he is trying to reach. The gift of tongues is as remote as unfallen Adam's power to name and hence to identify his world. As faith weakens, so does the belief in the world's ability to create presence. Yet this same loss seems to make the modern poet more desperate to discover a revelatory language with which to redeem himself and his world. Poetic language thus tries to return words to their lost incarnational status. As Harries notes:

> A longing remains to find words that would capture this mystery, words which, as the poet writes, were he to find them would force to their knees the cherubim in which he does not believe. For such words would close the gap between language and reality. They would be the creative words of God.[6]

At most, according to Harries, the poet can employ a form of Ricoeur's "limit-language" by using "metaphors of collision" that catapult the reader out of a world of dead metaphor and anticipated referentiality toward a new sense of presence.

In an early (1934) letter to Trevor Hughes, Thomas explains the poet's struggle with a dead language and expresses the need to create a new living language. Old ground, like dogmatic faith, needs to be ruptured to be renewed:

> We look upon a thing a thousand times; perhaps we shall have to look upon it a million times before we see it for the first time. Centuries of problematical progress have blinded us to the literal world; each bright and naked object is shrouded around with a thick peasoup mist of associations; no single word in all our poetical vocabulary is a virgin word, ready for our first love, willing to be what we make it. Each word has been wooed and gotten by a vast procession of dead litterateurs who put their coins in the plate of a procuring Muse, entered at the brothel doors of a divine language, and whored the syllables of Milton and the Bible.
> But consciousness of such prostitution need not lead us, as it has led

James Joyce, into the inventing of new words; it need not make us, as it made Gertrude Stein, repeat our simplicities over and over again in intricate and abstract patterns so that the meaning shall be lost and only the bare and beautiful shells of the words remain. All we need do is to rid our minds of the humbug of words, to scorn the prearranged leaping together of words, to make by our own judicious and . . . artistic selection, new associations for each word. Each word should be a basin for us to cough our individual diseases into, and not a vessel full already of others' and past diseases for us to play about with as a juggler plays with puddings. (*CL*, 93–94)

Thomas tackles the problem of an overused language by a direct assault on this "prearranged leaping together of words." Often mistakenly called a surrealist, he severs words and syntax from their common associations.[7] As he tells Pamela Hansford Johnson, "It is part of a poet's job to take a debauched and prostituted word . . . and to smooth away the lines of its dissipation, and to put it on the market again, fresh and virgin" (*CL*, 25).

At first this task seems to demand that Thomas assume the role of God or Adam. In his early poetry, he employs an inverted typology within which he seeks to return to an edenic state before the sullying of the Word. Such a search for original presence without self-sacrifice carries him back to prenatal and precreation imagery where he attempts to mime the creating Word. In such "genesis" poems as "Before I Knocked," "The Sun Burns," "Through These Lashed Rings," and "In the Beginning," he simultaneously recreates his own birth and that of the world. This equation of self and world or of world as microcosm of self is the hallmark of Thomas's early poetry. The equation is both medieval and modern. The medieval assumption that human beings were microcosms of the greater macrocosm was predicated on a belief in God as supreme creator. One was not responsible for the correspondence between his body and the external cosmos; one simply accepted the correspondence as proof of God's omnipotence. Unlike Donne who personalizes and internalizes biblical types to give his poems religious authority, Thomas uses religious imagery to magnify himself. Thomas posits his own body as ground of being and as proof of external nature's validity. In the early poems God seems an adjunct or a helpful metaphor through which the poet can project the authority of his own identity. It appears that the presence Thomas wishes language to call forth is his own, not that of God or Christ. Where Hopkins and Donne seek to reconcile their individuality with conformity to Christ, Thomas uses Christ to reinforce his own individuality, an act the earlier poets would have considered heretical.

Reduced to his own self-taste in his final sonnets, Hopkins can only hope for a spiritual presence to reemerge. With faith in its eventual reappearance, however, Hopkins refuses to despair. Knowing only self-taste from the start, Thomas builds outward, stretching Whitmanesque filaments toward nature, other people, and, most of all, toward death. Death in Thomas's poetry becomes the backdrop or absence against which the words at first fight and with which they finally collude. That he moves, like Donne, toward eschatological fulfillment along a Hopkinsian incarnational route becomes increasingly persuasive if one compares the religious language of certain early poems with that of his later "Ceremony after a Fire Raid," "Vision and Prayer," and "Author's Prologue." The key to this route is Thomas's gradual acceptance of the inevitability of sacrifice. Not surprisingly, the model for personal sacrifice is Christ.

Among the critics who view Thomas primarily as a religious poet, Elder Olson, Rushworth Kidder, and Aneirin Davies perceive a movement from darkness and doubt to light and faith—a steady progression toward a Christian sacramental vision. All three argue for a coherent set of religious symbols that, according to Olson, makes "immediate and factual what metaphor and analogue would have left remote and fanciful, to coerce the imagination and so coerce belief; he arouses our emotions before we have time to doubt."[8] Davies emphasizes the difficulty of constructing this symbology and blames it on the "erosion of Christian dogma":

> Every poet of any stature needs a solid superstructure of belief to sustain his imagination. The erosion of Christian dogma, which has been the foundation of Western civilization, has faced the modern poet with a double task, the first of which is to assemble or create a dictionary of relevant symbols, capable of sustaining his creative activity. Much of his energy, therefore, is taken up with this task of creating a superstructure of private dogma, with an attendant hierarchy of symbols.[9]

Yet up until "Ceremony after a Fire Raid" and "Vision and Prayer," Thomas's poems militate against such a superstructure. His religious allusions seem to tease the reader toward dogmatic coherence, but the syntax and juxtaposition of sacred and secular continually shatter any such cohesiveness.

Arguing less for a specifically Christian progression and more for an innate "animal faith" are Derek Stanford, W. S. Merwin, and Staurt Holroyd. Stanford regards Thomas's poetry as progressively pantheistic. He notes that pantheism allows Thomas reign to interchange matter randomly, yet still to acknowledge an immanent God as the authority for such random transubstantiation:

> When . . . the poet deals with matter of one kind or another, he is dealing with, partaking of, God; and when he substitutes for the image of this matter the image of matter of a different type, he is creating a sacrament, and establishing a sacramental view of the world.[10]

Yet the sacramental view, as Stanford concedes, is achieved without sacrifice or tension; it does not point beyond itself to a divine purpose nor to an eschatological conclusion. For this reason, Stanford does not rank Thomas with Hopkins; rather, he sees him as an "agnostic who has retained a naturally religious imagination."[11]

Similarly, Stuart Holroyd argues that Thomas's God is wholly immanent. Holroyd pushes beyond Stanford to assert that only through descent into his own body and its sexual processes can Thomas discover God:

> The god of Dylan Thomas is wholly immanent, felt along the bloodstream or in the sexual organs, buried in the unconscious. He possesses no attributes, is capable neither of love nor anger, but is conceived rather as a vague Force or Power which is responsible for the harmony of the world and is most clearly discernible in that harmony.[12]

According to Holroyd, the moment of orgasm is analogous to the moment of religious revelation because one surrenders one's identity and briefly moves beyond the confines of the flesh. Such an experience introduces the consciousness of death, a constant theme in Thomas's poetry:

> . . . sex, together with the process analogous to it in the natural world, was Dylan Thomas's god. The sexual act between man and woman was therefore invested with a grave significance. The act that created life was symbolical of the moment of death; for death was the entry into the womb of the universe, and as man and woman surrender their separate identities at the moment of union, so does man give up his identity when submerged by death.[13]

This serious emphasis on sex as a regenerative force in Thomas's poetry finds its counterpart in Donne's wittier love lyrics. The explosive syntax and juxtaposed images recall Hopkins's sensuous mimesis of the experience of uplifting grace. Yet, for both Donne and Hopkins, God is still the authorization for all "limit-experiences." He is both ontological ground and eschatological promise. Because rebellion against such a God is both inevitable and futile, Donne's and Hopkins's poems employ rebellious language like tigers lashed to posts. They are certain of their inability to uproot the posts but must nevertheless convey the agonizing drive toward self-assertion together with the equally agonizing but necessary pursuit of self-sacrifice.

For Thomas, however, the post has already been uprooted—hence, the struggle to be both God and rebel soul simultaneously. Such an effort actually mocks the dogmatic goal of Real Presence: instead of sacrificing himself as a tribute to the sacrificed Christ and merging with him at the moment of communion, Thomas extends himself in an attempt to absorb and appropriate nature, humanity, and God. As W. S. Merwin states, "he will see himself, man, as a metaphor or analogy of the world. The human imagination will be for him the image of the divine imagination; the work of art and the artist will be analogous with the world and its creator."[14]

Yet for Thomas, like Hopkins, human and divine do not stand in *metaphorical* relation to each other; they are mutually dependent and equally literal. It is this realization of a simultaneous secular and sacred presence that underlies both Thomas's early and late poems. What finally separates his genesis poems from his later ones is a deepening sense of the inevitability of sacrifice, both human and divine, in the creation of a sacramental universe. It is ultimately this emphasis on sacrifice that links him both thematically and linguistically to Donne and Hopkins. Like them, Thomas forces language to strain against itself to expose the wound of the poet who finds himself in a world of fallen speech. Not surprisingly, this image of wounding appears constantly throughout his poetry. It connects his earlier genesis poems with his later death-oriented ones, and it harks back both to Adam's wound—the loss of his rib—and to the wound in Christ's side. The act of writing is, for Thomas, a sacrificial wounding akin to the actual wounding of Christ at the crucifixion.

As early as 1933, Thomas had established his body as the central ground of his poetry. In the poems the body is lashed through two great sacrifices—birth and death. This original ground gradually expands to include identification with other wounded figures—Adam, Christ, Noah, and always with nature. In a section of a letter to Pamela Hansford Johnson entitled "Defence of Poesie," Thomas proposes Donne's *Devotions* as the great example of writing rooted in the physical:

> The greatest description I know of our own "earthiness" is to be found in John Donne's Devotion, where he describes man as earth of the earth, his body earth, his hair a wild shrub growing out of the land. All thoughts and actions emanate from the body. Therefore the description of a thought or action—however abstruse it may be—can be beaten home by bringing it onto a physical level. Every idea, intuitive or intellectual, can be imaged and translated in terms of the body, its flesh, skin, blood, sinews, veins, glands, organs, cells, or senses.
>
> Through my small, bonebound island I have learnt all I know, experienced all, and sensed all. All I write is inseparable from the island. As much as possible, therefore, I employ the scenery of the island to describe the scenery of my thoughts, the earthquake of the body to describe the earthquake of the heart. (*CL,* 39)

Later in the same year, this apocalyptic imagery shifts to specifically eucharistic imagery. Thomas announces his desire to resurrect the "dead flesh," a theme that gradually grows more insistent in his poetry:

> For the time at least, I believe in the writing of poetry from the flesh, and, generally, from the dead flesh. So many modern poets take the *living* flesh as their object, and, by their clever dissecting, turn it into a carcase. I prefer to take the *dead* flesh, and, by any positivity of faith and belief that is in me, build up a *living* flesh from it. (*CL,* 72–73)

Here he proposes to become consecrator and reviver, focusing, like the priest, on the sacramental power of words to transform death to life.

Coexisting with the role of resuscitator is that of absorber. Both fuse to create an image of a godlike poet who can vanquish death and human inferiority by sheer will and self-assertion. In the early letters and poems, Thomas wrestles with God from the position of a superior being; instead of denying God's existence, he subordinates it to his own. The reciprocal process of instress-inscape or *kenosis-pleroma,* so prevalent in Hopkins, is absent in Thomas. Thomas senses the potential danger of usurping God's place, yet he defends his own poetic ability to appropriate nature to himself:

> But I defend the diction, the perhaps wearisome succession of blood and bones, the neverending similes of the streams in the veins and the

lights in the eyes, by saying that, for the time at least, I realise that it is impossible for me to raise myself to the altitude of the stars, and that I am forced, therefore, to bring down the stars to my own level and to incorporate them in my own physical universe. (*CL*, 90)

Instead of "meeting" and "greeting" God in nature like Hopkins, or reaching toward Him at death like Donne, Thomas must pull Him down and cover spirit with flesh in a mimesis of the Incarnation. His vision is immanent, often irreverent, his poetic imagery and syntax semantically discordant but aurally rhythmic. The building rhythms stand in contrast to the destruction of logical syntax. This gap between melodic rhythm and disruptive imagery marks much of the early poetry and announces one of Thomas's most persistent themes—the paradox of destruction and creation occurring every-where simultaneously.

In 1933 this paradox leads to an explicit poem about faith. To believe in God, the poet must kill Him, then resurrect Him. "No Man Believes" records the confrontation of faith with death and illustrates the need to "wound" the former to make it firm. There are subdued echoes of both Christ at the Crucifixion and Job at the height of his despair on the dung hill, though Thomas does not assume those personae directly. The poem introduces the death-resurrection theme of much of the later poetry and employs favorite linguistic devices of repetition and oxymoron to push the point home. As in Hopkins's early poems, syntax does not yet mime semantic action. The repetition is imitatively biblical and heavy-handed, the style prescriptive instead of presentational.

After describing man's confrontation with natural death, Thomas asserts that "No man believes who . . . does not make a wound in faith / When any light goes out, and life is death."[15] The final paradox of the first stanza—"life is death"—is unexpected and dogmatic; it reverses and echoes the traditional Christian teaching that "death is life." Yet this reversal is more a shift of emphasis than a perverse denial. Throughout his early poems Thomas tends to equate birth with death. Only later does he come to the es-chatologically-oriented belief in death and resurrection. Here the death-resurrection process is more a metaphor for abstract faith than a literal equation. Hence it does not *activate* presence; it *explains* the process by which presence may be realized.

The poem operates through negatives reminiscent of the prohibi-tions of the Ten Commandments; in fact, it contains ten basic assertions couched in negatives. These assertions lead to a final affirmative faith reached through the process of "breaking and making," analogous to the eucharistic fraction and communion. In the final stanza, Thomas graphically spells out the death-resurrection dilemma on which faith hinges:

> And this is true, no man can live
> Who does not bury God in a deep grave
> And then raise up the skeleton again,
> No man who does not break and make,
> Who in the bones finds not new faith,
> Lends not flesh to ribs and neck,
> Who does not break and make his final faith.
>
> (ll. 18–24)

In "Presence and Absence in Modern Poetry," James Hans notes that "descent into the world of absence is linked to the ascent of presence."[16] For Thomas, this descent involves a confrontation with death and a realization of a presence beyond death. Although this confrontation recalls both the crucifixion-resurrection and its eucharistic recreation, it differs from them in its attitude toward the victim-communicant. Instead of submitting himself will-lessly to death to be reborn, the poet actively kills the natural objects of his world and presumes to resurrect them himself. As Hillis Miller explains:

> it is the act of returning upon the world of created things after their deaths, assuming them all sacrificially, dying their deaths again for them, and by this doubling saving them, affirming them as alive in the midst of their deaths.[17]

At this early point of "No Man Believes," the sacrificial quality is absent; the poet kills and resurrects but does not die himself. There is no sense of reciprocity, only a desire to control and through controlling to affirm belief on the poet's terms, not on God's. This is the opposite of Donne's pleas for grace or Hopkins's desire for instress in which both earlier poets understand the need to relinquish control to God.

The central poetic device in the poem is the assonance of the long "o" words, expressed primarily in the repetition of "No," "Not," "God." As Thomas mentions in a letter, "God moves in a long 'o'" (*CL*, 73). The aural equation of God with the negatives "no" and "not" reinforces on a syntactical level the thematic statement "life is death." It also hints that faith must be achieved by a negative and rebellious route, not through blind affirmation.

Thomas continues in several early poems to emphasize this simultaneous creation-destruction based on his observation of the body and its "limit-experiences" of birth and sex, both of which he equates with death. Admitting to Pamela Hansford Johnson that "the equilibrium between flesh and non-flesh can never be reached by an individual" (*CL*, 70), he opts for the former, although he realizes its artistic limitations. Yet he seems to believe that by absorbing and expressing different speakers, he can break out of a purely solipsistic confinement. This assumption of multiple personae, as well as the increasing emphasis on biblical imagery, provides a route from the self to the outside world in such poems as "Before I Knocked," "The Sun Burns," "Through These Lashed Rings," and "In the Beginning." As Rushworth Kidder points out, however, the imagery is still allusive and referential, not yet thematic. The biblical personae and allusions are still subordinated to the poet and poem, not the reverse. The felt presence is that of the poet and his own vocabulary, not that of God or Christ.[18]

"Before I Knocked" employs one of Thomas's favorite doubling devices—that of multiple speakers. Like the natural elements, the individual and people are interchangeable. Human beings are no longer rooted in a Christian scheme—hence, their peculiar mobility and Thomas's fluid imagery. Here Thomas is alternately or simultaneously himself and Christ. As in "No Man Believes," he is determined to subordinate spirit to flesh to control and believe in the incarnational process. Sex paradoxically unites with divine annunciation in a poem that has parodic overtones. Unborn, the persona, Thomas or Christ, can transcend or avoid human time, death, and sex until the moment of birth. Here, the first explicit hint of personal sacrifice enters Thomas's poetry. Here too he reinforces his earlier assertion that "life is death."

Just before birth, he depicts entrance into life as a crucifixion:

> My veins flowed with the Eastern weather;
>
> . . . .
> As yet ungotten, I did suffer;
> The rack of dreams my lily bones
> Did twist into a living cipher,
> And flesh was snipped to cross the lines
> Of gallow crosses on the liver
> And brambles in the wringing brains.
>
> (ll.17–24)

The crucifixion is twofold. Not only is the child born to death, but its birth is a physical crucifixion for the mother whose dreams are twisted into reality ("living cipher") and whose womb is split ("crossed") during the birth. By doubling the speaker's identity, Thomas can combine the literal physical level with the spiritual or, more accurately, force the latter into the service of the former. Christian imagery, specifically that of the Passion and Resurrection, underlies the poem. Yet Thomas transforms the nouns "lily" and "gallow" to adjectives that modify his own body in an effort to make even the syntax and grammar support his emphasis on the physical and personal over spiritual and universal.

The confusion of speakers becomes especially apparent in the last two stanzas as the persona nears death:

> I, born of flesh and ghost, was neither
> A ghost nor man, but mortal ghost.
> And I was struck down by death's feather.
> I was a mortal to the last
> Long breath that carried to my father
> The message of his dying christ.
>
> You who bow down at cross and altar,
> Remember me and pity Him
> Who took my flesh and bone for armour
> And doublecrossed my mother's womb.

(ll.37–46)

To insist on the double identity of the speaker Thomas purposely confuses uppercase and lowercase letters. In stanza 3 he capitalizes "Eastern" weather, thereby hinting at both east and Easter, but emphasizing the latter. In these final two stanzas he chooses to keep the trinitarian *ghost, father,* and *christ* in lowercase and to capitalize "Him" in the last stanza. Stanza 7, consequently, places the emphasis on Christ's subordination to the human speaker, and stanza 8 *appears* to emphasize Christ at the moment of the Incarnation. Derek Stanford perceives this stanza as a reversal of the communion supplication to God to pity the communicants who remember Christ.[19] It seems more plausible, however, that Thomas has cleverly introduced a third presence into the poem—God. If so, one could read stanza eight as a united rebellion by Christ and Thomas against God. Is Christ-Thomas asking the reader to pity a god who has to assume "flesh and bone for armour" against mankind and who "doublecrossed" or cheated a mother out of sexual satisfaction? The possibility for multiple interpretations is rife in this confusion of speakers and is supplemented by the transformation of uppercase and lowercase letters. Also, "doublecrossed" is

packed with both profane and religious connotations. In addition to
echoes of Christ's crucifixion, it could mean crossed twice—once at
conception and again at birth; technically, it means cheated; pun-
ningly, it could serve as a key to the double nature of the speakers
who seem to cross paths throughout the poem.

"The Sun Burns the Morning" offers "Before I Knocked" an
interpretation of "doublecrossed." After alluding to the Old Testament episode of the appearance to Moses of the Angel of Jehova
(Exod. 3:2–4) and the New Testament interpretation of the burning
bush as a type of the Virgin Mary—"The sun burns the morning, a
bush in the brain" (l.1), the first two stanzas continue to embed
biblical imagery in often obscurely inverted syntax. Stanza 1
echoes Adam exiled to the wilderness and Christ as the second
Adam at the Crucifixion: "Here in my wilderness wanders the
blood; / And the sweat on the brow makes a sign, / And the wailing
heart's nailed to the side" (ll.3–5). Stanza 2 hints at Christ's birth—
"a saviour who sings like a bird" (l.7) and "the stable under the
skin" (l.10).

The final stanza interprets the Crucifixion as already inherent in
both the Christ child and, by extension, in all children and their
mothers. Here, as in "Before I Knocked," the mother in labor is
presented as double-crossed:

> Under the ribs sail the moon and the sun;
> A cross is tattooed on the breast of the child,
> And sewn on his skull a scarlet thorn;
> A mother in labour pays twice her pain,
> Once for the Virgin's child, once for her own.
>
> (ll.11–15)

The mother, a type of "all women" or of the Virgin, as the child is a
type of Christ, begets a child doomed to suffer like Christ. Birth
carries with it the stigmata of torture—"scarlet thorn"—and
death—a tattooed cross. The mother, like all believers, has already
suffered spiritually for Christ; now she must suffer physically at the
birth-death of her own child.

Instead of confusing personae, the poem merges people and
nature by implanting the human in the natural. Here Thomas's main
feat, like that of Hopkins in the Terrible Sonnets, is severe compression of biblical images and their absorption into the body:
"bush in the brain," "stable under the skin." By internalizing
biblical episodes, Thomas moves beyond Donne's equation of himself with biblical types. Thomas forces spiritual significance to

incarnate itself in physical sensations; likewise he makes intellectual comprehension dependent on physical sensation. This tactic is not unlike that of the eucharistic sacrament where one must literally *eat* the spiritual bread and wine that have been transformed into body and blood. Absent, however, from both "Before I Knocked" and "The Sun Burns" is any hope of resurrection. Crucifixion and incarnation are ends in themselves. Both pervade persons and nature and unite them in the same process, but neither guarantees immortality.

"Through These Lashed Rings" represents a departure from the previous two poems. It internalizes God instead of Christ or nature, and forces God to serve the speaker. Although Donne and Hopkins both move to an affirmation of faith through sensuous identification with God, they would strongly dispute Thomas's subordination of God to a human body:

> And through these eyes God marks myself revolving,
> And from these tongue-plucked senses draws His tune;
> Inside this mouth I feel His message moving
> Acquainting me with my divinity;
> And through these ears He harks my fire burn
> His awkward heart into some symmetry.

(ll. 12–17)

Here, in a radical departure from dogma, Thomas has forced God to praise a human being, not the reverse. God's function is not only to acquaint the speaker through language with the speaker's own divinity but also to derive "His tune"—from the speaker's "tongue-plucked senses"—eyes, mouth, and ears. Here self-knowledge, although still relying on God, replaces faith. The last two lines recall Blake's "The Tyger," which asks the nature of a God who would frame an animal with such "fearful symmetry." Yet in Thomas's poem the speaker himself becomes the symmetrical framer of God's heart. Having presumably framed man, God is now dependent on man to reshape His divine plan in poetry. The synesthetic "He harks my fire burn / His awkward heart" disrupts ordinary semantic interpretation and recalls biblical revelations in which divinity is mysteriously manifested to humans through a mixture of physical sensations. Even if the poem seeks to reinterpret God's Word through the speaker's senses, one would have to concur with Stuart Holroyd that, for the modern poet, "Religion is not so much man's attempt to know God as his attempt to know himself."[20]

"In the Beginning" fuses the Old Testament account of the creation with the New Testament doctrine of the Incarnation. In so doing, it dispenses with chronological time and makes the moment of creation and the moment of Christ's Incarnation simultaneous. The poem finds its cornerstone in the trinitarian combination of God, Christ, and the Holy Ghost. The star in the beginning is "three-pointed"; the "pale signature" is "Three-syllabled"; and the "mountain fire"—the son-sun—is "three-eyed." Here Thomas travels backward as he does in "Before I Knocked" to affirm the existence of Christ before the Incarnation. The last stanza disrupts chronological and biblical time in its insistence on the temporal "before." It places the sacrifice and resurrection of Christ *before* the creation of either the world or the birth of Christ:

> Before the pitch was forking to a sun;
> Before the veins were shaking in their sieve,
> Blood shot and scattered to the winds of light
> The ribbed original of love.

(ll.27–30)

Thomas evinces here a tendency both to scramble and compress time in the poem. A possible motive for this ploy is his desire to reverse the reader's logical and linear thinking. One result of this reversal is a realization of the coterminous quality of divine events. Thomas urges one to regard secular events as sacred. Here the doctrine of the Real Presence provides a viable analogy. In the Real Presence of the Eucharist both linear time and geometrical space disappear or are no longer applicable. Likewise, in all divine events, time and space transcend one's limited linear perspective. Stanza 2 announces the spiritual fuse—blood—that makes all time coterminous: "The blood that touched the crosstree and the grail / Touched the first cloud and left a sign" (ll.11–12). Here again, the element of sacrifice is implicit in the allusion both to the Crucifixion and the Eucharist. The sign on the first cloud is a warning of Christ's impending sacrifice. The blood image extends to unite creation with destruction.

With "This Bread I Break," Thomas shifts to a specifically eucharistic subject away from speculations on human birth and death. Although the imagery recalls the eucharistic sacrament, the order of events, like that of the genesis poems, is scrambled and reversed. Unlike the early eucharistic poems of Hopkins, Thomas absorbs Christ and priest into himself. By doubling the personae and confusing their roles, Thomas is able to articulate the eucharistic sacrament from different vantage points. Such confusion of speaker

and stance jolts the reader into an unorthodox view of the ceremony. At the same time the juxtapositions allow for a doubling or
tripling of presence. Not only is Christ's presence felt, but also that
of the elements and the priest-poet become equally urgent. What
binds all three, aside from the multiple voices, is the element of
sacrifice implicit in each speaker.

On one hand, the poem mocks the dogmatic belief in transubstantiation by reversing the process and moving from body and
blood to bread and wine. Conversely, it reinforces belief in consubstantiation by granting identity and equality to all the elements—both natural and divine. Natural is not subordinated to
supernatural. Yet both natural and supernatural are destroyed in the
fraction that precedes the actual communion. Thomas still cannot
see past destruction to resurrection.

Christian interpretations of this poem proffer it as testimony of
Thomas's increasing sacramentalism. Both Davies and Spender
argue for Thomas's orthodox belief in the Catholic Eucharist.
Spender notes:

> At his best, one really has the impression of the word becoming flesh. In
> a poem like "This Bread I Break" the mystery of the transubstantiation
> seems to be hidden within the changes going on in the words them-
> selves. If one completely understood what was happening with these
> verbs and nouns, one would have a deeper knowledge of the Christian
> mystery.[21]

More likely, however, this early poem is a reinterpretation of the
Eucharist from Thomas's own viewpoint. It incorporates an ambiguous persona, a descent of the spiritual into the physical, and a
literal description of a human being's inseparable relationship to
nature. Although Derek Stanford suggests that the poem is a "sort
of 'pantheistic' eucharist," he goes on to aver that it is addressed to
a lover, not to a congregation.[22] Given Thomas's penchant for
rooting much of his imagery in bodily processes, this may be
plausible, but it is certainly secondary to the literal nature imagery.
Kidder's reading seems more to the point. He sees the poem as a
prototype of later thematic poems and an early instance of language
giving way to theme instead of obscuring it.[23]

The imagery demonstrates the disruption of the eucharistic sacrament. By the end of the poem, the body and blood are returned to
bread and wine in a typological reversal of the actual Eucharist. The
speaker in the first two stanzas looks backward to the natural

origins of the elements instead of forward to their spiritual antitypes:

> This bread I break was once the oat,
> This wine upon a foreign tree
> Plunged in its fruit;
> Man in the day or wind at night
> Laid the crops low, broke the grapes' joy.
>
> Once in this wine the summer blood
> Knocked in the flesh that decked the vine,
> Once in this bread
> The oat was merry in the wind;
> Man broke the sun, pulled the wind down.
>
> This flesh you break, this blood you let
> Make desolation in the vein,
> Were oat and grape
> Born of the sensual root and sap;
> My wine you drink, my bread you snap.

(ll. 1–15)

Thomas anthropomorphizes nature to make man's destruction of it
almost cannibalistic. The eucharistic imagery acts subversively; it
lends seriousness and sanctity to the original oat and grape. The
staccato syllabic verses are propelled by short, destructive verbs,
primarily versions of "break."

In stanza 1, either man or the wind has harvested or destroyed
the oat and grape. Here harvesting and natural destruction are
equal evils. In stanza 2, this destruction is intensified by allusion to
"summer blood" and "flesh" of the vine. Furthermore, man has
broken the "sun," a thinly veiled allusion to the Son, and controlled
the wind. In other words man, not Christ, exacts the sacrifice.
Stanza 3 reverts to the present tense and addresses an ambiguous
you—the reader, a lover, a congregation? It fuses the allusions of
the previous two stanzas and causes an almost dizzy series of
transformations: flesh and blood hark back to oat and grape, then
become wine and bread in a return to the present tense. Thomas
adds a living element to the ceremony by introducing man-made
wine and bread in their pristine forms of grape and oat. The entire
poem operates on the principle of decomposition.

The full rhyme "sap" and "snap" of the final two lines is unusual
for Thomas and stresses the now static quality of nature over-
whelmed by man's violent action. All in all, this eucharist is a

violation, not a restitution. The real presence is that of the living oat and grape, not of Christ. Significantly, Thomas avoids the word "body" throughout the poem and limits it to the synecdoche "flesh," thereby intensifying the visceral focus on natural over spiritual elements.

Finally, one again encounters the problem of the ambiguous persona. Is the "I" of stanza 1 the same "I" of stanza 3? If so, both "I" and "you" are complicit in their plot to destroy nature. If not, the second "I" would appear to be Christ equating himself with "the sensual root and sap." The "desolation in the vein" would then signify man's participation in the sacrificial part of the sacrament, his *kenotic* self-surrender and his fusion with Christ and Christ's Passion. In either case, "This Bread I Break" heralds a movement away from the more personal "I" of the genesis poems toward a sustained exposition of sacramental imagery. It remains for "Altar-wise by Owl-light" further to untangle (entangle) Thomas's religious stance.

"Altarwise by Owl-light," a series of ten sonnets written in 1935 and 1936, marks a midpoint in Thomas's effort to make a religious theme speak through language instead of having the linguistic tex-ture obscure the theme. Here both content and verbal texture merge, at times clouding each other, at others creating an almost shocking sense of presence. The title is an accurate indicator of the complexity one encounters throughout the poem. It contains sev-eral of Thomas's favorite tropes of amplification—tmesis (transposi-tion of the words "wise" and "light"), paradox ("Owl-light" equals darkness), and homonymic pun ("Altarwise" equals close to the altar or wise as to the sacrificial meaning of the altar). Most of all, the title indicates the "halfway" quality of the entire poem: much of the imagery is paradoxical and disconnected as if the speaker were writing in doubt as to which way to turn. "Altarwise" in this sense could mean lacking any wisdom of the sacrifice, remaining near the altar in doubt and darkness.

Although several critics have argued that the sonnet sequence moves from doubt to faith, several others focus on the density of language that threatens to cloud content.[24] One cause of this cloud-iness, as Bernard Knieger suggests, is that Thomas "simulta-neously denies and affirms Christ's divinity."[25] Indeed, the lan-guage seems to mime this conflict; it staggers backward and for-ward without an identifiable pattern of imagery. Part of this con-fusion may be, as Kidder suggests, due to the uncertainty of a narrative framework that "gives the impression of an emphasis on Biblical specifics to the exclusion of religious commitment."[26] Kidder goes on to note the absence of any coherent thematic imagery as the central problem of the poem.[27]

Yet this lack of a thematic thread may be precisely Thomas's point. Refusing as he has said to raise himself to the stars or to orthodox Christian dogma, he chooses to pull the stars down to his own level. In fact, this level has various surfaces, each of which contains its own cluster of imagery and evokes its own tone. These tones—variously sarcastic, bitter, and revelatory—change with the choice of persona who seems alternately to be Christ, Thomas, and an obscure prophet, or perhaps a mixture of the three. As in his earlier poetry, Thomas incorporates Old and New Testament allusions and twists them into morbidly visceral images. At times the sonnets parody both Incarnation and Resurrection and posit a person's obstinate confrontation with death as the ultimate reality. "Death is all metaphors, shape in one history" (l.15), he says in sonnet 2, affirming his persistent equation of birth and death in the genesis poems.

In "Altarwise," as in "This Bread I Break," however, Thomas moves past this simple equation by tackling the problem of sacrifice. One must be wounded with the Word to experience redemption. The sonnets almost literally wound the ear in their often ugly straining against the confinement of the sonnet structure. Here Thomas approaches Donne and Hopkins both thematically and linguistically. He deranges ordinary perception, as Jacob Korg suggests, to reach a reality beneath linear syntax.[28] Thomas frequently speaks of this elusive reality as "the magic beyond definition," and the "attempt at an expression of the summit of man's experience."[29] In his "Poetic Manifesto" he avers that poetry is "figures of sound expressing some lyrical impulse, some spiritual doubt or conviction, some dimly-realized truth I must try to reach and realise."[30]

Like the beginning of Donne's "Godfriday," "Altarwise" tries to speak doubt and conviction simultaneously by transforming Christ into a degraded "penny-eyed . . . gentleman of wounds, / Old cock from nowheres and the heaven's egg, / With bones unbuttoned to the half-way winds" (ll. 7–9). This dubious figure will not leave the Thomas persona alone; he "Scraped at my cradle in a walking word / That night of time under the Christward shelter" (ll.11–12). The counterpart to the Christward shelter in the first sonnet is the halfway house in which the gentleman lies "graveward with his furies," descendent of Abaddon (angel of death) and Adam (instigator of death). Although Kleinman argues that sonnet 1 is a "transformation of the Nativity story according to St. Luke," it is difficult to perceive even a semiorthodox treatment of the Incarnation here.[31] Rather, the extension of the Incarnation into the present is more like a curse than a blessing, for it reminds one of the sacrifice ("gentleman of wounds") and the uncertain origin ("Old cock from nowheres") of Christ, not his promised Resurrection nor redemption of mankind.

The salient doubling device of sonnet 1 that serves as a thematic key is the repetition of "half-way" and its echoes throughout in such words as "graveward," "hangnail," "Christward," and hyphenated compounds. The directional markers, "graveward" and "Christward," mean pointed toward, not accomplished. "Hangnail," in addition to its literal meaning as a painful piece of flesh, also conjures up Christ's flesh hanging nailed to the cross, a painful reminder to man of his own impending death. "Owl-light," "atlas-eater" and "penny-eyed" all provoke almost impossible contradictions; "owl-light" and "penny-eyed" simultaneously suggest and deny sight, and "atlas-eater" indicates a physical impossibility—a creature eating the world. Finally, the "long world's gentleman," transformed from "that gentleman of wounds," foreshadows the climactic assertion of the ambiguous poet-Christ persona of sonnet 8: "The world's my wound" (l.102). Christ, not Adam, has imposed his wound on the entire world. Instead of resting complacently in Adam's sin, one must now contend with the problem of sacrifice to be redeemed.

In addition to the syntactical and thematic dislocations, the sonnet form is violated by lines of eleven beats, and the meter does not scan smoothly in iambic pentameter. As Kleinman notes, "We are cut adrift from syntax."[32] This severing of form and syntax mimes the halfway quality of the Thomas persona who is loath to fasten himself to one specific structure but must drift midway between doubt and faith. The halfway quality of the imagery, syntax, and rhythm in sonnet 1 indicates a failure to recreate a "limit-experience" in "limit-language," perhaps because the truth and nature of that experience are still uncertain. Language is neither referential nor revelatory; sound and sense cannot harmonize.

It falls to sonnets 8 and 10 to create some kind of coherence and in so doing to break the words open to sacramental presence. Both sonnets operate by compression; they fuse images synesthetically and introduce ambiguous personae. Sonnet 8 compresses time to expose the fallacy of human chronology. It announces both Crucifixion and Resurrection and transforms Christ to "Time's nerve in vinegar" (a temporal echo from sonnet 1—"That night of time under the Christward Shelter"):

This was the crucifixion on the mountain,
Time's nerve in vinegar, the gallow grave
As tarred with blood as the bright thorns I wept;
The world's my wound, God's Mary in her grief,
Bent like three trees and bird-papped through her shift,
With pins for teardrops is the long wound's woman.
This was the sky, Jack Christ, each minstrel angle
Drove in the heaven-driven of the nails
Till the three-colored rainbow from my nipples
From pole to pole leapt round the snail-waked world.
I by the tree of thieves, all glory's sawbones,
Unsex the skeleton this mountain minute,
And by this blowclock witness of the sun
Suffer the heaven's children through my heartbeat.

(ll. 1–14)

Of all the sonnets and the earlier poems, sonnet 8 comes closest to merging secular and divine time in the "mountain minute"—the moment of Christ's death and the promise of his Resurrection and consequent redemption of mankind. Christ's death catapults human beings into a new dimension of eschatological time. The "gallow grave" in line 2 compresses both Crucifixion and tomb; it unites death and burial by alliteration, semantic proximity, and grammatical equality (the two words are both nouns).[33]

In line 3, blood and tears fuse through the thorns, a simultaneous image of sacrifice and grief. The "I" here is ambiguous: Are the mourners or Christ weeping, or both? At death, the "gentleman of wounds" from sonnet 1 transfers his wounds to the world where the speaker, now seemingly Thomas, inherits that wound at the moment of Christ's death.[34] The second half of the line is ambiguous— "God's Mary in her grief." It either modifies wound or "God's," and also acts like a contraction in which God becomes Mary in her grief as the world becomes the speaker's wound. The two possibilities illustrate Thomas's technique of exploding meaning through two equally plausible interpretations of the same phrase. The teardrop pins echo the thorns and nails as teardrop crosses back to "the bright thorns I wept" of line 3. The unexpected "minstrel angle" for "minstrel angel" seems a purposeful slip and indicates the multiple angles of the singer-speaker as well as arousing a visual image of angels at the four angles of the cross.

The persona of the final four lines is again uncertain. Kleinman perceives the "I" as Christ unsexing death,[35] though another possibility suggests that the "I" is God who, by the witness of the sun (Son), affords mankind entrance into eternal life. The unsexing of the skeleton echoes the early poem "No Man Believes" where one must first kill an anthropomorphic God and reduce Him to a skeleton in order to raise and clothe Him. Here God must perform the same action on Christ to ensure mankind's belief. Again Thomas asserts that there is no faith without sacrifice. Finally, the "I" may be Thomas himself who "unsexes" the skeleton through the revelatory words of the poem.

The final two lines recall the proclamatory saying of Christ, "Suffer little children, and forbid them not, to come unto me: for of such is the kingdom of heaven" (Matth. 19:14), reinterpreted and internalized in a transformation similar to "My camel's eyes will needle through the shroud" in sonnet 4 (l.52). Both allusions refer to Christ's parabolic statements about life after death in the "other" kingdom. Like Christ, Thomas disrupts ordinary logic by borrowing the eschatological language of the parables and proclamations. He goes further, however, and disrupts the accepted sense of the parables by scrambling syntax and transforming parts of speech. As Paul Ricoeur notes, parables "disorient" us to "reorient" our imagination "to new possibilities, to discover another way of seeing, or acceding to a new rule."[36] Thomas twists parables not only to thrust the reader into a new way of seeing but also to make him question the freezing of parabolic language into dogma. He plays with "limit-language" in the "Altarwise" sequence to displace dogma and renew active faith. He degrades parable to rhetorical riddle; he distorts the speaker's stance and denies the reader a visual image. By this disruptive process, Thomas shows how traditional syntax reinforces dogma—the "peasoup mist of associations"—that obscures true divinity.

As M. J. Hammerton states:

Thomas's originality appears in a favorite device of his which consists in taking a well-known phrase, using enough of it to provide recognition, and just when we are about to settle comfortably on the cushion of a well-established formula, we find ourselves sitting on something sharp and unaccustomed, for he has deftly deflected the ending of the cliche to provide the shock and surprise that all original writers can create.[37]

Such abruption, characteristic of Donne and Hopkins as well, creates a temporary mental block in which the mind harks back to the original (in this case, parable), then darts forward to the discrepancy or gap between the original and the actual text. By this device, Thomas succeeds in forcing the reader back toward familiarity and forward to unforeseen revelation. These distortions of the familiar slice through time and space simultaneously to push together and pull apart associations. Furthermore, because parable and kingdom saying carry within them a disruption of human time, the reader is already predisposed to see beyond temporal logic.

The final sonnet, as Kleinman notes, echoes and subtly transfers many of the words in sonnet 1. "Altarwise" is now "Atlaswise"; the globe is balanced, not eaten; the word blown, not walking. Compression is again evident in line 6—"December's thorn screwed in a brow of holly"—fuses allusions to Incarnation and Passion. There is here also a remnant of the random transubstantiation of "This Bread I Break" as well as the metonomy of "December's thorn" and "brow of holly." The persona is submerged, save for the "I" of the first five lines, the teller of the tale "from a Christian voyage." This teller is a survivor who balances "Time's [a periphrasis for Christ] ship-racked gospel" atlaswise on the globe. The teller still has to balance time with Christological time; he has not yet reconciled the two. "Ship-racked" recalls the more traditional word shipwrecked and also images a ship stretched in two or a person (Christ?) split on a rack (cross?). It also, perhaps inadvertently but temptingly, echoes Hopkins's line in the *Deutschland*: "Is the ship-wrack then a harvest?" (1.248). Likewise, the gospel (Christ's words) is "racked" and held "half-way off the dummy bay," (again an echo of the *Deutschland's* wrecked position off the Welsh coast), still not given directly to prospective believers. "Dummy" as an adjective means fictitious, a definition that adds further ambiguity to the gospel's destination.

Line 4 uses hyperbaton and synesthesia—"So shall winged harbours through the rockbirds' eyes / Spot the blown word" (ll.130–31)—to emphasize the flux and chancy reception of the gospel. The counterpart to "winged harbours" is the flying garden" of line 10— allusions, respectively, to eschatological kingdom and ontological Eden. The transformation of flying garden to diving garden, while it captures the darting and soaring of the rockbirds, also links Christian ontology and eschatology through the images of the "two bark towers"—tree of knowledge (death) and cross (Resurrection).

The sonnet pushes beyond the temporal transformations of "This Bread I Break" to illustrate the Christian concept of redeemed time. Here elements are not randomly transubstantiated; instead, a clear pattern of descent and ascent, absent from the former poem, emerges. The final two lines, however, are puzzling. Clearly referring to Judgment Day, they state, "When the worm builds with the gold straws of venom / My nest of mercies in the rude, red tree" (ll.139–40). Perhaps the threat of the worm or of death's poison is preparatory to the realization of mercy through sacrifice. "Rude, red tree" recalls the homonym rood or cross as well as Christ's blood on the cross. The tree of knowledge and its consequent sin foreshadow both Christ's bloody sacrifice and his redemption. Judgment Day will abolish death and sacrifice for those who have received mercy.

Unlike Hopkins's *Deutschland*, "Altarwise by Owl-light" seems to stop short of actually asserting redemption. Though it refers to Judgment Day and though its imagery appears redemptive—"blown word," "sown," "flying," "soar," "build"—the final sense is of the necessity of sacrifice, not of rebirth. The "nest of mercies"—symbol of suffering, not joy—is built in the tree. The straws, though golden, are venomous. The presence here is not clearly analogous to the Real Presence of the Eucharist where Christ and communicant are mutually sacrificed and united. It seems that such presence, contingent on sacrifice, is still only anticipated, not achieved. It falls to the later poems, specifically to "Ceremony after a Fire Raid" and "Vision and Prayer," to realize sacramental presence through human sacrifice.[38]

In "Ceremony after a Fire Raid" and "Vision and Prayer," Thomas attempts to fuse language and theme into sacramental ritual. Here syntax finally supports rhythm, and a central theme arises from this collusion. In these two poems, he moves beyond the biological consubstantiation of elements in the genesis poems to a specifically religious typology. The poems are erected on an inherently Christological framework; they posit Christ as the nexus of temporal and eternal. Like Hopkins's *Deutschland*, they use Christ as the route from death to rebirth. Christ offers a release from Adam's mortality, yet Christ must die to redeem mankind. As John Nist notes, "The blood of Christ is that final light which the dark in man cannot ultimately escape."[39] Like Davies and Kidder, Nist argues that Thomas finally subordinates himself to the religious myth instead of subsuming the myth to himself. Davies sees "Ceremony" as "bringing together . . . the legend of Adam, and the Mass of the 'broken body' of Christ the second Adam."[40] Though less inclined to acknowledge a strictly typological movement, Kidder perceives a transformation from hollow ritual to fleshed-out sacrament where words and theme conspire:

> Ritual . . . may be taken to mean language that refers to some form and order of worship. Sacrament, involving ritual, goes farther and calls attention to the poem itself—to the process of poetic creation and to the very words on the page—as symbol of a deeper religious realm.

The sacramental "rises from words about things towards things in themselves."[41]

Although "Altarwise" appears to rise "towards things in themselves," it ultimately fails to make form analogous to content. There is always a gap between the ritualistic rigidity of the sonnet form and the seemingly random juxtaposition of images. "Ceremony after a Fire Raid" departs from Thomas's longer syllabic lines to emphasize the jagged, nonlinear process of faith. Unlike the denser "Altarwise," the persona and progression are guided by verbs that propel the progress instead of retard it. Similarly, the prepositional phrases designate direction; they do not disrupt it.

The doubling devices begin with the "Myselves" of the persona, a boldly ungrammatical assertion of communion, in which the dead child, Christ, poet, and mourners are fused. Throughout the poem this double persona allows personal and public to merge in a mimesis of the eucharistic ceremony where communicants and priest are united through the language of the Mass. Here the language of the poem, like that of the Mass, activates the vision in each stanza. Part 1, guided by the verbs "grieve," "sing," and "forgive," moves like a formal communion prayer addressed not to Christ but to the child who by stanza 4 is equated with Christ in the image of "Child beyond cockrow." Like the crucified Christ, denied by Peter before the cock's third crow, the child is now beyond the denial of the living.

Stanza 3 moves like the "flesh-burst" stanza 8 of *The Wreck of the Deutschland*: It explodes the communion wafer in a violently hyperbolic image. The ritualistic repetition begins with a penitential prayer and ends in a celebration of the death-life paradox similar to the last line of "Altarwise's" sonnet 8: "Suffer the heaven's children through my heartbeat." Like "No Man Believes," the persona, "myselves the believers," needs the sacrifice of death to experience true faith:

> Forgive
> Us forgive
> Us
> Your death that myselves the believers
> May hold it in a great flood
> Till the blood shall spurt,
> And the dust shall sing like a bird
> As the grains blow, as your death grows, through our heart.
>
> (ll.17–24)

The supplicatory "Forgive" introduces a new *kenotic* element absent from the earlier poems. With faith and forgiveness—the necessary *kenotic* ingredients for grace—the persona can understand the sacramental significance of the child's (Christ's) death as it grows through "our heart," another paradoxical doubling device in which many hearts are emptied into one communal one. Here too is a subtle typological movement from the Old Testament allusion to the "flood" to the New Testament sacrifice of "blood," as the internal rhyme stresses the transition. The "blow" / "grow" rhyme of line 24 furthers this movement and pushes toward the resurrection from death and its realization in the communal "our heart."

Another doubling device that operates *kenotically* or sacrificially in "Ceremony after a Fire Raid" is reverse typology in which the grievers are advised to sing back to a synesthetic beginning before the Word when "the caught tongue nodded blind." The child's "decreation" has (however blasphemously) dictated a sympathetic decreation of the Word in an effort to recreate a new faith and a new language in which to express that faith. This typological reversal— New Testament collapsing back to Old—underscores part 2. Here the speaker speculates which holy figure—Adam, Eve, Christ, Mary—was the first to die in the child's skull. He then offers his own interpretation: He fuses Old Testament with New in a feat of compression where the words strain both forward and backward:

> I know the legend
> Of Adam and Eve is never for a second
> Silent in my service
> Over the dead infants
> Over the one
> Child who was priest and servants,
> Word, singers, and tongue
> In the cinder of the little skull,
> Who was the serpent's
> Night fall and the fruit like a sun,
> Man and woman undone,
> Beginning crumbled back to darkness
> Bare as the nurseries
> Of the garden of wilderness.
>
> (ll.46–59)

The white "skeleton / Of the garden of Eden" of the first verse has become the bare "nurseries / Of the garden of the wilderness,"

as original sin begets barrenness or death. If, as in "Altarwise,"
death is still "all metaphors, history in one shape," then Old and
New Testaments are identical, each hedged by death. Yet part 2
does not wholly support such despair. The child, both itself and
Christ, is the serpent's "Night fall," Satan's death, as well as Satan's
institution of death. If Christ vanquishes Satan and death, however,
it is only after his own and that of mankind. This is the great lesson
with which the poem struggles to come to terms. As Thomas will
aver later in "Poem on His Birthday," "Dark is a way and light is a
place," but "dark is a long way" (ll.49, 64). Likewise, in his final
sonnets and letters, Hopkins lives in a nighttime world where he
realizes that to the living, light is more a promise than a reality.

Part 3 of "Ceremony after a Fire Raid" employs repetition of the
kenotic "into" and *pleromic* "over" to announce the sacrifice of
death and the victory of resurrection. Here Genesis unites with the
Revelation to St. John in a resounding declaration of light:

> Into the organpipes and steeples
> Of the luminous cathedrals,
> Into the weathercocks' molten mouths
> Rippling in twelve-winded circles,
> Into the dead clock burning the hour
> Over the urn of sabbaths
> Over the whirling ditch of daybreak
> Over the sun's hovel and the slum of fire
> And the golden pavements laid in requiems,
> Into the bread in a wheatfield of flames,
> Into the wine burning like brandy,
> The masses of the sea
> The masses of the sea under
> The masses of the infant-bearing sea
> Erupt, fountain, and enter to utter for ever
> Glory glory glory
> The sundering ultimate kingdom of genesis' thunder.

(ll. 60–76)

The brutal burning of the child has been transformed into a
gloriously sacramental burning that will become the scalding purgation of "Vision and Prayer." The earthquake imagery of the last
stanza not only recalls the biblical Revelation but also catches the
moment of communion—the Mass—when the bread and wine assume living properties and force the communicant into a realization
of a new presence united with his own. This presence connects both
the creation of Genesis and the eschatological kingdom of St. John's

Revelation by vanquishing death. Thomas has used the occasion of the child's death to force an odyssey through and beyond death in "Ceremony after a Fire Raid." Unlike the "half-way" gospel held off the "dummy bay" of "Altarwise," "Ceremony" enacts and commemorates a sacrifice that was previously regarded askance with fear and skepticism. The explosive quality of repeated words thrusts meaning forward instead of restricting it. The reader is pushed by sound instead of lulled or distracted by it.[42] Yet Thomas must still realize presence through a human, not a divine, tragedy. The act of coming to grips with the child's death pushes him toward reconciliation with God. As he must in the early poems descend into himself to realize presence, he now moves into an empathic identity with the dead child.

Refusing to acknowledge any sacramental fusion of language and belief in "Ceremony after a Fire Raid," Jacob Korg argues that the poem is a "ritualistic rehearsal of established articles of faith." He goes on to state, "The spiritual victory of the poem, encountering too little resistance, is too easily won . . . it moves, like a ceremony, among symbols divorced from their sources of value."[43] Yet this divorce is precisely Thomas's intention. As in "Altarwise," he dislocates symbols to jar the reader out of complacent orthodoxy. He then reassembles these symbols into a new pattern to suggest a new meaning. As he says in his letters, first to Charles Fisher in 1935 and later to Henry Treece in 1938, a poem should "work from words from the substance of words and the rhythm of substantial words set together, not towards words. Poetry is a medium, not a stigmata on paper" (CL, 182). Korg is anxious to view Thomas's work as either hermetic—a self-referential artifact—or as purely referential—a hollow mimesis of an orthodox ceremony. To Henry Treece Thomas justifies his dialectical method of composition, which makes the two poles of Korg's view converge:

Each image holds within it, the seeds of its own destruction, and my dialectical method . . . is a constant building up and breaking down of the images that come out of the central seed, which is itself destructive and constructive at the same time. . . . an image must be born and die in another; and any sequence of my images must be a sequence of creations, recreations, destructions, contradictions. Out of the inevitable conflict of images—inevitable because of the creative, recreative, destructive and contradictory nature of the motivating centre, the womb of war—I try to make that momentary peace which is a poem. . . . A poem of mine is a watertight section of the stream that is flowing all ways, all warring images within it should be reconciled for that small stop of time. (CL, 281–82)

"Vision and Prayer" literally illustrates this dialectical method both in its concrete appearance and in its extension of this creation-destruction theme. Like *The Wreck of the Deutschland,* it is a conversion poem, moving from birth to death to rebirth in twelve patterned stanzas. Of the numerous interpretations of the stanza shapes, one fact is clear: the diamonds of part 1 are reversed to hourglasses in part 2 as if to mark two contrasting times—the first ebbing away from, and the second fulfilling the first.[44] A further interpretation would insist on the personal visionary quality of part 1 and the public prayerlike quality of part 2. The self-enclosure of part 1 and the expansiveness of part 2, as Sister Roberta Jones suggests, may mark the descent and metaphorical death of the persona and the ascent of the convert, or, as Kidder suggests, the death of the poet and the birth of the convert.[45] The emblematic hourglass stanzas of part 2 visually reinforce the *kenotic* emptying and *pleromic* fulfillment of the eucharistic service.

Like the genesis poems and like parts 1 and 2 of "Ceremony," part 1 of "Vision and Prayer" is concerned with a birth that Thomas equates with death. There is no way out of this world, both shape (womb = tomb) and statement—"And the heart print of man / Bows no baptism / But dark alone / Blessing on / The wild / Child" (ll. 12–17)—suggest. Birth foreshadows crucifixion: ". . . the shadowed head of pain / Casting tomorrow like a thorn" (ll. 24–25). "And the winged wall . . . torn / By his torrid crown (ll. 29–30). Although the imagery is familiar (see "Before I Knocked"), the shape and speaker are more formal than in the earlier poems. No longer is the ground of the poem exclusively based on the poet's body and its biological functions. Instead, like "Ceremony after a Fire Raid," the foundation rests on a human child who is equated with the Christ child, not on Thomas himself. In both poems, however, the child, not the grown Christ, spurs the poet's conversion. Here Thomas, like Donne, has designated an external event as a type of internal event and has reversed his earlier tendency to view the world as a microcosm of himself. Self-absorption has been transformed to self-sacrifice.

Stanza 4 insists on the necessity of self-sacrifice as a prerequisite for redemption. Like part 3 of "Ceremony after a Fire Raid," the imagery recalls that of St. John's Revelation. The slightly varied repetition of lines 6 and 11 adds liturgical formality to a vision whose swirling imagery threatens to break out of its tightly controlled form:

In
The spin
Of the sun
In the spuming
Cyclone of his wing
For I was lost who am
Crying at the man drenched throne
In the first fury of his stream
And the lightnings of adoration
Back to black silence melt and morn
For I who was lost who have come
To dumbfounding haven
And the finding one
And the high noon
Of his wound
Blinds my
Cry.

(ll.52–68)

Synesthetic recognition of the wound that blinds and makes dumb ("dumbfounding haven") paves the way for the culmination of the vision in which the speaker ascends from "the vultured urn / Of the morning / Of man" (ll.81–83) to "The world winding Home" (l.98). The diamond shape of part 1 has become an equation of Genesis with Revelation, Alpha with Omega, through the speaker's participation in the wound: "And the whole pain / Flows open / And I / Die" (ll.99–102). One is reminded of Donne's insistence on personal crucifixion as a requirement for God's grace. The pun on "dumbfounding" illustrates the paradox of language and vision in part 1. To surrender the self to the wound of Christ's crucifixion means to lose one's voice, hence Kidder's assertion that part 1 indicates the death of the poet.

Part 2 does not immediately announce the resurrection attendant on the sacrifice. Instead, the voice prays "In the name of the lost" from "the centre of dark," not in the name of God, nor from heaven. It asks that Christ let the dead lie in darkness, for "Forever falling night is a known / Star and country to the legion / Of sleepers whose tongue I toll" (ll.154–56). Because Christ's martyrdom demands a reciprocal martyrdom from humans, Thomas asks that human beings be allowed to avoid the pain, that Christ return to "a grave grey / And the colour of clay" (ll.184–85). The final stanza, however, like that of "Ceremony after a Fire Raid," heralds a sudden reversal. Unexpectedly, the speaker experiences a revelation in which sun and Son fuse to mark the climax of the vision and the answer to the prayer:

> I turn the corner of prayer and burn
> In a blessing of the sudden
> Sun. In the name of the damned
> I would turn back and run
> To the hidden land
> But the loud sun
> Christens down
> The sky
> I
> Am found.
> O let him
> Scald me and drown
> Me in his world's wound.
> His lightning answers my
> Cry. My voice burns in his hand.
> Now I am lost in the blinding
> One. The sun roars at the prayer's end.
>
> (ll. 199–215)

Here the cry is not, as in part 1, blinded or muted. Rather it is heard and answered. Prayer and poetry coincide, or rather poetry is transformed into prayer, as wordless vision gives rise to praise— "my voice burns in his hand." Reciprocity finally replaces assertion and appropriation.

Recognition of the necessity of sacrifice pervades Thomas's later poems. "Poem on His Birthday" and "Author's Prologue" act as sacramental responses to the vision achieved in "Vision and Prayer." This underlying realization of sacrifice allows Thomas to view death without rancor and with hope for salvation. "Poem on His Birthday," written two years before his death, recapitulates the doubt and lostness of "Vision and Prayer" until the last three stanzas. The prayer, like the prayer in the name of the lost, is "Faithless," but the final enumeration of blessings pierces through the unreconciled "brambled void" of Heaven to announce a victorious voyage toward death:

> That the closer I move
> To death, one man through his sundered hulks,
> The louder the sun blooms
> And the tusked, ramshackling sea exults;
> And every wave of the way
> And gale I tackle, the whole world then,
> With more triumphant faith

Than ever was since the world was said,
    Spins its morning of praise,
    I hear the bouncing hills
Grow larked and greener at berry brown
    Fall and the dew larks sing
Taller this thunderclap spring, and how
    More spanned with angels ride
The mansouled fiery islands! Oh,
    Holier then their eyes,
And my shining men no more alone
    As I sail out to die.

(ll.91–208)

Having given himself over to death, he is able to "inscape" the sacramental quality of nature in which he can now participate. Despite Karl Shapiro's caveat against this sacramental view, Thomas is able both to celebrate and enter his own death through the poetic process.[46] As mourning shifts to rejoicing, he has gained, like Hopkins before the Terrible Sonnets, a sense of the consubstantiation of man and nature through Christ's example of sacrifice.

The final stanza converts fall to spring through synesthetic images of growth. Thomas "hears" the hills grow greener and "sees" the larks "sing taller" in "this thunderclap spring," a possible reminder of the thunder of Revelation. The last two stanzas are filled with comparative adjectives that directly equate proximity to death with expanding life. It is as if Thomas has assimilated Judgment Day into his own personal life and death. By internalizing the imagery of Revelation, he at once makes his own death more divine and the Eschaton more human. Like Donne in his final "Hymne to God My God," Thomas is now able to assert his identity with divinity at the moment of death. His "sundered hulks" have been transformed to "shining men" surrounded by angels. Like the "myselves" of "Ceremony after a Fire Raid," the speaker is no longer isolated but infused with both natural and spiritual presence. Like Coleridge's Ancient Mariner, he learns that prayer and blessing—a specific type of prayer—can effect a consecration of self and nature. From "Ceremony after a Fire Raid" to "Vision and Prayer" through "Poem on His Birthday," Thomas becomes a consecrator, invested with the ability to make the relationship between words and their referents sacramental.

"Poem on His Birthday" is a subtler evocation of sacramental presence than either "Ceremony after a Fire Raid" or "Vision and Prayer." Although some critics perceive Thomas's late poems as a failing of poetic power, the reverse seems to be true.[47] This poem and "In Country Sleep," for example, do not take the reader abruptly by storm. They do not pinpoint the revelation of a sacramental universe; rather they survey the effects of what Hopkins might term "after-gracing" or a kind of resignation to a limited time on earth. Instead of recalling Genesis, they push toward a typological and eschatological view of life. Allusions to Christ are muted; stanzas are regular and strictly syllabic. The rhythm *flows* through the words instead of *bursting* through them or acting against them. Assonance and internal half-rhyme contribute to the steady softer beats. Once accepted, the wound imagery too fades in anticipation of the final wound of death.

Thomas's final finished poem, "Author's Prologue," gathers up the selves of "Poem on His Birthday" and "Ceremony after a Fire Raid" as well as his other chosen *Collected Poems* into a metaphorical ark that he sends out on the flood to his readers. Its form—two stanzas of 51 lines each rhyming backward from the middle—recalls the hourglass shape of part 2 of "Vision and Prayer."[48] Its progression, however, is more linear and chronological. Choice of the typological image of Noah building his ark is unusual for Thomas who generally avoids such a sustained single analogy. Unusual too at first glance are the simple syntax and short lines that, in a sentence of 33 lines, operate by listing and thereby accumulating sea life. Yet both theme and form are carefully wrought to enclose the *Collected Poems* in a timeless present—the *now* of the first and last lines and the *sun* of "God speeded summer's end" (2nd and 101st lines). If one regards the poem as a sacrificial offering to the reader as Thomas indicates in a parenthetical insertion one should do—"(though song / Is a burning and crested act, / The fire of birds in / The world's turning wood, / For my sawn, splay sounds)" (ll.24–28), the "Prologue" reinforces the movement toward a sacramental vision of nature the earlier poems had promised.

The tropes of amplification—often full, identical rhymes, mirrored reverse stanzas, onomatopoeia, direct address, exclamation, parenthetical asides—move away from the tight paradoxical compression of such poems as "Altarwise" toward a less conflicted vision, a "poor peace," as Thomas states in the poem and in his letter to Bozman. Noting the intricacy of the rhyme and the difficulty of composition, he says, "Why I acrosticked myself like this, don't ask me" (*CL*, 838). The pun's closeness to the Crucifixion is unmistakable and provides a clue to the poem's sacrificial character.

M. J. Hammerton argues that for Thomas writing was the su-
preme sacrifice. He implies that such a sacrifice united him with
Christ and allowed him a sacramental view of man and nature.[49]
"Author's Prologue" spells out this sacrifice to the reader:

> At poor peace I sing
> To you strangers (though song
> Is a burning and crested act,
> The fire of birds in
> The world's turning wood,
> For my sawn, splay sounds),
> Out of these seathumbed leaves
> That will fly and fall
> Like leaves of trees and as soon
> Crumble and undie
> Into dogdayed night.
>
> (ll.23–33)

Poetry is a wound, the act of writing a self-wounding as such poems
as "On No Work of Words" assert.[50] Though it may purport to
preserve life by praising it, the process of writing is itself life
draining, not life sustaining for Thomas. The imagery of the "Prologue" makes this clear as it equates building (preserving) with
wounding and hacking:

>   as I hack
> This rumpus of shapes
> For you to know
> How I, a spinning man,
> Glory also this star, bird
> Roared, sea born, man torn, blood blest.
>
> (ll.36–41)

And again:

>   my flood ship's
> Clangour as I hew and smite
> (A clash of anvils for my
> Hubbub and fiddle, this tune
> On a tongued puffball)
>
> (ll.69–73)

Thus in a very literal sense, the "Prologue" and the other *Collected Poems* are bloody sacrifices transformed into sacramental
songs. Though the recreation of Noah's ark in the "Prologue"

would seem to introduce a new life as it sails out on the flood, its images recall particularly the end of "Poem on His Birthday" where the sun blooms as the men sail out to die:

> We will ride out alone, and then,
> Under the stars of Wales,
> Cry, Multitudes of arks! Across
> The water lidded lands,
> Manned with their loves they'll move,
> Like wooden islands, hill to hill,
> Huloo, my proud dove with a flute!
> Ahoy, old, sea-legged fox,
> Tom tit and Dai mouse!
> My ark sings in the sun
> At God speeded summer's end
> And the flood flowers now.

(ll. 91–102)

Both Stephen Spender and J. Hillis Miller recognize the dilemma of poets like Thomas who struggle with their own rebellious wills under the shadow of a larger cosmic will. Hopkins and Donne believed in the necessity of subduing their individual wills to the will of God, whereas Thomas had no such direct path. His obssession with wounding and sacrifice throughout his poetry attests to an intuitive belief in the efficacy of sacrifice as a prerequisite for sacramental presence. As he sloughs off his godlike persona, he moves toward the embodiment of this sacramental presence in his poems. The price of this achievement is, as Miller notes, agonizing. Either one can absorb the world, or he can surrender himself to it: "The act by which man turns the world inside-out into his mind leads to nihilism. This can be escaped only by a counter revolution in which man turns himself inside-out."[51] The turning inside out perhaps epitomized by the visual hourglass of "Vision and Prayer" and the aural hourglass of "Author's Prologue" requires death as a prelude to resurrection.

In a late letter to Marguerite Caetani, Thomas refers to himself as a miraculous Houdini bent on submerging himself, then rising in a parody of Christ's death and resurrection:

I see myself down and out on the sea's ape-blue bottom: a manacled rhetorician with a wet trombone, up to his blower in crabs. Why must I parable my senseless silence? my one long trick? my last dumb flourish? It is enough that, by the wish I abominate, I savagely contrive to sink lashed and bandaged in a blind bag to those lewd affectionate

racous stinking cellars: no, I must blare my engulfment in pomp and
fog, spout a nuisance of fountains like a bedwetting what in a blanket,
and harangue all land-walkers as though it were their shame that I
sought the sucking sea and cast myself out of their sight to blast down
to the dark. It is not enough to presume that once again I shall weave up
pardoned, my wound din around me rusty, and waddle and gush along
the land on my webbed sealegs as musical and wan and smug as an
orpheus of the storm: no, I must first defeat any hope I might have of
forgiveness by resubmerging the little arisen monster in a porridge
boiling of wrong words and make a song and dance and a mock-poem of
all his fishy excuses. (*CL*, 915–16)

Gone is the "found" persona of "Vision and Prayer," the "shining
men" of "Poem on His Birthday." As Thomas stated in a prophetic
letter to Pamela Hansford Johnson in 1933, a writer must choose
between the world of flesh and the world of nonflesh:

> . . . under the philosophy . . . which declares the body to be all and the
> intellect nothing, and . . . limit(s) the desires of life, within the walls of
> the flesh; or under the philosophy which, declaring the intellect and
> reason and the intelligence to be *all*, denies the warmth of the blood and
> the body's promise. You have to class yourself under one heading . . .
> for the equilibrium between flesh and non-flesh can never be reached by
> an individual. While the life of the body is . . . more directly pleasant, it
> *is* terribly limited, and the life of the non-body, while physically un-
> satisfying, *is* capable of developing, of realising infinity, of getting some-
> where, and of creating an artistic progeny. (*CL*, 70–71)

Both Donne and Hopkins struggle with this equilibrium in their
poetry. Strongly orthodox Anglican and Roman Catholic, they have
in the Real Presence of the Eucharist a precedent for this balance
between flesh and nonflesh. Dylan Thomas and Geoffrey Hill lack
faith in such a model, yet they try to achieve an analogous presence
through words that echo the eucharistic Prayer of Institution.
Thomas falls heavily into the way of the flesh or what Stephen
Spender terms the "way of the self," whereas Hill pursues the
opposite route. Spender notes in an essay on Auden and Thomas
that applies equally well to Hill and Thomas:

> The way of the self or the way of the not-self: the way of intensively
> living the contemporary experience, turning it into the flesh and soul of
> the poet's own personality, out of which closed world he hammers his
> romantic poetry; or the way of knowledge, analysis, depersonalization
> and bringing into the area of poetic symbolism the instruments of

science and religion which can dissect the modern world. The way of intuition or the way of learning.[52]

Together, the fleshed sacramental vision of Thomas and the skeletal skepticism of Hill mark two divergent routes open to the modern religious poet. Although Donne and Hopkins could combine voluptuous and ascetic in their poetry, Thomas and Hill lack the orthodox foundation that would permit such a tension to exist. In the absence of an integrating belief, they rely on language itself to revive this tension. Whether they work from word to idea or from idea to word, they have not inherited the spiritual thread that would mend the two. As both Thomas and Hill admit, the world has been tarnished beyond recognition. The task of reclaiming it entails a search for a new ground in which to plant their poems. Although this ground is for Thomas most often like the shifting uncertainty of the sea, his poetry nevertheless identifies a process of sacrificial death and resurrection modeled on the Christological myth: One must first drown before being scalded or saved, a process that Thomas's later poems constantly enunciate.

5

Signs of Presence and Absence: Geoffrey Hill's Way of Dissent

> I cannot turn aside from what I do;
> You cannot turn away from what I am.
> You do not dwell in me nor I in you.
>
> —"Lachrimae Verae"

In choosing what Stephen Spender terms the way of the "not-self," Geoffrey Hill offers an alternative to the early self-absorption of Dylan Thomas. As Hill says in his essay, "Poetry as Menace and Atonement" (1978): "From the depths of the self we rise to a concurrence with that which is not-self."[1] In an interview with John Haffenden in 1981, Hill agrees with T. S. Eliot's statement in "Tradition and the Individual Talent" about the necessary extinction of personality. Hill thinks poetry should have no truck with "the display of the personality of the writer."[2] Again, following Eliot, he argues later that "The transcendence of personality in art presupposes an intensity and richness of personality in the creator."[3]

Hill's search for presence in his poetry is fraught with conflict and self-conscious suspicion. He is unable, like Cardinal Newman or Newman's disciple Hopkins, to assent to an incarnational faith that would secure the bond between language and theology. Instead, he hovers between admiration and scorn for the leap of faith demanded by martyrdom (one of his most persistent themes).[4] He remains detached, hidden behind the disparate historical voices projected from his often elaborately formal poetic structures. This suspicion of faith, combined with and perhaps engendered by a guilty cultural consciousness, prevents Hill from realizing—like Donne, Hopkins, and Thomas—a sacramental presence in his poetry. At the same time, Hill's preoccupation with exposing cultural crimes reinforces the power of language to evoke what might oxymoronically be called the presence of absence or a longed-for

147

presence analogous to that of Donne's Holy Sonnets or Hopkins's Terrible Sonnets.

Speaking of Hill's "uncommon tongue," Vincent Sherry remarks that the poetry "is a purging, a *kenosis* or emptying, rather than a *pleroma,* a filling with the grace of redemption."[5] This emphasis on *kenosis,* or self-sacrifice, links Hill with the more overtly religious voices of Donne, Hopkins, and Thomas. Yet, unlike his three predecessors, Hill is less concerned with personal self-sacrifice as a prerequisite for identification with Christ and more insistent on probing the integrity of sacrifice as a response to political and cultural tyranny. His personae are frequently figures who stand in a symbolically sacrificial relation to their country or their cause. Surveying the sacrifices of war and specifically those of religious martyrs, Hill concludes that there must be a reciprocity between faith and action, or, for the poet, between imagination and action.[6] Hill's poems set out to expose the fraudulent quality of reciprocity without true assent. For Hill there can be no revelatory presence without true assent. On this point he is in agreement with Hopkins who hinges the ability to inscape God's presence on one's *"doing-agree"* or active assent to God's will.

In an instructive early essay on Yeats, " 'The Conscious Mind's Intelligible Structure': A Debate," Hill borrows Newman's title, *A Grammar of Assent,* to explain that a poet's assent involves "a reciprocity between imagination and action," in which the mind is " 'enriched and deepened by action.' " Failing a "grammar of assent," Hill says a "way of syntax will do." Such syntax will naturally be tortured; fully conscious of its own inadequacies, it will not make false promises. Instead it will evince

> the tune of a mind distrustful yet envious, mistrusting the abstraction, mistrusting its own mistrust, drawn half-against its will into the chanting refrain that is both paean and threnos, yet, once drawn, committed utterly to the melody of the refrain.
>   It is not Newman's real assent. . . . One can only say that it is a paradigm of the hard-won "sanctity of the intellect."[7]

Though Hill is speaking here of Yeats, the definition applies to his own poetry. He commits himself, as one essay's title—"Our Word is Our Bond" (1983)—indicates, to language in lieu of faith. Whether such a commitment can evoke a presence analogous to the sacramental Real Presence is arguable.[8] Nevertheless, both the poet's and the priest's search for presence involves a belief in the potentially transfiguring power of language. This power, according to Hill, comes from discovering and acknowledging the recurrent, underlying rhythms of language. On rare occasions when rhythm is perfectly suited to semantics, the poet achieves a "way of syntax" that might deepen to a "grammar of assent."

In "Redeeming the Time" (1984), Hill praises Wordsworth's Immortality Ode for transforming a fractured world. Leaning on Hopkins's discussion of the Ode in an 1886 letter to Canon Dixon, Hill adds:

> If language is more than a vehicle for the transmission of axioms and concepts, rhythm is correspondingly more than a physiological motor or a paradise of dainty devices. It is capable of registering, mimetically, deep shocks of recognition. (*LL*, 87)

Hill terms the collusion between rhythm and semantics a vital relationship as opposed to an inert structure (*LL*, 95). A vital rhythm (and here Hill refers to Hopkins's use of sprung rhythm) allows poetry to step out of stride while still progressing. (*LL*, 98). These steps out of stride serve, not unlike Ricoeur's discussions of Christ's parabolic sayings, to disrupt ordinary linear logic, to detect at least the strains of a deeper logic beneath the common rhythm. According to Hill, a poet has an obligation to step out of stride, to register his antiphonal voice against the common and often debased language of his age. In "Our Word is Our Bond" Hill describes the ethical importance of this antiphonal voice. Referring to Felix Holt's *Address to Working Men,* Hill deplores George Eliot's inability to step out of stride, to record "the antiphonal voice of the heckler": "George Eliot has denied us the cross-rhythms and counterpointings which ought, for the sake of proper strategy and of good faith, to be part of the structure of such writing. Felix's argument is fair enough but it ought to be fairly heckled" (*LL*, 90). Consequently, Hill frequently returns to the older English rhythms—to the language of the *Anglo Saxon Chronicle* and the Anglican liturgy—but always interrupts these rhythms with his own heckling voice. If he cannot redeem language and so redeem the time, Hill refuses to allow either to rest in complacency.

Hill offers Hopkins as the primary example of a poet's attempt to redeem a time. In his explanation of the final line of "Carrion Comfort" in which Hopkins depicts himself as the heckler, Hill gives his own definition of language's ability to evoke presence. One's own language *communes* with the language of God as one communes with Christ in the Eucharist:

> What we have termed the ambivalent power of the short words is most eloquently realized in the final line of "Carrion Comfort": "(my God!) my God." The abrupted experiences once more commune with each other; the expletive of a potentially filthy bare forked animal ("I wretch," "carrion") and the bare word of faith. (*LL*, 102)

This clash, according to Hill, produces a "shock of recognition" when the physical and spiritual seem to meet in the syntax of human language. Hill admires Hopkins above the latter's contemporaries George Eliot and Matthew Arnold for resisting the "inertial drag of language," for redeeming the time "both ethically and rhythmically" (*LL*, 103).

In "Our Word is Our Bond," Hill continues his search for a language that would enforce communion between word and deed, and would thus raise language above a purely referential and often hypocritical status. Conceding that "Modern poetry . . . yearns for this sense of identity between saying and doing" (*LL*, 153), Hill pulls Hopkins's concerns into the twentieth century. He pits Ezra Pound's "disjunction of the aesthetic and the ethical" (*LL*, 155) against Hopkins's religious struggle for right will, translating the latter into an ethical and linguistic struggle for right words and right action:

> There is an essential "freedom of pitch" (which is when "I instress my will to so-and-so") and there is "accident[al]" "freedom of field." If, however, language as medium is a prime manifestation of "freedom of field" and the right-keeping of will manifests "freedom of pitch," Hopkins's theological crux is necessarily a linguistic crux. The abrupt and ugly phrasings (*"the doing be, the doing choose, the doing so-and-so . . ."*) excessively, even absurdly, concentrate the sense of pitch. It is a consciousness which accepts that the determining of grace necessitates at times a graceless articulation. (*LL*, 157)

Hill restricts Hopkins's theological definition of pitch as the highest cleave of being, or the "determination of right and wrong" (*Sermons*, 148), toward which one can reach to its literal, aural definition. He considers "freedom of field," defined by Hopkins as "the object, the field of choice" (*Sermons*, 149) and "choice of alternatives" (*Sermons*, 152) to be choice of words. Pitch then becomes an acknowledgment of right rhythm, a poet's ability to maintain a stride and to step out of that stride. For Hill, however, correct pitch demands an ethical commitment to a particular course of action. This commitment demands a language ("freedom of field") that must be faithful to its source, a language not necessarily rhythmical. In fact, it is often harsh and brutal as it reflects the violence and corruption of its society. It is the poet's way of implicating himself in his guilty culture. By refusing to soothe himself with traditional poetic cadences, he tries to reinstate a language true to the ideas it expresses. Hill praises Hopkins for stepping out of stride to preserve a committed will; conversely, he condemns Ezra Pound for stepping out of stride, then retracting that misstep.[9]

Hill translates Hopkins's discussion of human and divine will into a moral and secular concern and places the burden for finding both the right action and the right words on the poet:

> The ethical and the esthetic come together at those points where "freedom of pitch" and "freedom of field" perfectly intersect or perfectly coincide. (*LL*, 158)

According to Hill, a poet in a postincarnational age must respect language in the same way he reveres (or should revere) right action. The spiritual dimension of language has been transformed to ethical obligation on the part of the speaker. Consequently, the poet with the correct pitch may transmute language into right action. "Bond" carries a double meaning: Between the poet with correct pitch and his language, it symbolizes a tie; for a poet who does not commit himself to words, it signifies imprisonment.

Hill oscillates between both meanings of "bond." At times language is the tool with which the poet may transfigure a fractured world and, like Wordsworth, make it new. At others, language is an enemy, refusing to open itself to the poet, refusing presence. At those times, the modern poet (and especially Hill) finds himself in Hopkins's final dilemma—unable to inscape God in nature and thus unable to locate the words to enact the experience.

For Hill, however, the modern poet's inability to inscape presence involves more than a sense of personal unworthiness. Hopkins's sense of failure is a direct and personal one, whereas Hill expands his to include historical guilt. One is now both passive victim (inheritor of guilt) and active purveyor—by virtue of living and writing in a guilty culture—if not participant. Such a position makes the poet particularly vulnerable because he is compelled to dredge up historical sins, yet is unable to exonerate himself. Thus for Hill, poetry does not act like confession or the Prayer of Consecration. It does not purge the communicant and prepare him for communion. Instead, it exposes criminal deeds but lacks the healing power to forgive those deeds. Still, by reviving historical atrocities, Hill tries to achieve a presence that slices through time and unites history with the present. His primary aim is to force one into a bloody communion both with one's own guilt and also with that of one's ancestors. Such a cannibalistic communion is a prerequisite for any spiritual transcendence. Hill would differ with Thomas's "No Man Believes" where man must kill God to resurrect Him. Hill would aver that we have already committed the slaughter but lack the grace (Hopkins's definition of "freedom of pitch") to beg for the resurrection.

The modern poet has inherited a guilty language, and Hill is too conscious of that guilt to adopt Thomas's method of absorber and namer. This historical guilt severs Hill from Thomas and prevents him from asserting any sacramental presence in his poems. Still, he is not unmoved by the temptation to play prophet or priest. As he mentions in an interview:

> I think there's a real sense in which every fine and moving poem bears witness to this lost kingdom of innocence and original justice. In handling the English language the poet makes an act of recognition that etymology is history. The history of the creation and the debasement of words is a paradigm of the loss of the kingdom of innocence and original justice.[10]

Conversely, Merle Brown sees Hill as masochistic in his desire to explore the ugly side of history: "Hill's joy comes from exposing the unexamined terror in the examining experience, in the poetic act of resuscitating the past."[11] Exhuming the corrupt past entails a careful examination of words and syntax. If the word was once creator and redeemer, it is now also deceiver. Most of Hill's critics point to his battle with a suspicious language as the main problem and ultimate victory of his poetry. Of Hill's reluctance to use lavish imagery, Jon Silkin notes, "it is as though the image whereby one object is enriched by the verbal presence of another, combined with it, and a third thing made—as though such a creation were recognized as so potentially powerful, and so open to abuse, that he was especially careful to use it sparingly."[12]

Others mark the dichotomy to which Hill's "Bond" essay addresses itself: the discrepancy between word and action. Summing up Hill's first three books, Edward Hirsch states,

> The relentless paradox at the center of Hill's work is the sense of a linguistic responsibility to a reality that evades language. Speech may be impotent and bereft of meaning, but it is the only weapon that the poet-as-bewildered-survivor can rely on. And so he is left with the irony of

his own helplessness, the promethean task of reinfusing the shod Word.[13]

As Robert Richman notes, "To Geoffrey Hill, the faintest whisper of possible consummation cheats life of its despair."[14] Consummation would be communion, realization of presence. According to Hill people are not worthy of such an achievement until they can expiate historical sins. Hill cannot partake of a communion already sullied by centuries of hypocrisy. Accordingly, his language cannot elicit an incarnational presence.

Defending himself against the criticism that his poems "lack a true feeling for the passion of religion," Hill states, "Since a failure to truly grasp experience and substance is one of the characteristic failings of human nature, I would have thought that the lyric poet with any psychological and dramatic sense is quite properly involved with that kind of distancing and failure."[15] Hill borrows a phrase of Joseph Cary's to speak of himself and his poetry: " 'a heretic's dream of salvation expressed in the images of the orthodoxy from which he is excommunicate.' "[16] His long poem, "The Mystery of the Charity of Charles Peguy" (1983), deals with another alienated figure who "remained self-excommunicate [from Roman Catholicism] but adoring."[17]

The theme of excommunication runs throughout much of Hill's poetry. Taken beyond its specifically theological definition of "An ecclesiastical censure imposed by competent authority which excludes those subjected to it from the communion of the faithful and imposes on them other deprivations and disabilities" but significantly adds, "it is not impossible for a man to be excommunicated and yet to be and remain in a state of grace,"[18] it extends to the plight of the contemporary poet who possesses a historical sense that distances him from both his fellow poets and his audience. It also applies to the gap between words and experience. Physically, Hill is excommunicated from historical atrocities, a position Igor Webb is too quick to criticize. Webb accuses Hill of ignoring "a dialectical interaction between poetry and lived experience . . . he implies an aesthetic which perceives as *practical* resolutions which are actually made within the realm of poetry alone."[19] Yet Hill's poetry intentionally *avoids* resolutions; it capitalizes on language's ability to contain multiple meanings without choosing one. In so doing, it opens up events for evaluation, not blessing.

Webb does, however, identify the ground on which much of Hill's poetry stands: "History has become the terrain of meaning, the concreteness which permeates consciousness and impresses its

shape on language and literary form."[20] In other words, history and
its atrocities have replaced God as the ground of being. God has
receded in the face of such global horrors as World War I and the
holocaust of World War II. The presence Hill is forced to elicit is a
negative one.

Although Hill's poetry adopts many of the doubling devices of
Donne, Hopkins, and Thomas, it employs them toward different
ends. Hill uses language as a weapon to wound himself and the
reader and to create an intentional fissure between the word and its
promised fulfillment. Instead of tropes of amplification, Hill uses
figures of diminution. Conversely, Donne, Hopkins, and Thomas
use amplified and exaggerated imagery to expose their own wounds
and to beg grace from such exposure. The four poets converge,
however, in their belief in the necessity of personal self-sacrifice as
a prerequisite for any grace or redemption.

Only Hill, while acknowledging and even dwelling on instances of
sacrifice, refuses to assent to an eschatology that would promise
redemption. Without this eschatological goal, his poetry moves
through the dark. Light is not a place, nor death a hoped-for
culmination where one is typologically fulfilled by Christ's Passion.
Yet throughout his five books from the ironic title of *For the
Unfallen* (1958) to *The Mystery of the Charity of Charles Peguy*
(1983), Hill's poetry combines passion with restraint, often almost
destroying the former with the latter. The poetry is like an inverted
communion service. It offers the sacrifice, but denies the sacramental transformation of wafer and wine into Body and Blood. The
clash between passionate outburst and restrained form recalls most
vividly the more overtly religious conflict of Donne and Hopkins—
the problem of the human will lashing itself into obedience to the
divine will. Hill's "way of syntax" adapts the other poets' spiritual
conflict between self-assertion and self-abnegation to a more detached struggle within language.

Hill's critics see this struggle variously as one of "direct mind"
versus "indirect utterance," one of confinement versus release, or
one of withdrawal and return.[21] Yet Calvin Bedient and Thomas
Getz come closest to pinpointing the relationship between language
and faith that is the central crux of much of Hill's poetry. Both see
in the poems a conflict between sensuously carnal imagery and
severely restrained form (an echo of Thomas's distinction between
poetry of the flesh and poetry of the spirit). Bedient argues for a
split in the psyche where "Hill's imagination enjoys what his judgment deplores."[22] Bedient regards *Mercian Hymns* as Hill's best
attempt to merge intellect and sense and, consequently, to create a

language of presence: "The language is dignified while trying to be what it says: both self and other, judgment and participation."[23] Unfortunately, this presence is only momentarily achieved because Hill's ascetic conscience cannot long indulge itself in such poetic luxury. As Getz succinctly states, "The language of verbal incarnation falters and is replaced by a more formal language which establishes a sort of autonomy for the poet."[24]

In Hill's vocabulary, the "pitch of attention" subordinates itself to the "freedom of field." The personal voice of the antiphonal heckler retreats behind the public form only occasionally to burst out in discordant notes. Hill loads words with passionate presence, then *kenotically* empties them of that presence. He introduces complex personae, then forestalls their description by restricting rhyme and aborting punctuation and syntactical flow. Any discussion of doubling devices in Hill must consider the reverse of these devices—distancing techniques—in which the poet "refines himself out of existence" to make the language speak for itself. Paradoxically, these distancing tactics force the reader toward direct confrontation with the words themselves instead of with the poet behind those words. Hill admits that form plays a central role in such achievement:

> I would find it hard to disagree with the proposal that form is not only a technical containment, but is possibly also an emotional and ethical containment. In the act of refining technique one is not only refining emotion, one is also constantly defining and redefining one's ethical and moral sensibility. One is constantly confronting and assessing the various kinds of moral and immoral pressures of the world, but all these things happen simultaneously in the act of self-critical decision.[25]

One can translate Hill's preoccupation with form as "ethical containment" into liturgical terms to examine the semantics of the poetry. Like church ritual, poetic form provides both a boundary and an entrance. It contains collective emotions and lends individual faith a sanctuary, a familiar rhythm. This rhythm roots and secures the faith; it also helps to articulate it. Speaking of the "liturgical prose" of the Anglican collects, Hill notes that their " 'familiar rhythm' is both liturgical and extraliturgical, telling of a rhythm of social duties, rites, ties and obligations from which an individual severs himself or herself at great cost and peril, but implying also the natural sequences of stresses and slacks in the thoughts and acts of a representative human being" (*LL,* 93). When one taps this rhythm either in the liturgy or in a poem, one approaches a communion between words and sound. Such rhythmic communion underlies the meeting of the individual voice with the public liturgical one in Holy Communion. It also unites the poet with a poetic tradition. In the work of a good poet, according to Hill, rhythm generates form; the poem becomes a grammar of assent. A lesser poet works backward, hoping form will discover rhythm. Hopkins and Wordsworth belong to the former; Hill aligns himself with the latter but aspires to the former.

In three early poems from his first collection *For the Unfallen* (1959)—"Genesis," "The Bidden Guest," and "Canticle for Good Friday"—Hill shows how form (and ritual) are inadequate replacements for the rhythm of true faith. The three poems from his first book are tragic expositions of the failure to achieve real presence. "Genesis" pits personal will against the impersonal rhythm of nature and concludes that creation of a world (or of a poem) is always self-defeating. Its persona moves from a briefly ecstatic affirmation of God's works—"Against the burly air I strode / Crying the miracles of God"—to the irreconcilability of human passion with Christ's Passion:

> On the sixth day, as I rode
> In haste about the works of God,
> With spurs I plucked the horse's blood.
>
> By blood we live, the hot, the cold,
> To ravage and redeem the world:
> There is no bloodless myth will hold.
>
> And by Christ's blood are men made free
> Though in close shrouds their bodies lie
> Under the rough pelt of the sea;
>
> Though Earth has rolled beneath her weight
> The bones that cannot bear the light.

(ll. 36–46)

Death and destruction undo creation, although the Christian myth insists that Christ's death redeems mankind. Although Hill assents to the inevitability of sacrifice and death, he cannot comprehend the irony of their necessity, nor understand how they guarantee redemption. In "Genesis" the monotonous iambic tetrameter and the full rhymes reinforce the heavy fatalism of Hill's version of creation.

Yet Hill "steps out of stride" to indicate that the victory of the physical over the spiritual is not without struggle. The rhymes are often half or slant; iambic tetrameter is broken by spondees so that one is forced to pause at specific words. The "blood" of stanzas 2, 4, and 5 connects the stanzas, and clinches the paradox of creation and destruction. People live by acts of physical cruelty—drawing horses' blood—as well as by acts of faith—believing in Christ's blood. Between these two poles is the simple biological fact of stanza 5: "By blood we live." Here, in one word, Hill compresses the themes of much of his later work: bestial, biological, and spiritual wrestle for dominion in humans. Hill's abrupt breaking apart of phrases at the line's end syntactically postpones fulfillment until the beginning of the next line. The semantic antithesis of "ravage" and "redeem" reacts against the words' alliterative and rhythmic placement. The promise of redemption has supposedly sanctioned the slaughter, yet such close placement emphasizes their ironically antagonistic relationship. Nevertheless, a "bloodless myth," like mere ritual or a purely formal poetic structure, will deny the possibility of presence. The last two lines represent the capitulation of the individual voice to the formal structure. Regularly iambic, they breathe resignation. Earth and its mechanistic processes have vanquished the redemptive myth of Christ's bloody sacrifice.

The single long stanza of "The Bidden Guest" reinforces "Genesis's" denial of spiritual presence. This poem, more than any of Hill's, details the despair of the would-be communicant who cannot assent to the "bloody myth" of Christ's Passion. It conflates the Pentecostal gift of tongues (one of Hill's favorite liturgical allusions) with the sacrament of Holy Communion, but uses similes to stress the distance between the wished-for sacramental state and the actual one void of presence in which the persona finds himself:

> The starched unbending candles stir
> As though a wind had caught their hair,
> As though the surging of a host
> Had charged the air of Pentecost.
> And I believe in the spurred flame,
> Those racing tongues, but cannot come
> Out of my heart's unbroken room;
> Nor feel the lips of fire among
> The cold light and the chilling song,
> The broken mouths that spill their hoard
> Of prayer like beads on to a board.

(ll. 1–11)

The rest of the poem sketches the speaker's will to believe, but his failure to feel and hence to overcome his excommunication:

> There, at the rail, each muffled head
> Swings somberly. O quiet deed!
> This is the breaking of the bread;
> On this the leanest heart may feed
> When by the stiffly-linened priest
> All wounds of light are newly dressed,
> Healed by the pouring-in of wine
> From bitter as from sweet grapes bled.
>
> (ll.12–19)

The priest is transformed into a surgeon who heals wounds by covering, not cauterizing them. The synesthetic feeding heart and "wounds of light" displace presence by distorting the images. The wounds are healed superficially by wine, not blood. Like Thomas's "This Bread I Break," the poem suggests that the true sacrifice comes from the "bleeding" of the grapes or man's ravaging of nature, not from the mimetic recreation of Christ's Passion in the Eucharist. The hyperbaton, "From bitter as from sweet grapes bled," creates a further depletion. The simile is *in*serted but not *as*serted. The reward is not a sweet one. Such a device—suggested and withdrawn fulfillment—makes the ceremony and the assertion "From bitter grapes bled" all the more unrelenting.

Sacrament and ritual have parted company here. Having witnessed the ritual, the heart remains, like the cold altar, isolated and intact, unmoved:

> The heart's tough shell is still to crack
> When, spent of all its wine and bread,
> Unwinkingly the altar lies
> Wreathed in its sour breath, cold and dead.
> A server has put out its eyes.
>
> (ll.34–38)

For the skeptic there has been no consecration. The extra beat of the next-to-the-last line falls heavily on "dead" and rhymes with "bread" that has turned sour. Likewise, the emphasis on the polysyllabic "unwinkingly" modifying "altar lies" creates an ambiguous persona, neither human nor divine. The poem is a mockery of the Eucharist. The personification is ironic: The altar is given breath and eyes in a synecdotal parody of the Body and Blood of the sacrament. This is not even the half-light of "Altarwise by Owl-light"; it is a total denial of light.

"Canticle for Good Friday" continues the theme for darkness and denial of real presence. Here the irregular stanza structure and uneven line length with the strong stress meter undercut the regularity of the liturgical chant. Hill shows through the persona of St. Thomas, the doubter, that mere desire for faith cannot secure faith. Witnessing the crucifixion, the disciple Thomas is "As yet unsearched, unscratched":

> And suffered to remain
> At such near distance
> (A slight miracle might cleanse
> His brain
> Of all attachments, claw-roots of sense)
>
> In unaccountable darkness moved away,
> The strange flesh untouched, carrion-sustenance
> Of staunchest love, choicest defiance,
> Creation's issue congealing (and one woman's).
>
> (ll. 11–19)

"Carrion-sustenance / Of staunchest love" suggests not only the crucifixion but also its extension in the Eucharist. Carrion here, however, disturbingly echoes Hopkins's use of the same word in "Carrion Comfort" with its cannibalistic connotations. St. Thomas, doubting the efficacy of miracle—of Christ's resurrection and transubstantiation—cannot partake of the eucharistic meal in true faith. Consequently, he can neither realize the Real Presence of Christ in the Eucharist on the altar nor in himself. If St. Thomas, witnessing the crucifixion, still remains untransfigured, what hope is there for modern beings separated by such distance from the actual event, Hill seems to ask.

Hill makes ample use of parentheses in this poem—a doubling device Christopher Ricks remarks in other poems. Ricks terms such bracketing a "creative disjuncture" in which speech and silence are juxtaposed.[26] In this poem the parentheses also suggest the "antiphonal voice of the heckler" (perhaps the poet) that insists didactically that the disciple Thomas, by now a metaphor for everyman, is not transfigured by watching the crucifixion. The second set of parentheses stresses the absence of the miracle of transfiguration to one dependent on sense. "Sense" assumes both meanings of physical sensation and commonsense logic, both of which would be contradicted by a miracle. In both cases, the parentheses, like the hyperbaton of "The Bidden Guest," refer to a spiritual transformation that has *not* occurred and that, consequently, does not belong to the secular narrative.

The final set of parentheses—"Creation's issue congealing (and one woman's)" (l.19)—adds a further touch of irony. If the earlier parenthetical statements suggest what has not occurred, the final phrase calls into question the validity of the Annunciation and Mary's participation in Christ's saga.[27] The parenthetical comments introduce a persona who is dissatisfied with the linear narrative and who wishes paradoxically to stress the spiritual implications of the scene by alluding to the absence of spirit.

The poem presents the carnal nature of the crucifixion devoid of its spiritual significance. The hard "c" alliteration—"carrion," "choicest," "Creation's," and "congealing" (as well as "Canticle")—aurally supports that carnal presence. Like "The Bidden Guest," "Canticle for Good Friday" empties ritual of its sacramental quality by focusing on the material and temporal. There is no mystery, no Real Presence, because the eyewitness cannot bring himself to believe and testify. Hill reduces St. Thomas (and by implication mankind) into a beast who "stamped, crouched / Watched / Smelt vinegar and blood" (ll.7–9), and who finally retreated, leaving the "prey" untouched. Donne's "Goodfriday" still preserves the image of Christ in human beings even though that image is tarnished with sin. Consequently, Donne is able to recreate the crucifixion as a really present physical and spiritual event. Hill's modernized disciple no longer possesses the faith that would restore Christ's image to its spiritual status. The ironic title, "Canticle"—a nonmetrical hymn taken directly from the Bible—insults its biblical source by erasing the intended anagogical meaning.

In his second book, *King Log* (1968), Hill moves toward a more obsessive concern with the perversion of religion by history. The poems in this book reflect his desire to expose the sullying and subsequent defeat of the Word by successive centuries of killing and hypocrisy. They also worry at the gap between professed and lived faith. Too often, Hill insinuates, poetry masquerades as false faith and preaches messages to which it is not committed. "Annunciations," "History as Poetry," and "An Order of Service" arraign this false faith. The rhyme schemes are more complex and subtle, the statements more sardonic than in the first book. Despairing of the poet's ability to "redeem the time," Hill forces his language to wound the ear and the eye in an attempt to recreate "history's atrocities." Donne and Hopkins appeal to God to wound them into *grace,* whereas Hill asks history to wound one into recognition of the *impossibility of grace*.

"Annunciations," like a cannibalistic Eucharist, reverses the promise of figural or typological fulfillment. Descending to flesh in the Incarnation, the Word loses all traces of its redeeming spirituality in the common language of society. Here Hill condemns in synecdotal language the perversion of the original spiritual intention:

> The Word has been abroad, is back, with a tanned look
> From its subsistence in the stiffening-mire.
> Cleansing has become killing, the reward
> Touchable, overt, clean to the touch.
> Now at a distance from the steam of beasts,
> The loathly neckings and fat shook spawn
> (Each specimen-jar fed with delicate spawn)
> The searchers with the curers sit at meat
> And are satisfied. Such precious things put down
> And the flesh eased through turbulence the soul
> Purples itself; each eye squats full and mild
> While all who attend to fiddle or to harp
> For betterment, flavour their decent mouths
> With gobbets of the sweetest sacrifice.
>
> (ll. 1–14)

The first sonnet condemns all those, particularly poets, who have spawned words irresponsibly. Hill mercilessly plays on the double meaning of "spawn"—eggs of aquatic animals and numerous human progeny—as a metaphor for the perversion of the Incarnation. Likewise, he forces words like "Purples" and "Harp" to "spawn" various connotations. Does the soul smugly clothe itself in royal purple, or does it bruise itself? Do the "curers" (of meat? social evils?) and "searchers" (hunters? philosophers?) simply attend to ritual, or do they "harp"—beg continuously—for "betterment"? These puns reveal Hill's expressed dichotomy between passive acceptance of historical crimes and active rebellion against them. The oxymoron, "gobbets of the sweetest sacrifice," mocks the swallowing of the Word in false humility. What Hill despises in both poetry and history is the self-righteously false piety with which the participants clothe themselves. The original Word (Christ), intended to cleanse people of sin, has been appropriated by those same people as a sanction for killing. The wordmongers, just as responsible as warmongers, remove themselves from direct contact with the killers and in so doing are guilty of irresponsibly

sanctioning violence: "flavour[ing] their decent mouths / With gobbets of the sweetest sacrifice."

Sonnet 2 further demonstrates the parody of the Incarnation. The
Word, apostrophized as Love, has dwindled to lust:

> O Love, subject of the mere diurnal grind,
> Forever being pledged to be redeemed,
> Expose yourself for charity; be assured
> The body is but husk and excrement.
> Enter these deaths according to the law,
> O visited women, possessed sons. Foreign lusts
> Infringe our restraints; the changeable
> Soldiery have their goings-out and comings-in
> Dying in abundance. Choicest beasts
> Suffuse the gutters with their colourful blood.
> Our God scatters corruption. Priests, martyrs,
> Parade to this imperious theme: "O Love,
> You know what pains succeed; be vigilant; strive
> To recognize the damned among your friends."
>
> (ll.15–28)

Like the Word in sonnet 1, this Love (lust) spawns equivocal
references both to God and to a human lover. Furthermore, it is
conditional, "Forever being pledged to be redeemed." Paradoxically, redemption is negative, contingent upon recognizing "the
damned among . . . friends." Those who kill under the protective
guise of religion, Hill suggests, are the true whoremongers of the
Word. "Annunciations" (divine impregnations) are "spawned,"
multiplied into proclamations, devoid of spirituality. Mary has been
denigrated to "visited women," Christ to "possessed sons." Here
Hill parallels the perversion and fragmentation of the one Word
with the historical perversion of the Incarnation. Common words
have robbed the Word of its spiritual presence. Instead of con-
centrating on and personalizing biblical legend like Donne and
Thomas, Hill here as in "Canticle for Good Friday" diffuses it,
empties it of sacramental power, and reduces it to secular story.

"History as Poetry" further rejects poetry's ability to purify
language or history. Where Donne, Hopkins, and Thomas would
elevate poetry to sacrament, Hill parodies such pretension:

> Poetry as salutation; taste
> Of Pentecost's ashen feast. Blue wounds.
> The tongue's atrocities. Poetry
> Unearths from among the speechless dead

Lazarus mystified, common man
Of death. The lily rears its gouged face
From the provided loam. Fortunate
Auguries; whirrings; tarred golden dung:

"A resurgence" as they say. The old
Laurels wagging with the new: Selah!
Thus laudable the trodden bone thus
Unanswerable the knack of tongues.

(ll. 1–12)

Depleting the Pentecostal gift of tongues, the poem reduces the tongues of flame from the Holy Ghost to ashes. This Pentecost echoes the degenerate "spawning" of words from "Annunciations." The wounds it inflicts are blue, bloodless. Poetry can unearth, but in Auden's words, "Poetry makes nothing happen" because words have lost their ability to persuade people toward faith or action. The Hebrew word "Selah," signaling a pause at the end of a Psalmic verse, is as foreign and ironic as is "Lazarus mystified." Words have been reduced to mere sounds: "Auguries," "whirrings," or, worse, to "tarred golden dung," excrement preserved and valued like gold. The poet's "knack of tongues" is futile because unanswerable; it is more reminiscent of the "waggings" of Babel than of Pentecost. Again, Hill as in "The Bidden Guest" and "Annunciations" robs words of their spiritual connotations in a reversal of figural fulfillment. The implied resurrection—the lily rearing "its gouged face / From the provided loam"—rises from its "provided" historical material. Thomas and even Donne force spiritual words to praise profane ones, whereas Hill debases spiritual to profane, then condemns both.

As in "Annunciations," words and physical sensation are intimately connected. Words taste, are eaten, feasted on, as in Holy Communion. This sensuousness adds to these two poems a further touch of irony. Those who feast without faith, as Donne warns, are in danger of damnation. For Hill, those who relish words without concern for their meanings are as guilty as hypocritical communicants. Syntactically, Hill relegates poetry to a realm of fragments. The only two active verbs—"unearths" and "rears"—counter sentences driven downward by fragments. The fragments abbreviate the action and halt ascent or resurrection.

"An Order of Service" briefly presents Hill's second major concern in the book—the efficacy of martyrdom. It harps not on presence but on absence of faith and life after death. "Order" becomes double-edged. Ostensibly referring to liturgical service, it also suggests a militaristic command about how to "dismiss" the martyr who dies without belief:

> Let a man sacrifice himself, concede
> His mortality and have done with it;
> There is no end to that sublime appeal.
>
> In such a light dismiss the unappealing
> Blank of his gaze, hopelessly vigilant,
> Dazzled by renunciation's glare.

(ll.4–9)

In "light" of the "sublime appeal" of sacrifice, other potential victims are encouraged to ignore the reality of death as final. Ironically, renunciation becomes a negative presence, an ideal that dazzles or blinds one to the absurdity of self-sacrifice. "An Order of Service" appears to hinge on a Christian myth, but then undercuts that myth to expose the futility of dying for a false cause.

The long sequence "Funeral Music" affords Hill more expansiveness to rail against another equally negative aspect of martyrdom—the posturing faith of those who aspire to be saints. The Wars of the Roses provide the setting and the characters for a battle between "saying" and "doing," or "assent" and denial of assent. Like "Canticle for Good Friday" and "An Order of Service," "Funeral Music" is ironically titled. As Hill states in an appendix to the poem:

> In this sequence I was attempting a florid grim music broken by grunts and shrieks. . . . Admittedly, the sequence avoids shaping these characters and events into any overt narrative or dramatic structure. The whole inference, though, has value if it gives a key to the ornate and heartless music punctuated by mutterings, blasphemies and cries for help. (*CP*, 200)

In this sequence of eight sonnets Hill again evokes the "antiphonal voice of the heckler." That presence is bitterly sardonic. Formal ritual clashes with dissenting voices to expose the hollowness of the former and the ineffectiveness of the latter. What might force the content to fulfill the form is missing—a belief in an ontological-eschatological reality. Such a belief would knit the individual voice ("pitch of attention") with the language of formal ritual ("play of field") in a figural relation; it would constitute a "grammar of assent." Hill, however, condemns the desire to impose such a salvation schema on history. He sees the concept of typological fulfillment as a false justification of history's crimes. Like many of the *Unfallen* poems, the entire sequence maintains a tension between formal vessel and bloody content. By juxtaposing the two instead of having the latter fill the former, Hill jolts the reader out of an anticipated response. Even his choice of the sonnet form sets up expectations of sequence and fulfillment and deliberately undercuts those expectations. It is as if he had offered the hope of communion and withdrawn the cup and wafer at the last moment.

Throughout the sequence as he details the beheadings of English noblemen during the Wars of the Roses as well as the battles, Hill sets up a dialectic between sanctimoniousness and sanctity. He undermines ritual with synesthesia—the "voice fragrant with mannered humility" and paradox—"feasts of unction and slaughter," "a composed mystery," "fastidious trumpets." Here ritual is a bloodless artifact that masks the bloodiness of the acts it praises.

Naturally, Hill suspects the motives of the English martyrs who make of their sacrificial deaths "lingering shows of pain, a flagrant / Tenderness of the damned for their own flesh" (ll.69–70). Like Dylan Thomas in "Altarwise by Owl-light," Hill struggles and fails to come to grips with the connection between sacrifice and redemption. Instead, however, of recreating Christ's sacrifice and probing its efficacy, Hill examines inadequate human emulations of Christ's Passion like that of Tiptoft, Earl of Worcester, who demanded that he be beheaded with three blows " '*in honorem Trinitatis*' " (l.5). He concludes sonnet 1 by exposing the vacuousness of ceremony and the doubtful spiritual reward for such slaughter. Hill juxtaposes the liturgical Latin phrase with the actual bloody event of the beheading: "Crash. The head / Struck down into a meaty conduit of blood" (ll.5–6) to undermine the ideal with the physical fact.

Although the funeral sequence is freighted with historical and theological allusions, Hill again assumes the guise of the heckler to undercut the formal theology with abrupt ruptures of rhythm and with "grunts and shrieks" of the syntax. This heckling presence even manages to undermine the doctrine of the eucharistic Real Presence. It marks the spiritual expunged by the carnal, not the carnal ascending to the spiritual, nor the copresence of the two. The mystery, like the poem, is "composed" by human voices, not by God. In sonnet 2, Hill questions:

> For whom do we scrape our tribute of pain—
> For none but the ritual king? We meditate
> A rueful mystery; we are dying

To satisfy fat Caritas, those
Wiped jaws of stone.

(ll.15–19)

The oxymoronic "fat Caritas"—Christian love and charity—has
been transformed into a lustful beast demanding homage. The mystery of the crucifixion is "rueful," pitiful or sardonic, not filled with
awe and spiritual presence. Hill seizes a sacramental situation and
sacramental language and depletes them of mystery to condemn
the perversion of a Christian ideal. His vision reverses the typological thrust of the sequence instead of reinforcing it.[28]

The third sonnet recalls the Battle of Towton, according to Hill's
sources, a holocaust not unlike that of the Jews in Europe (*CP*,
200–1). Here he forces several doubling devices simultaneously to
elicit the presence of death and the irony of faith. His use of clichés,
for instance, works both to call up familiarity and to twist the
familiar back to its literal meaning.[29] Hill accomplishes this task in
lines 1 and 2 by separating "by / God" over two lines so that one
pauses both after "by" and after "God": "They bespoke doomsday
and they meant it by / God, their curved metal rimming the low
ridge. / But few appearances are like this" (ll.29–30) God is brought
into battle as witness and as empty pledge. He is both present and
absent. The cliché, "by God," illustrates syntactically what it
means semantically: The preposition and its object are separated as
if to emphasize the uncertain relationship between the human and
the divine, or to demonstrate the inability of the human to appropriate the divine to its use. This is the opposite of Hopkins's "(my
God!) my God" of "Carrion Comfort" where Hopkins fully realizes
and submits himself to the linguistic power of God.

Similarly (ll.32–33), Hill speaks of a "comet's / Overriding still-
ness" where here he evokes the gap between the clichaic abstraction (dominant) and the motion of riding over or surveying. The
oxymoron of the literal meaning creates a momentary fissure in
which an unearthly horror is revealed: "men / In such array, livid
and featureless, / With England crouched beastwise beneath it all"
(ll.33–35). Here Hill compresses cliché, oxymoron, and personification to jolt the reader into a nightmarish vision of a bloody war. In
the next line, however, he retracts that vision and assumes the
collective voice of the historian who terms it euphemistically "that
old northern business." Abstracted to ritual, the collective voice
dismisses the individual emphasis on slaughter. The anonymous
quotation exposes the hollowness of a collective voice that can thus
easily absolve itself of responsibility.

The sonnet ends with a scathing comment on the irony of blind sacrifice:

> A field
> After battle utters its own sound
> Which is like nothing on earth, but is earth.
> Blindly the questing snail, vulnerable
> Mole emerge, blindly we lie down, blindly
> Among carnage the most delicate souls
> Tup in their marriage-blood, gasping "Jesus."
>
> (ll. 36–42)

The rude juxtaposition of "carnage" and "delicate," "marriage" and "blood" reinforces Hill's horror of "blind" slaughter. As in "An Order of Service," any revelatory presence at the moment of death is illusory; humans are equated with the snail and the mole, not with Jesus. The gasp is a word turned back on itself, a renunciation of presence. The sonnet offers a cannibalistic self-mutilation in lieu of a eucharistic sacrament.

Here Hill raises the old Augustinian quarrel between sign and signified. Augustine questions, "If it is a carnal slavery to adhere to a usefully instituted sign instead of to the thing it was designed to signify how much is it a worse slavery to embrace signs instituted for spiritually useless things instead of the things themselves?"[30] Hill asks in "Funeral Music" whether there are such things as usefully instituted signs and whether we are justified in attributing spiritual significance to "religious warfare" and to the slaughter it implicitly sanctions.

Sonnet 4 summarizes Hill's attitude toward "expediency of assent." It is straightforward and philosophical, devoid of the sensuous slaughter of sonnet 3:

> Let mind be more precious than soul; it will not
> Endure. Soul grasps its price, begs its own peace,
> Settles with tears and sweat, is possibly
> Indestructible. That I can believe.
> Though I would scorn the mere instinct of faith,
> Expediency of assent, if I dared,
> What I dare not is a waste history
> Or void rule.
>
> (ll. 43–50)

The remonstrance at a "waste history" and "void rule" intensifies throughout the sequence. Hill continues to castigate the

"minds" responsible for such destruction. Such minds, he states in
sonnet 5, are incapable of begging forgiveness:

> When we chant
> "Ora, ora pro nobis" it is not
> Seraphs who descend to pity but ourselves.
> Those righteously-accused those vengeful
> Racked on articulate looms indulge us
> With lingering shows of pain, a flagrant
> Tenderness of the damned for their own flesh.
>
> (ll.64–70)

Here there is no reciprocity between faith and action. Like
Hopkins's late despair at God's withholding of presence, Hill views
prayer as twisting back on itself unanswered. As Craig Raine per-
ceptively notes in a review of *Tenebrae,* Hill's later book, "Christ's
indwelling presence cannot be guaranteed by prayer or the rejection of sin."[31] Here, too, Hill omits the expected punctuation in line
11, eliding the "righteously-accused" with "those vengeful," victim
with actor, to underscore the martyr's responsibility for his own
death.

Hill's refusal of expedient assent breaks through again in sonnet 6
where he announces the agony of belief without object:

> Some parch for what they were; others are made
> Blind to all but one vision, their necessity
> To be reconciled. I believe in my
> Abandonment, since it is what I have.
>
> (ll.81–84)

One cannot force reconciliation. Though abandonment signals absence of God, it is preferable to false acquiescence and shows of
belief. As Hill admits in an interview, "I would answer that the
grasp of true religious experience is a privilege reserved for very
few, and that one is trying to make lyrical poetry out of a much
more common situation—the sense of *not* being able to grasp true
religious experience."[32]

The final sonnet of "Funeral Music" assumes the personae of the
martyred saints as they regard their worshipers. Implicit in the
speakers, however, is the voice of the poet who has capitulated to
the demands of his readers and has, consequently, lost his own
identity. The poem is a meditation on the way people (as Augustine
warns) attribute false presence to signs. The syntax carefully balances being and seeming through repeated phrases. In this sense

the poem serves as a fitting end to the sequence that has attempted, but failed, to destroy this false presence. Repetition levels both the semantic and grammatical difference—"all echoes are the same":

> Not as we are but as we must appear,
> Contractual ghosts of pity; not as we
> Desire life but as they would have us live,
> Set apart in timeless colloquy:
> So it is required; so we bear witness,
> Despite ourselves, to what is beyond us,
> Each distant sphere of harmony forever
> Poised, unanswerable. If it is without
> Consequence when we vaunt and suffer, or
> If it is not, all echoes are the same
> In such eternity. Then tell me, love,
> How that should comfort us—or anyone
> Dragged half-unnerved out of this worldly place,
> Crying to the end "I have not finished."
>
> (ll. 98–112)

History has frozen martyrs and events into postures of reverence. Ritual, Hill will suggest more strongly in *Tenebrae*, has done the same. Both have robbed their subjects of identity. The last three lines erupt out of the semantic and syntatctical composure to protest against this theft. The quoted (hence distanced) cry, " 'I have not finished,' " bitterly refuses to close the sequence. It registers Hill's final antiphonal protest against attempts to reconcile words and actions into formal, ceremonial patterns. The voice pulls the reader into the present to make the martyrs and the slaughtered of the Wars of the Roses contemporaneous with poet and reader. The real presence evoked is that of our kinship with the slaughtered and slaughterers of the fifteenth century. Rhythmically, the presence is that of the liturgical chant, undercut by the antiphonal voice in quotations, a voice that does not respond or obey as it is instructed to do in the traditional chants and psalms.

Mercian Hymns heralds a radical departure in form for Hill. The book resurrects the eighth-century King Offa of Mercia to comment on historical corruption. Like "Funeral Music," *Mercian Hymns,* ironically titled, sounds more like cymbals crashing than church hymns. As in "Annunciations," the Word has descended to flesh and corruption; it is preserved in Offa's titles, his coins, his base actions. Throughout, the imagery blends eighth-century Mercia with the twentieth-century Worcestershire of Hill's childhood. There is no hint of transcendence nor spiritual presence. Hill dredges up the gore and slime of the landscape and of human greed with no attempt to glorify it.

The doubled presence in this book comes from the merging of eighth- and twentieth-century themes and language. Hill mixes archaic Anglo-Saxon words with formal Latinate constructions. Hymn 23 is a particularly good example of the two vocabularies. Stanza 1 lures the reader into a false view of luxurious spirituality. Titled *"Opus Anglicanum,"* it also contains a criticism of Catholic opulence:

> In tapestries, in dreams, they gathered, as it was enacted, the return, the re-entry of transcendence into this sublunary world. *Opus Anglicanum,* their stringent mystery riddled by needles: the silver veining, the gold leaf, voluted grape-vine, masterworks of treacherous thread.
>
> They trudged out of the dark, scraping their boots free from lime-splodges and phlegm. They munched cold bacon. The lamps grew plump with oily reliable light.
>
> (ll. 1–10)

Like the final sonnet of "Funeral Music," this hymn mocks the supposedly religious artist's tendency to transform carnage into art and thereby to distance himself from personal guilt. The glorification of war is a "mystery riddled by needles," a phrase immediately recalling the clichaic "riddled with bullets." The true mystery of Christianity has been punctured by the artist's egotistical notion that he or she could actually restore revelation by simply representing revelatory moments in tapestries. By implication, this idea indicts the poet as well in his similar search for a way to pattern events in words and so reduce history to mere icon. Stanza 1 elevates this euphemistic art into a long formal sentence, whereas stanza 2 mocks the mystery in three bluntly declarative sentences. Again syntax mimes semantic content: At first it elevates the role of the artist and then presents the remoteness and irrelevance of art in contrast to the factual brutality of war. The short, earthy words of stanza 2 effectively undercut the lavish imagery and musical cadences of stanza 1.

Though some critics read *Tenebrae* (1978) as a retraction and a return to Hill's earlier religious concerns, others view it as a spiritual advance.[33] If *Mercian Hymns* exposes bloody myths to public view, *Tenebrae* internalizes the myths and explores their psychological effect on the aspiring believers. More than any of Hill's earlier books, *Tenebrae* is concerned with the problem of assent and grace, and specifically with the ultimate failure of real presence. Unlike Donne and Hopkins, Hill cannot accept the paradox of death as a prerequisite to spiritual rebirth. Nor can he, like Thomas and Hopkins, open himself to the sacramental quality of nature as long as he suspects that quality might be false. In this book he still differs markedly from his precursors while seeming most closely to capture their language of faith.

"Pentecost Castle," the first poem in the book, abjures punctuation and allows for a plurality of speakers and an open-ended form.[34] The lines, often only four or five beats, are unusually short for Hill. Likewise, the rhymes, frequently abab and full, are deceptively simple. The simplicity of the form, however, contrasts sharply with the difficulty of assent. Yet the absence of punctuation allows for ambiguity among words and phrases. Because punctuation between paradoxes is absent, the reader hears those paradoxes more distinctly as in section 8:

> And you my spent heart's treasure
> my yet unspent desire
> measurer past all measure
> cold paradox of fire
>
> as seeker so forsaken
> consentingly denied
> your solitude a token
> the sentries at your side
>
> fulfillment to my sorrow
> indulgence of your prey
> the sparrowhawk the sparrow
> the nothing that you say

(ll.85–96)

Spent presence gives way to absence—"the nothing that you say." One suspects the title, "The Pentecost Castle," gives a clue to the way to read or not read the poem and especially section 8. If the poem is itself a "Pentecost Castle," the words are pent up inside it, awaiting release. Although the lack of punctuation might open the poem, the paradoxes, unlike the scriptural gift of tongues to the apostles (Acts 2:1–6), make the message untranslatable. There is no reciprocity between speaker and listener, and the absence of punctuation reinforces this absence of reciprocity.

"The Pentecost Castle" at first seems to recall Dylan Thomas's sacrificial stance in "Vision and Prayer" and "Poem on his Birth-day." The familiar image of dying to live is, however, slightly skewed in section 9: "I die to sleep in love" (l.98). The action reverses the traditional Christian assertion of dying to wake in love or in God. Likewise, Thomas's assertion that "dark is a long way" is shifted in part 11 to "If the night is dark / and the way short / why do you hold back / dearest heart" (ll.121–22). Like the conversion poems of Donne, Hopkins, and Thomas, "The Pentecost Castle" seeks conversion. Unlike its forerunners, however, it withholds the actual experience. Although it seems in part 13 to lull the reader into belief, the rhythm is deceptive; the words are hollow para-doxes, like those of section 8:

> Splendidly-shining darkness
> proud citadel of meekness
> likening us our unlikeness
> majesty of our distress
>
> emptiness ever thronging
> untenable belonging
> how long until this longing
> end in unending song
>
> and soul for soul discover
> no strangeness to dissever
> and lover keep with lover
> a moment and for ever

(ll. 145–56)

The word "long," wedged between "belonging" and "longing" in stanza 2, links the two words aurally while it pushes them apart semantically. The poem seduces through rhythmic repetition and distances through semantic content, the opposite of Hopkins's defi-nition of poetic counterpoint in which rhythm and semantics ul-timately reinforce each other. Hill stresses such seduction and separation on a linguistic level as a metaphor for the relationship between faith and the skeptical believer.[35]

By the final stanza, Hill equates this relationship with a wound that will not heal:

> I shall go down
> to the lovers' well
> and wash this wound
> that will not heal

beloved soul
what shall you see
nothing at all
yet eye to eye

depths of non-being
perhaps too clear
my desire dying
as I desire

(ll. 169–80)

The "nothing that you say" has become the nothing that the soul sees. Sound and sight are both quenched in the lovers' well, that acts like an impenetrable moat around the castle. The sacrificial wound does not secure grace; instead, Hill reaches an intentional ambiguity in the last two lines. "As I desire" could refer to motive, intention, or to the act of desiring, or both. If "desire" means "act of desiring," one sees the paradox of the seeker suddenly cut off from the act of seeking. In either case, desire or assent is not achieved, although the ambiguity lends a tension to the desire for faith and the rejection of that desire.

In "Lachrimae" Hill moves beyond the ambiguity of "The Pentecost Castle" to a ritualistic search for and criticism of Christian faith. In this poem he realizes a presence similar to that of "Funeral Music," yet here the persona is more intimate and immediate, the subject less rooted in a specific historical context. Merle Brown explains "Lachrimae's" "withheld quality of fulfillment":

> As in "Funeral Music," the "Lachrimae" builds from one poem to the next, and yet, once the sixth sonnet is reached, the others are pulled up into simultaneity with it, so that, what had seemed like hollowness during the experience of building is felt to be folded inside-out so as to manifest the withheld quality of fulfillment.[36]

Yet the entire poem reverses typology as if to empty each successive sonnet. Each sonnet seems to wage an internal battle between desire for faith and denial of that desire. Such conflict, as Thomas Getz notes, impedes both syntax and semantics. Getz states that Hill's halfway faith "does not show him God fully figured in Christ, and so his own language and imagery are half-given."[37] This halfway faith allows Hill a degree of anonymity; instead of purposely disrupting the cadence as in the heckling voices of "Funeral Music," he masks his own personal voice beneath formal liturgical cadences. Ritual affords a temporary escape from personal heresy.

Defending himself against the biographical implications of *Tenebrae*, Hill evasively argues that a fascination with religion and ritual do not make him a religious poet:

> I think that the poems in *Tenebrae* are fascinated by the existence of religion as a historical fact, as a power in the lives of men and women. This is rather different from being a religious poet in the way that term is generally understood.[38]

He concedes, however, that ritual can act as a form behind which one may deal with personal concerns:

> *Tenebrae* is a ritual, and like all rituals it obviously helps one to deal with and express states which in that particular season of the church's year are appropriate—suffering and gloom. *Tenebrae* does at one level mean darkness or shadows; but at another important level it clearly indicates a *ritualistic*, formal treatment of suffering, anxiety, and pain.[39]

This withdrawal from statements of personal faith or doubt paradoxically characterizes Hill's ability to create several presences in a poem. The personal voice speaks behind the formal structure as if from behind a rood screen. Whereas Thomas's religious poems operate in an opposite fashion—the multiplication into the "myselves" of "Ceremony after a Fire Raid," for instance, Hill partitions off his own dissenting voice and allows it to rankle off stage.[40] This rankling takes the form of retracting lines of faith. Hill employs tropes of diminution; he undercuts one word by slightly altering it in the next line (paronomasia), provides anticlimactic epigraphs, and pits words oxymoronically against each other so that the second word depletes the first in a reversal of the communion process.

Sonnet 1, "Lachrimae Verae" (Tears of Truth), conjures up the picture of the first "passionate Pavan" or sixteenth-century stately court dance, itself an oxymoron:

> Crucified Lord, you swim upon your cross
> and never move. Sometimes in dreams of hell
> the body moves but moves to no avail
> and is at one with that eternal loss.
>
> You are the castaway of drowned remorse,
> you are the world's atonement on the hill.

This is your body twisted by our skill
Into a patience proper for redress.

I cannot turn aside from what I do;
You cannot turn away from what I am.
You do not dwell in me nor I in you
however much I pander to your name
or answer to your lords of revenue,
surrendering the joys that they condemn.

(ll.1–14)

The expectations of resolution set up by the Italian sonnet form mock the speaker's inability to turn toward faith. The sestet literally denies the anticipated turn and resolution. Apostrophized at first through the speaker's tears, Christ seems to move until one realizes that the movement is a projected illusion. The presence is delusive. In the octet Hill tries to revive that presence by twisting words as tearful eyes twist vision. By the sestet, however, he realizes the same "depths of non-being" as the speaker of "The Pentecost Castle." In a series of negatives, the tercet acknowledges the irreconcilable division between the speaker's defiant action and Christ's witness of that action. In almost direct counterpoint to Donne's persona in "Goodfriday," Hill's speaker can neither turn aside (renounce his sins) nor beg for the grace to repent. Frozen in this position, he realizes that the Real Presence for him is a myth. Furthermore, pandering to a name and answering to "lords of revenue" are hollow repetitions of ritual. Even highly wrought artistry cannot revive faith. Unlike the exuberantly parabolic imagery of Thomas's "Altarwise by Owl-light's" sonnet 7, "Lachrimae Verae" descends to the cold asceticism of its final word, "condemn."[41]

Sonnet 2, "The Masque of Blackness," condemns the irresponsibility of the self-infatuated writer (Dylan Thomas?) who "models new heavens in his masquerade / its images intense with starry work, / until he tires and all that he has made / vanishes in the chaos of the dark" (ll.24–28). Images of stone and imprisonment in the octet continue the theme of artifice announced in the first sonnet. Lavish words are "contained" in the poet's or the martyr's actions; there is no hope of transcendence: "Splendour of life so splendidly contained" (l.15) and the synesthetic "stony hunger of the dispossessed / locked into Eden by their own demand" (ll.21–22) provoke simultaneously the hope of presence, transcendent communion, and the denial of such presence. The writer who would try to "contain" such splendor does not allow doubt or self-sacrifice to penetrate his world. By defending against sacrifice, he reduces his poems to false icons like the historian who euphemistically smooths over history's atrocities.

"Martyrium" ironically comments on the frozen opulence of sonnet 2. Here, the poem becomes a martyr's shrine, preserving in the octet the actual brutality of unconscious martyrdom, a "Jesus-faced man walking crowned with flies / who swats the roadside grass or glances up / at the streaked gibbet" (ll.29–31). The ugly reality of the martyr's march to the scaffold is, like Christ's body in sonnet 1, twisted into a fading tapestry and abstracted, glorified. The sestet compactly sums up Hill's ambivalent attitude toward sacrifice and the celebration of sacrifice in art:

> Clamorous love, its faint and baffled shout,
> its grief that would betray him to our fear,
> he suffers for our sake, or does not hear
>
> above the hiss of shadows on the wheat.
> Viaticum transfigures earth's desire
> in rising vernicles of summer air.

(ll.37–42)

The poem turns on the ambiguity of "suffers." Do Christ or the martyr simply *endure* the "clamorous love" of their admirers, or do they intentionally *suffer* "for our sake"? Here, as in the end of "The Pentecost Castle," one encounters the conflict between passive acceptance and active participation. If Christ is merely passive and if one attributes sacred characteristics to him to allay one's own fear of death, then the final stanza is ironically secular. "Viaticum" is simply money for a journey, "vernicles" herbal flowers with no curative powers. If, however, Christ actively suffers, "Viaticum" assumes its sacred definition of Extreme Unction—the offering of the Eucharist at death—in which earth's desire is transfigured by the image of Christ's face on St. Veronica's handkerchief. In this sonnet, Hill achieves a disturbing presence closely analogous to the eucharistic Real Presence, yet he continually questions that sacramental presence by depleting sacred words of their biblical and liturgical status and embedding them in a purely carnal context. Hill fuses orthodox definitions of sacred words with the anger of excommunication, or the denial of communion. In "Our Word is Our Bond," he refers to Spenser's *Amoretti* as "a form of troth-plight between denotation and connotation" (*LL*, 144). In "Lachrimae" and elsewhere, Hill experiments with this "troth-plight" and with its opposite—divorce, severance—to make one word unravel numerous contradictory meanings. He confesses that both writer and reader are often at the mercy of these various meanings; they are alternately victims and participants:

> It is [writing poetry], in a peculiar way, the most oxymoronic art: its very making is its undoing. In a poet's involvement with language, above all, there is, one would darkly and impetuously claim, an element of helplessness, of being at the mercy of accidents, the prey of one's own presumptuous energy. (*LL*, 146)

This conflict between active choice and passive acceptance lies at the heart of Hill's problem with martyrdom and assent. Throughout "Our Word is Our Bond," Hill insists, citing Donne among others as proof, that a writer is both active and passive, "exhibiting the symptom at the very moment that we diagnose the condition" (*LL*, 152). If so, the dialectic between symptom and diagnostician helps to quell the criticisms that Hill mercilessly withdraws fulfillment or presence while appearing to offer it. Hill's poetry evokes both the surgical or critical exposure of personal flaws and also the artistic symptoms—the attempts to repress or disguise the flaws beneath religious and poetic imagery.

Such self-repression leads, according to Hill, to the seduction or " 'menace' " of poetry for which the poet must " 'atone.' " In "Poetry as 'Menace' and 'Atonement,' " Hill stresses the guilty poet's *kenotic* endeavor to perfect the poem's form. He defines atonement as "at-one-ment," "a setting at one, a bringing into concord, a reconciling, a uniting in harmony" (*LL*, 2). Such a task pushes beyond poetry as representation or artifact. It marks the poet's struggle with language, which for Hill is analogous to the doubter's struggle with faith:

> It is one thing to talk of literature as medium through which we convey our awareness, or indeed our conviction, of an inveterate human condition of guilt or anxiety; it is another to be possessed by a sense of language itself as a manifestation of empirical guilt. (*LL*, 6–7)

According to Hill, "empirical guilt" has replaced sin. Instead of asking for grace from God, the modern poet must strive to purge himself through a self-lacerating language. Words have become the elements of communion, offering both the possibility of real presence and the knowledge of real absence if taken lightly, in bad faith.[42] In a telling conclusion, Hill equates his own "agnostic faith" with that of Wallace Stevens. He offers a dim hope for poetry's ability to redeem the poet caught in such a paradox:

> It is . . . conceivable that a man could refuse to accept the evident signs of grace in his own work; that he himself could never move beyond that "sorrow not mingled with the love of God" even though his own poems might speak to others with the voice of hope and love. (*LL*, 16)

One hears both these voices in "Lachrimae"—that of the skeptical poet and the rhythmic language that echoes the liturgy, traditionally an instrument of grace. Yet the two voices are not in "at-one-ment"; such an accomplishment would be the actual achievement of Real Presence between the poet and God through the medium of language. Hill's essay undercuts itself in suggesting a sacramental definition of atonement but realizing only a sacrificial one.

The sacrificial stance is embodied in sonnet 4, "Lachrimae Coactae" (Collected or Constrained Tears). Like sonnet 1, it is addressed to Christ, the "Crucified Lord" whom the speaker desires alternately to confess himself to and to condemn. The poem maps out the no-man's land in which the would-be believer finds himself. Like stanza 3 of *The Wreck of the Deutschland*, ("The frown on his face / Before me, the hurtle of hell / Behind, where, where was a, where was a place?" [ll.17–19]): Hill's speaker can find no foothold:

> I fall between harsh grace and hurtful scorn.
> You are the crucified who crucifies,
> Self-withdrawn even from your own device,
> Your trim-plugged body, wreath of rakish thorn.
>
> (ll.47–50)

Unlike Hopkins, however, Hill fails to make the leap, to "tower from the grace to the grace": "You are beyond me, innermost true light" (l.53), and he blames that failure not on himself but on Christ. For the speaker, the crucifixion is a withdrawal of presence, not a eucharistic offering. Consequently, like the Roman soldiers, he mocks Christ—"trim-plugged body, wreath of rakish thorn." The sestet, however, resumes a tone of serious self-interrogation— "What grips me then, or what does my soul grasp?" (l.51)—but by the final tercet the speaker again accuses Christ of withdrawal— "uttermost exile for no exile's sake, / king of our earth not caring to unclasp / its void embrace, the semblance of your quiet" (ll.54–56).

Embittered by his failure to believe, the speaker must pitch a battle between his own active will and the unresponsive Christ his sonnet has invoked. A potential dialogue turns into a dialectical argument between the speaker's will to believe and his disgust at that will, between an urge for transcendence and a recognition of empirical experience that exposes such an urge as hopelessly idealistic. The self-division is finally dissolved by the realization that Christ is an ineffective icon, a collection of poetic words. The poem itself has failed to create the longed-for presence. Instead it has exposed the real absence, "the semblance of your quiet," not even the actual quiet or purposeful absence. Unlike Hopkins's Terrible Sonnets that lament Christ's withdrawal but never question his existence, the Lachrimae sonnets display Christ as the fictitious creation of a distracted speaker. Without faith, this speaker cannot participate in the ceremony; he can only atone continually for his inability to assent.

Sonnet 5, "Pavana Dolorosa," continues to ridicule both "self-wounding" martyrs and the "self-seeking hunter of forms"—the artist. It fuses the apparent passivity of martyrdom with the egotistical activity of the poet. Both lend too much attention to outward displays of emotion to the detriment of what Hill terms in his essays the "pitch of attention" characteristic of such poets as Hopkins and Southwell. Hill suggests that poets and martyrs emphasize ritual over committed belief or true assent. Subtly reversing Southwell's epigraph—"Passions I allow and loves I approve"—the poem turns "Ash Wednesday feasts" and "self-wounding martyrdom" into human passions and shifts Southwell's spiritual intent earthward—to "the decreation to which all must move" (l.64).

Hill's frequent use of the reflexive prefix "self" throughout the sequence and twice in sonnet 5, underscores his warning of solipsism in both martyr and poet. As he remarks, the poet is often caught between a subjective solipsism and an objective adherence to hollow forms. Both extremes represent the " 'menace' " of poetry:

> . . . a considerable danger for the poet lies at either extreme. If he pretends to be wholly unaware of any other mind or spirit with whom he would communicate, then he's in peril of lapsing into a dangerous solipsism. At the other extreme, if he trims his work in any way to some real or supposed expectation, then it seems to me that the danger is just as great.[43]

The "selfs" in the sequence point toward the solipsistic position, the solemn liturgical cadences and formal language toward the public position. The clash between the two paradoxically creates both void and excess, and strikes at the heart of Hill's poetics of real presence. The self can choose to withdraw, to wound itself, to love itself, to seek forms; it can also choose to dance to the liturgical pavans, to participate in the eucharistic ceremony.

Unlike Donne and Hopkins, Hill cannot resolve the conflict between these two options. His own heckler's voice can neither harmonize with the public voice nor with formal liturgy. It can only register protest like an intermittent series of wrong notes. Yet he still believes strongly enough in the efficacy of formal poetic structures and the appearance of ritual not to discard either altogether. He cannot adopt the Whitmanesque stance of the American Beat or Confessional poet who eschews traditional forms as societal constraints. Like Donne and Hopkins, Hill wrestles with an individual will perversely caught in a language of religion and history, a language turned away from action toward hollow form. Unable to force his will to assent to God, Hill spurs it to puncture the hollow forms of language. He uses traditional poetic devices—synecdoche, paronomasia, paradox, oxymoron—to shock the reader into a new sense of linguistic presence. In this light he justifies his assertion that in the absence of "a grammar of assent," a "way of syntax will do."

Sonnet 6, "Lachrimae Antiquae Novae," specifically addresses the deterioration of religion to ritual. Christ is cheapened, "consigned by proxy to the judas-kiss / of our devotion, bowed beneath the gold, / with re-enactments, penances foretold" (ll.73–75). Wedded to form, people have lost the meaning of Real Presence; Christ is consigned to betrayal by dogma that allows symbols to substitute themselves for presence. The entire sonnet spells out the consequences of a Eucharist celebrated for the wrong reasons without true faith:

> Beautiful for themselves the icons fade;
> the lions and the hermits disappear.
> Triumphalism feasts on empty dread,
>
> fulfilling triumphs of the festal year.
> We find you wounded by the token spear.
> Dominion is swallowed with your blood.

(ll.79–84)

The words reverse the communion. Mere celebration of communion replaces the actual triumph of Christ's Resurrection. The sign is mistaken for the event it signifies. In effect, the sign has effaced the event. Hill mocks the perversion of Holy Communion into a justification of war and dominion. Those now partaking of Christ's blood have reduced a religious feast to a carnal, self-aggrandizing activity. The last line's passive voice spreads the blame over all who partake of communion merely for form's sake. The passive voice at once distances the reader from targeting specific persons and also makes him complicit in the act. [44]

The final sonnet, "Lachrimae Amatis," avoids specific mention of Christ by assuming the mask of a secular lover. Like Donne in "Batter my Heart," Hill merges secular and divine through an ambiguous persona who seems to secularize religious allusions. By now, one expects a revelation but receives another retraction or postponement. As in the early poem, "The Bidden Guest," the "heart's tough shell is still to crack" (l.34). It "keeps itself religiously secure" (l.90), a pun on the double meaning of "religious" as holy and tightly guarded. The octet announces the sacrifice, seen as a withholding of the self. The "passion's ancient wounds" literally refer to the lover who keeps suing for love but who is continually rebuffed. On another level (though passion is not capitalized), the wounds refer to Christ's Passion, that "must bleed anew" to be believed in by the speaker.

The final sestet lulls the reader in Keatsian fashion into an anticipated vision, then quietly aborts the vision with the speaker's postponement of presence:

> So many nights the angel of my house
> has fed such urgent comfort through a dream,
> whispered "your lord is coming, he is close"
> that I have drowsed half-faithful for a time
> bathed in pure tones of promise and remorse:
> "tomorrow I shall wake to welcome him."
>
> (ll.93–98)

The sequence ends with a scathing indictment of the seductive quality of language—its ability to arouse a half-faith "bathed in pure tones" that promises presence. It also targets the persona who, unable to assent fully, must lamely promise assent in sleep. Like Keats's "Ode to a Nightingale," Hill's poem flirts with faith and death. Both poems revel in the hypnotic quality of language, then abruptly retract the state that quality induces. Keats, however, appears (albeit momentarily) to achieve his ecstatic vision, whereas Hill's speaker never realizes it.

Although all the poems in *Tenebrae* emphasize Hill's battle between ritual and true assent, "A Pre-Raphaelite Notebook" and "Tenebrae" express the rage that leaps forth from the satirical juxtapositions of sacred and secular images. Such rage engenders a cannibalistic communion in "A Pre-Raphaelite Notebook":

> Primroses; salutations; the miry skull
> Of a half-eaten ram; viscous wounds in earth
> opening. What seraphs are afoot.
>
> Gold seraph to gold worm in the pierced slime:
> greetings. Advent of power-in-grace. The power
> of flies distracts the working of our souls.
>
> Earth's abundance. The God-ejected Word
> resorts to flesh, procures carrion, satisfies
> its white hunger. Salvation's travesty
>
> a deathless metaphor: the stale head
> sauced in original blood; the little feast
> foaming with cries of rapture and despair.
>
> (ll. 1–12)

Reminiscent of both "Annunciations" and "History as Poetry" in *King Log,* stanzas 1 and 2 denounce the artist's attempt to elevate mundane to sacred: "The power / of flies distracts the working of our souls." The seraph is indistinguishable from the worm in "the pierced slime." "Advent of power-in-grace" ironically recalls the liturgical season of Advent—the awaiting of Christ's birth which will prove the efficacy of "power-in-grace." All this desanctified Advent proves, however, is the power of flies to distract one from religious endeavor.

Stanza 3 parodies both the Incarnation and the act of writing poetry. Neither inculcates presence; both feed on themselves, producing a "deathless metaphor," deathless because both metaphorical and perpetually remembered and enacted in ritual. Christ, the "God-ejected Word," has descended to metaphor or worse—He now seeks "carrion,"—dead bodies—but does not save souls. The echo of John the Baptist—"the stale head / sauced in original blood"—further depletes the hope of salvation through baptism. Herod's cannibalistic feast and the Eucharist are conflated into an image that evokes rapture and despair, but not real presence. Again, as in *Mercian Hymns* and his previous books, Hill despairs of redeeming faith through language, although he insists on the sacrificial quality of both. Consequently, Holy Communion has become "the little feast," its communicants either enraptured by ritual or despairing of true faith.

"Tenebrae" continues the ambivalent quest for faith. As its title ironically indicates, the journey is through deepening shadows to total darkness. In its secular definition, *tenebrae* means darkness, mental obscurity—specifically, a Stygian darkness. In Anglo-Catholic doctrine, it denotes the ceremony of extinguishing the candles on the altar during Holy Week to commemorate Christ's death and consequent resurrection. The sequence has the same halfway quality of Thomas's "Altarwise by Owl-light," yet it concludes in a more pessimistic darkness. By the end, all that survives is music, inhumanly the "Angel of Tones, Medusa, Queen of the Air" (l.62). Words and "real cries" have vanished.

Even the public chanting of the psalms that accompanies the ceremony is subsumed by the artifice of the music and the poem that, like the music, composes its own sphere. The poem (sections of which were part of a cantata-text set to music) moves like a psalm in its rhythmic repetition. But, as in many of Hill's previous sequences, the meaning of the words undercuts the rhythm. Stanza 2, a Petrarchan sonnet, appears to address Christ as a lover and personifies faith as a seductress:

> And you, who with your soft but searching voice
> drew me out of the sleep where I was lost,
> who held me near your heart that I might rest
> confiding in the darkness of your choice;
> fulfilled in you I sought no further quest.
> You keep me, now, in dread that quenches trust,
> in desolation where my sins rejoice.
> As I am passionate so you with pain
> turn my desire; as you seem passionless
> so I recoil from all that I would gain,
> wounding myself upon forgetfulness,
> false ecstasies, which you in truth sustain
> as you sustain each item of your cross.
>
> (ll.9–22)

Having almost assented to a connection that would realize real presence, the speaker finds himself in darkness and desolation, confronted with the conflict between human passion and self-sacrifice. "Passion" is the ambiguously full word around which the poem revolves. Sensual passion is wounded, or diverted, as in the end of "The Pentecost Castle." A desire for passionate assent meets a seeming passionlessness or indifference. In addition, the Christ-like addressee seems "passionless"—shorn of his sacramental death. Without receiving a response to or an interpretation of passion, the speaker, like Hopkins in the Terrible Sonnets, recoils on himself, though here into a world of forgetfulness and false ecstasies. Because he knows the paradox of passion—obdurate will versus self-sacrifice—he is unable fully to assent to either. Hopkins accepts passion as sacrifice, whereas Hill's speaker remains in a darkness that blindly and falsely promises eschatological redemption:

> Veni Redemptor, but not in our time.
> Christus Resurgens, quite out of this world,
> "Ave" we cry; the echoes are returned.
> Armor Carnalis is our dwelling-place.
>
> (ll.23–26)

Hill criticizes both "Amor Carnalis"—love of the flesh—and the spiritual hollowness of religious festivals. Because he fails to perceive the sacramental intersection between carnal and spiritual love, the speaker distorts the eucharistic ceremony, parodying the first line of the Nicene Creed:

> O light of light, supreme delight;
> grace on our lips to our disgrace.
> Time roosts on all such golden wrists;
> our leanness is our luxury.
> Our love is what we love to have;
> our faith is in our festivals.
>
> (ll.27–32)

The periphrasis for God—"light of light," not God himself—is the "supreme delight." By subtle antithesis and anticlimax, Hill forces the end of each line to mock its beginning. Light shifts to an ironic *de*light, a pun on lack of light. Grace of communal presence becomes personal *dis*grace. Oxymoronically, leanness is luxury because of the hope of eucharistic fulfillment. Yet love is loved for its own sake, not as a route to God. The festival substitutes itself for the actual event and thereby exacts a false faith.

Here Hill reinforces St. Augustine's distinction between enjoyment and use. Augustine distinguishes between objects loved for their own sakes and those loved as a means to a spiritual end:

Those things which are to be used help and . . . sustain us as we move toward blessedness in order that we may gain and cling to those things which make us blessed. If we who enjoy and use things, being placed in the midst of things of both kinds, wish to enjoy those things which should be used, our course will be impeded and sometimes deflected, so that we are retarded in obtaining those things which are to be enjoyed, or even prevented altogether, shackled by an inferior love.[45]

Hill criticizes people's love of ritual and festival as an inferior one which prevents true assent or faith. Rituals have ceased to signify; they are temporal, temporary. As Augustine states:

. . . a temporal thing is loved more before we have it, and it begins to grow worthless when we gain it, for it does not satisfy the soul, whose true and certain rest is eternity; but the eternal is more ardently loved when it is acquired than when it is merely desired.[46]

Stanza 5 resumes the conflict between willful and sacrificial passion. Like Dylan Thomas, Hill considers the act of writing to be a continual sacrifice, analogous to the sacrificial life of Christ. Both poets seem to believe that by willfully wounding themselves, they will avoid allegiance to the temporal for its own sake. It is as if wounding (or writing) could prepare one for the reception of grace.

Hill queries in stanza 5, "Can my own breath be hurt / by breathless shadows groaning in their game? / It can" (ll.39–41). The shadows, or griefs and guilts, are both breathless with passion and dead or illusory, literally without breath. As in "The Pentecost Castle," desire is killed by desire. In willing not to will, one wounds the actively writing self into a passive victim. In Augustine's terms, one's words are figurative tools, breathless themselves because they work only to capture a faith beyond their realization. As the candles are extinguished, so words work themselves into shadow, "reeling with sensual abstinence and woe" (l.46). Once again, Hill uses oxymoron ("sensual abstinence") to turn words against themselves and deny figural fulfillment. He pits sensuous rhythm against a retreating language so that, as Calvin Bedient remarks, "his lines curl up against us, having been touched by irony or a Pyrrhonistic distrust of every appearance of virtue. Constriction and revulsion recur."[47]

Stanza 7 responds to stanza 2, transmuting false ecstasy into ecstatic wounding. Through his own wounds, Christ has earned the power to wound people into faith. Yet such power has been obscured by "motley" definitions of Christ:

> He wounds with ecstasy. All
> the wounds are his own.
> He wears the martyr's crown.
> He is the Lord of Misrule

He is the Master of the Leaping Figures,
the motley factions.
Revelling in auguries
he is the Weeper of the Valedictions.

(ll.53–60)

Because Christ supposedly dwells in human beings (although Hill has explicitly denied this presence in "Lachrimae"), human wounds are Christ's wounds. Yet people have made Christ the master of ritual and augury, not of indwelling presence. The metaphoric epithets reduce Christ's divinity to the secular role of coach or master of ceremonies. This is the crux that Hill's poetry cannot overcome. It longs for presence to enrich ritual, but it can only lament the lack of presence by mocking ritual, by undercutting it with linguistic presence. Disturbingly, this linguistic presence seems to fill the cadences and to substitute itself for a spiritual presence.

Noting the modern poet's tendency to unsettle language, Derek Attridge pinpoints a central element in Hill's poetry: "a formal pattern may contradict patterns of meaning, and some modern poetry uses rhythmic and sonic cohesion as the major unifier of semantically unrelated or conflicting elements."[48] One might see in this conflict the orthodox liturgical rhythms demanding assent while the poet's actual words deny that assent. In this sense, Hill's poems act as containers, not conveyers of a perverse presence. Because the modern poet cannot move through ritual into faith, he will turn ritual against itself to expose the irreverent contents.

Hill's long poem, "The Mystery of the Charity of Charles Peguy" (1983), recapitulates his favorite themes of historical guilt, martyrdom, and the search for spiritual presence by alternatiely praising and interrogating the dead socialist martyr Peguy. Although Hill derives his title from Peguy's "The Mystery of the Charity of Joan of Arc," he delves deeply into the actual religious meaning of mystery that cannot be logically understood—something that evokes a presence, the nature of which defies close inspection. Nevertheless, Hill inspects and dissects. He explores the central mystery of poetry—the connection between saying and doing— asking both Peguy and modern poets, "Must men stand by what they write / as by their camp-beds or their weapónry / or shell-shocked comrades while they sag and cry?" (ll.14–16). Throughout the poem Hill praises Peguy (who at times acts almost like an alter ego), for standing by his words, both on the battlefield and in his faith and political radicalism. According to Hill, Peguy, a radical socialist, was estranged, evidently not actually excommunicated, from the Roman Catholic church. In the poem, he "stood aside" from mass "to find salvation, your novena cleaving / brusquely against the grain of its own myth" (ll.204–6). Such faithful defiance Hill translates into charity, Augustine's supreme virtue—love of God for God's sake, not for that of others. The "Fat Caritas" of "Funeral Music" has become the true *caritas* of a modern martyr. If a poetic real presence is possible, it must combine words with actions. Words loved for their own sakes do not constitute the definition of charity.

Like Dylan Thomas's final poem, "Author's Prologue," "The Mystery of the Charity of Charles Peguy" is much closer to a coherent narrative than Hill's previous works. It is the antithesis of *Mercian Hymns* in its tight pentameter quatrains and its careful full and half-rhymes. Yet, like *Mercian Hymns,* it reaches for earthy and grotesque images in its refusal to raise Peguy to a bloodless abstraction. Like *Mercian Hymns* also, it adopts a persona behind which Hill may sketch his own attitude toward poetry, religion, and power. If Offa represents the netherside of Hill, Peguy symbolizes Hill's aspirations and his idealism.

Part 2 pits Hill against Peguy and decries the impotence of writers like Hill himself who have never witnessed active warfare: "Memory, Imagination, harvesters of those fields, / Our gifts are spoils, our virtues epitaphs, / Our substance is the grass upon the graves" (ll.48–50) against those who have: " 'Rather the Marne than the *Cahiers.*' True enough, / you took yourself off. Dying, your whole life / fell into place" (ll.57–59). Yet in the final two stanzas of part 2, Hill worries at history's tendency to freeze martyrs for voyeuristic tourists (Peguy died in the Battle of the Marne) into postures of "blank-eyed bronze," the antithesis of presence, like relics and icons.

Hill consigns Peguy to the same fate as the martyrs of "Funeral Music." He states that the manner of death or personal integrity will not matter to historians:

> This world is different, belongs to them—
> the lords of limit and of contumely.
> It matters little whether you go tamely
> or with rage and defiance to your doom.

(ll.109–12)

Such "lords of limit" confine language, rob it of transcendence and possibly deny the dead any shred of true identity. Hill employs repetition, anticlimax, and self-conscious cliché to embed words in their temporal and concrete connotations: "the guilt / belongs to time; and you must leave on time" (l.136). Hill also uses elision, sliding one phrase across stanzas and even across divisions into parts; as in "The Pentecost Castle," he defies expected pauses or formal constraints of punctuation.

The fifth section introduces the individual poet's tendency to spiritualize and eulogize the dead, to transform them and their actions into "images / of earth and grace" (ll.149–50). Here Hill plays, as in "Tenebrae," with seductive language; he briefly luxuriates in romantic imagery:

> Or say it is Pentecost: the hawthorn-tree,
> set with coagulate mangified flowers of may,
> blooms in a haze of light; old chalk-pits brim
> with seminal verdure from the roots of time.

(ll.161–64)

Just as quickly, however, he retreats from the lushness as if abashed at falling into the elegaic mode:

> Landscape is like revelation; it is both
> singular crystal and the remotest things.
> Cloud-shadows of seasons revisit the earth,
> odourless myrrh borne by the wandering kings.
>
> Happy are they who, under the gaze of God,
> die for the "terre charnelle," marry her blood
> to theirs, and, in strange Christian hope, go down
> into the darkness of resurrection.

(ll.165–72)

As in the "Funeral Music" sequence, death in battle is like a eucharistic sacrifice without actual communion with Christ. The tone is ironic. The dead *descend* into resurrection; merging their bodies with natural elements, they become literally what they have died for—their country. Hill satirizes the forces of patriotism and Christianity that collude to praise the dead in battle:

> The blaze of death goes out, the mind leaps
> for its salvation, is at once extinct;
> its last thoughts tether the furrows, distinct
> in dawn twilight, caught on the barbed loops.

(ll.313–316)

Reminiscent of "An Order of Service," the dying, hoping for salvation, are deceived; their minds descend to their flesh and disavow
the meaning of their action. Again, Hill ridicules the tendency to
transform slaughter to symbolic ritual. In Peguy's case, patriotism
and Christianity merge; assent to faith mingles with assent to
slaughter, a combination from which Hill still recoils. Nevertheless,
Hill admires Peguy's single-mindedness, his way of standing by his
words. As Hill claims in an appendix to the poem, "I offer 'The
Mystery of the Charity of Charles Peguy' as my homage to the
triumph of his 'defeat'" (*CP,* 207). The characteristic paradox allows Hill both to praise and condemn Peguy's actions. It also
captures the dilemma of the modern poet who cannot in good faith
praise his own skill. The final two stanzas insist on the "triumph" of
a poet's defeat as well:

> Low tragedy, high farce, fight for command,
> march, counter-march, and come to the salute
> at every hole-and-corner burial-rite
> bellowed with hoarse dignity into the wind.
>
> Take that for your example! But still mourn,
> being so moved: eloge and elegy
> so moving on the scene as if to cry
> "In memory of those things these words were born."
>
> (ll.393–400)

The poem undercuts the elegiac mode to the end as if Hill were
afraid of indulging in a romantic belief in poetry's power to resurrect the dead. Even the "hoarse dignity" fades as the last stanza
speaks ironically to Peguy's survivors—Hill's fellow poets: "Take
that for your example!" The "so moved" is ambiguous; it either
justifies mourning and emphasizes "so," or mocks it and makes "so
moved" into an indifferent expression of inclination. The second
"so moving" emphasizes physical motion while it also conveys the
emotional experience of Peguy's death. Yet one has the oddly ironic
picture of "eloge" and "elegy" gradually and formally pressing in
on the actual event and distorting it—"*as if* to cry." In fact, the final
line is not even Hill's but an adaptation of Marcel Raymond's.
Subtly and intentionally, Hill qualifies his homage by distancing
himself through simile, quotation, and an often sarcastic tone. Likewise, the liberal sprinkling of French words detaches both the
British poet and the English reader from intimate participation in
the events. The French words remind the reader that the action—

Peguy's life and death—occurs on foreign ground. Even when the words alliterate with the English, "eloge" and "elegy," for example, they emphasize difference more than similarity. Hill's penchant for the blunt Anglo-Saxon verb clashes with the longer and softer French phrases. As in his earlier, more overtly religious *Tenebrae,* Hill continues on both linguistic and semantic levels to offer presence, then retract it.

Although recent critics have somewhat vaguely praised "Peguy," Hill's strategy of defeat makes it difficult to recognize an actual presence in the poem.[49] Peguy is the nominal addressee, not a full-bodied presence. The constantly aborted imagery, the descent from abstract idealism to carnal pessimism, and the self-conscious criticism of the modern poet's passivity set up a dialectic instead of announcing fulfillment. Hill's own presence is not obviously enriched by his homage to Peguy, nor is Peguy's presence evoked by Hill's constant critique of meaningless death and false memorialization. One is tempted to agree with Bedient's survey of contemporary British poetry that the poets

> . . . have mythicized rather than tested the atmosphere of exhaustion, fatalism, sterility, disconnection. If so little of actual experience with its bewildering but vital variety breaks into their lines, the reason is that they have adopted the instant but limited pathos of diminishment as already the historical sense of things.[50]

This "pathos of diminishment" is the opposite of a "poetics of real presence." Yet Hill has not resigned himself entirely to such a bleak project. As his essays clearly illustrate, he is both in love with and suspicious of language, but the love is a menace for which he must atone. His failure to assent to faith fights against his desire for a real sacramental presence in poetry. He is, of the four poets—including Donne, Hopkins, and Thomas—the most equivocal, the most reluctant to assert personal belief and opinion. Yet he possesses their belief in the necessity of total commitment as well as their obsession with religious language. He can neither adopt Hopkins's route of self-sacrifice nor Thomas's path of self-absorption. Perhaps most like Donne, he tries to balance physical with spiritual but constantly fails to see the two as anything but antagonists. Donne's paradoxes (particularly in the Divine Poems) force an acknowledgment of the underlying similarity or simultaneity of physical and spiritual states, whereas Hill's paradoxes drive the two further apart. Donne achieves a startling presence based on this doubleness, whereas Hill highlights the absence or gap between physical and spiritual.

A sacramental vision that views physical reality (including words) as full of spiritual presence is a prerequisite for a poetics of real presence. If words remain hollow signs or if they become autonomous entities, they are equally divorced from such presence. Though Hill laments the hollowness of the signs and attempts to freight words with substance, the actual substance of his poetry is often, as he foresaw in " 'The Conscious Mind's Intelligible Structure,' " a "way of syntax" rather than a "grammar of assent."

6

The Word Dispersed: Possibilities of Presence in Poetry

And the whole earth was of one language and one speech.

—Genesis (11:1)

Therefore is the name of it called Babel; because the Lord did there confound the language of all the earth: and from thence did the Lord scatter them abroad upon the face of all the earth.

—Genesis (11:9)

In charting a subgenre of eucharistic poetry, I am aware of the analogical and therefore provisional nature of my methodology. I am aware that by urging a return to old-fashioned considerations of the text not only as a concrete and semantically viable entity but also as a potentially incarnational product, I am straining against all that is most "sacred" in deconstructionist and structuralist readings. Indeed as Eric Gould avers, seeming to recall Murray Krieger's warning, "Not only is the condition of the numinous highly controversial, but the intention to recover it is a defensive undertaking."[1] And yet if I must pursue a defensive strategy, I would argue that a deconstructionist approach posits an absence as radical in its denial of presence as an incarnational presence is in its assertion of sacramental reality.

Indeed, absence of any original source pradoxically suggests that source if only to demolish it, to deface it beyond recognition so all that remains is a series of fading images dissociated from any context or progenitor. The image is not merely tarnished like the Christ in Donne's "Goodfriday"; it is utterly divorced from its source like the Christ of Hill's "Lachrimae": "You do not dwell in me nor I in you" (l.145). This relation between word picture and its concrete referent, or icon and symbolic meaning, is still optimistically (if just barely) celebrated in Hopkins's "Pied Beauty" in which one can trace "All things counter, original, spare, strange" (l.7) back to their changeless Creator—God. It is ultimately reduced in the deconstructionist paradigm, however, to the "White My-thology" of Derrida's abolished origins. Here Real Presence be-comes a myth of absence. Talk about God is only metaphorical and therefore false. The Roman Catholic emphasis on eucharistic sub-stance over accidents is reversed. According to Derrida, because all language is metaphorical, this metaphoricity inevitably distances one from the essence or substance: "The 'space' of language, the field in which it may diverge, is precisely opened up by the dif-ferences between the essence, the 'proper,' and the accident."[2] A return to unmediated essence would require the abolition of the supreme mediator—language: "To be univocal is the essence, or rather the *telos* of language."[3]

Derrida fully recognizes that his deconstruction of metaphysics is opposed by persistent attempts to return language to its divine origins. Nevertheless he sees such efforts as pure wishfulfillment:

> if the play of metaphors could be reduced to a family circle or group of metaphors, that is, to a "central," "fundamental" or "principal" meta-phor [God-as-progenitor], there would no longer be any true metaphor: there would only be the guarantee of reading the proper sense in a metaphor that was true.[4]

In other words, if, as Hopkins believed, Christ is the foundation of language, all metaphors would lead back to this central source, to the final cry of the nun in *The Wreck of the Deutschland* calling to Christ. Such a push toward the condensation and contraction of language moves counter to Derrida's description of irreversible plurality: "But it is because the metaphorical does not reduce syntax, but sets out in syntax its deviations, that it carries itself away, can only be what it is by obliterating itself, endlessly con-structs its own destruction."[5]

Although it is perhaps unjust to pit a nineteenth-century Catholic priest against a twentieth-century French philosopher, it seems fair to juxtapose Derrida's view to that of his contemporary and fellow countryman Paul Ricoeur. Ricoeur's "hermeneutic of revelation" offers an antidote to the severity of Derrida's position. Ricoeur sees revelation arising from the same poetic tropes that Derrida dis-misses as false and misleading. According to Ricoeur, the text is a viable medium that "mediates between revelation in the broad sense of poetic discourse and in the specifically biblical sense."[6] Poetic language borrows modes of scriptural discourse—the pro-phetic, narrative, and hymnic specifically—to express a spiritual message that is absent from purely referential discourse. Though

Ricoeur acknowledges that poetic language is not empirically ver-
ifiable, he suggests that it reaches back to an earlier, more primitive
sense of reference.[7] This early referential correspondence between
word and object has been displaced by the prosaically linear language of fact and information. Through its "limit-language" of paradox, metaphor, and pun, poetry momentarily produces a new way
of seeing the world. Hence, for Derrida this "limit-language" signals its own death, a return to the unnameable where there is "no
syntactical differentiation," whereas for Ricoeur language is the
only instigator of presence in a world now devoid of miracle.[8]

Contemporary literary critics who tackle the connections between religion and literature tend to fall into two camps: those
allied more or less with Derrida's position or those on the side of
Ricoeur. In line with Derrida though inevitably giving more cre-
dence to the semantic text, Hillis Miller's *The Linguistic Moment*
(1985) seeks to "locate a ground beyond language for the linguistic
patterns present in [the poems]."[9] Defining the linguistic moment
as "catachresis," or disabled metaphor, Miller tries to show how
potentially revelatory moments in poets as disparate as Hopkins
and Stevens are actually self-reflexive examinations of the text,
recognitions of the priority of syntax over semantics. Thus defined,
these moments do not lead to Ricoeur's notion of participation in
the world; rather they force an alienation of the poet and his
language from that world.

Inching away from the Derridian camp but still with one foot
dangling in that abyss is Eric Gould in *Mythical Intentions in
Modern Literature* (1981). Though largely concerned with the form
of myth and fiction, Gould devotes his last two chapters to a
discussion of the numinous in literature. He credits D. H. Law-
rence and T. S. Eliot with straining to capture an ineffable moment
that inevitably lies outside any linguistic grasp. Although he does
not deny the possibility of such a presence, Gould insists that it
cannot be captured in language. Speaking of Eliot's endeavor in
"The Four Quartets," he says:

> The experience is made so interior, and yet it is so precise and diagram-
> matic, that though we might call it allegorical, we know we are pushed
> to a state where language is distinctly transparent.[10]

Yet, if Gould's reading of Eliot is accurate, the successful achievement of a spiritual moment makes language reduce itself to trans-
parency or tautology to close the gap between signifier and signified. The numinous can momentarily be grasped—but almost

despite language, not because of it. A transparent language is not an incarnational one. T. S. Eliot cannot finally be aligned with Donne, Hopkins, Thomas, or Hill (though the difference is less pronounced).

In ascending order toward a belief in poetic presence, though not necessarily in sacramental presence, Ashton Nichols's *The Poetics of Epiphany* (1987) seeks to secularize revelatory moments, to show how poets since the romantic period have made "words manifest the power of language to reify experience."[11] Nichols evades Ricoeur's religious stance by insisting that for most romantic, Victorian, and modern poets the immediate experience or the poet's individual perception is more important than any ultimate meaning. In effect, allegedly following James Joyce's lead, Nichols subverts the theological definition of epiphany in which an ultimate religious meaning is manifested through a specific individual's revelatory experience. Nichols occupies a middle ground between Derrida and Ricoeur in his avoidance of revelation as incarnated Word, but in his belief in language's ability to reify one's own consciousness.

More overtly theological literary critics tend to be less rigorous than Ricoeur in their dismissal of the debate between reason and revelation. They commonly argue for the position Derrida most disparages—a return to an original, often mystical Adamic source of language. Justus Lawler recognizes the conflict between reason and revelation that set in (he insists) not in the sixteenth or seventeenth centuries but earlier—in Genesis after the disaster of the tower of Babel: "The tower of Babel symbolizes the impossibility of any poem realizing what only the sacrament achieves."[12] Yet Lawler protests against this poetic debility and seeks to effect a restoration of the Word. Unlike Derrida, he views metaphor as a way back to a "fruitful union-with-the-object-in-mystery."[13] While simile posits an "as if" relation that stresses distance between objects, metaphor collapses that gap. Lawler's argument is essentially a debate between a sterile Aristotelian materialism and a Platonic idealism that would integrate pure forms with their earthly incarnations. Because he does not give the two sides equal weight, his conclusions are more pedantic, even mystical, than synthetic; the grounds of this premises lack a solid foundation.

Like Lawler's book, Michael Edwards's *Toward a Christian Poetics* (1984) rehearses the fate of a post-Adamic poetics and tries to suggest a return to origins. Edwards laments the prelapsarian "interpenetration" of world and words, and blames the serpent for the fall of language: "He opens, in language as in life, a terrible possibility. . . . The serpent's phrase is the beginning of semantic obscurity, and since it was effective it has left us a world in which meaning is no longer evident, and a language equally uncertain, as we interpret it and as we use it."[14] According to Edwards, the misapplication of language caused the fall, not the actual deed of eating the forbidden fruit. Moving in what he terms a "ternary pattern" similar to that of biblical history, Edwards explores—mainly in the poetry of T. S. Eliot—the poetic devices of paradox, pun, and oxymoron. Through these tropes he argues one approaches a "re-creative" language in which the internal speech of Adam and Eve meets the external chaos of a fallen language. Citing Eliot's "Four Quartets," Edwards optimistically sees the Pentecostal imagery of "Little Gidding" replacing the Babel of *The Waste Land*. Like Lawler, Edwards presumes the possibility of a typological fulfillment that would erase the gap between world and word.

Images of Pentecost prevade Geoffrey Hill's poetry as well. While Donne and Thomas look to the Crucifixion and the Resurrection as major emblematic sources and Hopkins leans toward the Incarnation, it seems that for the contemporary poet, steeped in the babble of technological language and caught among conflicting theories of interpretation, Pentecost offers a more plausible model. Yet Pentecost does not reverse the dispersal of languages at the tower of Babel to return language to the Word. Instead, Pentecost offers the apostles the ability to speak all the different languages to convey a spiritual message in many tongues, not to consolidate all those tongues into one language. The arrival of the Holy Ghost at Pentecost already recognizes the belatedness of the spirit, its inability to reverse time and deed. The apostles' task is not to restore language to its Adamic purity; rather it is to preach the words of Christ to the people and thereby to reintegrate spirit and language. They are translators and transcribers, not originators. Their example offers the modern religious poet the humbler and less tantalizing position of Hill's doubting disciple Thomas who stands "at such near distance" (l.12). Yet the role of translator, even of spiritual meaning, does not appear to satisfy the poetic craving for pure and unmediated linguistic presence.

If it is impossible to return language to its origin in the incarnated Word or even to relink words to their once spiritual dimensions, are the quests of these poets for a sacramental poetry doomed to silence? Or does the eucharistic sacrament offer an earthly model on which to base a poetics of presence? Two contemporary theorists who effectively suggest a middle ground between Derrida and Ricoeur are Murray Krieger and George Steiner. Both are wary of the mystical fallacy—acknowledging a true real presence in language—but both insist on the importance of reading "as if" true presence were possible.

Arguing against a poetics of absence yet recognizing, like Foucault, the Renaissance rupture between word and thing, Krieger advocates a poetry of presentation. He sees Renaissance love lyrics as first implementing such a poetics. The Renaissance poets sought to preserve love in a world of dissolution by an "act of . . . creative faith."[15] They based their poems on the analogy of the Incarnation: "Renaissance poets balance[d] their sense of the emptiness of words with their use of a verbal analogy to the divine miracle in order to fill those words with substance."[16]

By the twentieth century, Krieger asserts that this analogy has collapsed. Language is no longer safely referential; in fact, the outside world to which it would refer if it could is chaotic and relativistic. In such a world poetry entails a reactionary process of preserving its own hermetic presence against external absence: "The illusion is all; it is the seer's imaged reality, since there is no independently available reality against which the image can be seen as distorted or false, as a *de*lusion. Thus we become provisionally persuaded of the presence of the poem as our present world."[17]

Krieger recognizes that this thrust of the poem toward a self-contained presence is based on "theological metaphors of presence," yet he adamantly refuses to adopt the more essentialist stance of Ricoeur. His goal, like that of Ricoeur, is to offer the poem as an instigator of presence; the principal distinction between the two, however, is that for Krieger the presence is not real. Thus he skillfully, if provisionally, connects Derrida's idea of metaphoric language as illusory and false with Ricoeur's hope for a revelatory presence that would erupt from metaphor. The presence, however, is almost as diminished as the rubbed-out face of Derrida's coin. It has lost any ultimate value in a world that no longer knows how to attribute value. Against such a world a poem like Hill's "Pentecost Castle" can only close itself off and offer the reader a brief escape from chaos.

In *Language and Silence* (1967), George Steiner had questioned, "Can there be a coexistence other than charged with mutual torment and rebellion between the totality of the *Logos* and the living, world-creating fragments of our own speech?"[18] His answer at that point seemed to suggest Ricoeur's idea of revelation of divinity behind language, yet it stopped short of praising a "limit-language" as the vehicle of revelation:

It is just because we can go no further, because speech so marvelously fails us, that we experience the certitude of a divine meaning surpassing and enfolding ours. What lies beyond man's world is eloquent of God.[19]

In fact, Steiner warns against a eucharistic poetry that would "contract the *Logos* into the word."[20] The Logos is sacred precisely because it is untranslatable. Instead of trying to invoke presence, a "limit-language" should stress its own limits. It should demonstrate the impossibility of embodying divinity. So Steiner admires poets' silences more than their overreaching efforts at incarnation, (perhaps a reason for his exasperation at Dylan Thomas).[21]

In a later lecture delivered to Cambridge University students, "Real Presences" (1985), Steiner surveys the demise of the word by historical atrocity, applied science, and philosophy and concludes, "At decisive points, ours is a civilization 'after the word.' "[22] Given this postlinguistic state, Steiner proceeds to demonstrate how poetry and its readers together can revive such a civilization. He concedes the plausibility of the deconstructionist position: "the commonplace but cardinal verity that in all interpretation, in all statements of understanding, language is simply being used about language in an infinitely self-multiplying series."[23] As a way out of this self-consuming cycle, however, Steiner proposes an alternative that he locates outside of logic in ethics and morality. He reinstates the importance of the poem over commentary about the poem: "Its [the poem's] priority is one of essence, of ontological need and self-sufficiency."[24] In so doing he relegates criticism to the Aristotelian category of accident in relation to the substance of the poem: "The poem *is;* the commentary *signifies.*"[25]

From this point Steiner makes a case for what he calls poetry that "wager[s] on a transcendence" or a poetry of real presence.[26] Although his goal is antithetical to that of Derrida, it is more modest than that of Donne, Hopkins, Thomas, or even Hill. It entails, like Krieger's illusory presence, reading "as if the text before us had meaning."[27] Yet it effectively borrows sacramental terminology as its ground and in so doing describes a secular real presence that has unmistakable aspirations toward its theological roots:

Where we read truly, where the experience is to be that of meaning, we do so as if the text . . . *incarnates* (the notion is grounded in the sacramental) *a real presence of significant being.* This real presence, as in an icon, as in the enacted metaphor of the sacramental bread and wine, is, finally, irreducible to any other formal articulation, to any analytic deconstruction or paraphrase. It is a singularity in which concept and form constitute a tautology, coincide point to point, energy to energy, in that excess of significance over all discrete elements and codes of meaning which we call the symbol or agency of trans-parence.[28]

Steiner further extends the eucharistic metaphor to that of the relation between a host and guest, the latter producing an indwell-ing *"commonplace mystery of a real presence."*[29] Although he himself stops short of propounding a truly sacramental stance in regard to writing or reading poetry ("It may be the case that nothing more is available to us than the absence of God"), Steiner signals a way forward (doubtless deconstructionists would say backward) toward a renovated reading of sacramental poetry.[30] His "as if"—the necessary caution of the skeptical postmodernist intel-lect—still drives a wedge between wished-for and actual real pres-ence, between the text as illusion and the text as real. It still regards real presence as metaphorical and textual, therefore separate from the meaning the poet proposes to incarnate. Steiner's proposed poetics of real presence cannot resurrect God as the ground of being and so cannot reinstate Christ as the linguistic mediator between the poet and his reader, or between the poet and God.

It seems finally that only readers who, like Cardinal Newman, are able to answer "yes" to the question, "Can I believe as if I saw?" or who are able to read themselves into assent, can find in eucharistic poetry a real presence that eliminates the "as if.[31] In *The Force of Poetry* (1984), Christopher Ricks addresses Steiner's earlier posi-tion in *Language and Silence* in which poetry points toward but does not incarnate the ineffable. Ricks modestly suggests that "it may still be decent for a poet to seek the impossible ideal of a worded ineffability."[32] Eucharistic poetry—a poetry that grounds itself on the *literal* translation of Christ's words into the Real Presence of his Body and Blood—asserts that such an "impossible ideal" is indeed possible. It is more than possible; it is actual. "Worded ineffability" in this sense sheds its oxymoronic overtones as do the other oxymoronic tropes that Donne, Hopkins, Thomas, and Hill employ. These tropes transform ordinary words into ex-traordinary poetry where real presence breaks into language. It is the reader's task (to borrow Hopkins's term) to instress this pres-ence in the sacramental act of reading. This act requires a leap of faith that deconstructionists disparage as illogical; it requires a willingness to sacrifice ordinary linear and secular ways of reading and, most significantly, it requires a new humility (as Donne's rider learns in "Goodfriday") to face a language stronger and more resil-ient than any individual reader's or writer's monopoly on meaning.

Notes

Preface

1. *To Criticize the Critic* (New York: Farrar, Straus and Giroux, 1965), 127.

Chapter 1. Eucharistic Language and the Anglo-Catholic Poet

1. Murray Krieger, *Poetic Presence and Illusion: Essays in Critical History and Theory* (Baltimore: Johns Hopkins University Press, 1979), 152.
2. Ralph McInerny, *Studies in Analogy* (The Hague: Martinus Nijhoff, 1968), 22.
3. *Words and the Word: Language, Poetics and Biblical Interpretation* (Cambridge: Cambridge University Press, 1986), 224. Prickett surveys the field of biblical hermeneutics and blames this "disconfirmation" on the seventeenth-century split between literal and typological language: "The separation of the 'poetic' as a literary quality, to be distinguished from the actual metrical forms of poetry, begins historically to emerge as a direct response to this perceived need to account for certain statements and narratives as being 'true' in some *other* sense than the literal, scientific, or historical, on the one hand, or the allegorical and typological on the other" (200). Prickett concedes that drawing its origins from the Bible, religious language possesses an "inward and reintegrative power" that operates "as the vehicle of religious experience" (45).
4. "The Hermeneutics of Testimony," trans. David Stewart and Charles E. Reagan, in *Essays on Biblical Interpretation*, ed. Lewis S. Mudge (Philadelphia: Fortress Press, 1980), 147.
5. *Poetic Presence and Illusion: Essays in Critical History and Theory* (Baltimore: Johns Hopkins University Press, 1979), 26.
6. F. L. Cross and E. A. Livingstone, eds., *The Oxford Dictionary of the Christian Church*, 2d ed. (New York: Oxford University Press, 1974), 1162.
7. According to the decree of the thirteenth session of the Council of Trent in October 1551 in *Canons and Decrees of the Council of Trent*, trans. rev. H. J. Schroeder, O.P. (Rockford, Ill.: Tan Books, 1978), 75:

> But since Christ our Redeemer declared that to be truly His own body which He offered under the form of bread, it has, therefore, always been a firm belief in the Church of God, and this holy council now declares it anew, that by the consecration of the bread and wine a change is brought about of the whole substance of the bread into the substance of the body of Christ our Lord, and of the whole substance of the wine into the substance of His blood. This change the holy Catholic Church properly and appropriately calls transubstantiation.

8. According to Article Twenty-eight (1571) in Oliver O'Donovan, *On the Thirty Nine Articles: A Conversation with Tudor Christianity* (Exeter: Paternoster Press, 1986), 148:

> The Supper of the Lord, is not only a signe of the loue that Christians ought to haue among them selues one to another: but rather it is a Sacrament of our redemption by Christes death. Insomuch that to suche as ryghtlie, worthyly, and with fayth receaue the same the bread whiche we breake is a parttakyng of the body of Christe, and likewyse the cuppe of blessing, is a parttakyng of the blood of Christe.

The article goes on to deplore the Roman Catholic doctrine of transubstantation:

> Transubstantiation (or the chaunge of the substaunce of bread and wine) in the Supper of the Lorde, can not be proued by holye writ, but is repugnant to the playne wordes of scripture, ouerthroweth the nature of a Sacrament, and hath geuen occasion to many superstitions.

The forty-two articles drawn up by Cranmer in 1553 contain a more specific caveat against transubstantiation and even question Real Presence: "a faithful man ought not, either to beleue, or openlie to confesse the reall, and bodilie presence . . . of Christes fleshe, and bloude, in the Sacramente of the Lords supper" (149). Although interpretations of this article range from low-church Reformation concepts of Memorialism to Virtualism and Receptionism, the difficulty appears to be a semantic one. It hinges on the interpretation of Christ's words of institution at the Last Supper in the Gospels of Luke, Mark, and Matthew. According to E. J. Bicknell, "In eating and drinking by a deliberate and voluntary act we take into ourselves something that is outside ourselves, in order that it may become part of ourselves and so our bodies may be strengthened" (*A Theological Introduction to the Thirty-Nine Articles of the Church of England* [London: Longman, 1919; 3d ed. rev. H. J. Carpenter, 1955], 389).

9. J. Hillis Miller addresses the Eucharist as a poetic foundation in *The Disappearance of God: Five Nineteenth-Century Writers* (Cambridge: Belknap Press, 1975) but argues that by the nineteenth century this analogy had collapsed: "The Eucharist was the archetype of the divine analogy whereby created things participated in the supernatural reality they signified. Poetry in turn was . . . modeled on sacramental or scriptural language. The words of the poem incarnated the things they named, just as the words of the Mass shared in the transformation they evoked. The symbols and metaphors of poetry were no mere inventions of the poets. They were borrowed from the divine analogies of nature. Poetry was meaningful in the same way as nature itself—by a communion of the verbal symbols with the reality they named" (3).

10. The only other vehicle for participation in the divine according to Paul Ricoeur is poetic language that "alone restores to us that participation-in or belonging-to an order of things which precedes our capacity to oppose ourselves to things taken as objects opposed to a subject. Hence the function of poetic discourse is to bring about this emergence of a depth-structure of belonging-to amid the ruins of descriptive discourse" ("Toward a Hermeneutic of the Idea of Revelation" in *Essays on Biblical Interpretation,* 101).

11. William E. Addis and Thomas Arnold, *A Catholic Dictionary* (New York: The Catholic Publication Society, 1884), 315.

12. *The Shape of the Liturgy* (1945; reprint, New York: The Seabury Press, 1982), 267.

13. *Shape of Liturgy*, 633.

14. "The Specificity of Religious Language," *Semeia* 4(1975): 107. For further treatment of "limit-language" and "limit-experiences" see Carl A. Raschke, *The Alchemy of the Word: Language and the End of Theology* (Ann Arbor: American Academy of Religion, 1979), 7–17.

15. *Inscape: The Christology and Poetry of Gerard Manley Hopkins* (Pittsburgh: University of Pittsburgh Press, 1972), 98. Speaking specifically of Hopkins, Cotter outlines a poetics of sacrifice and replenishment, a process that for the Roman Catholic poet is rooted in the eucharistic action. For more general treatment of *kenosis-pleroma*, see Thomas J. Altizer, *Total Presence: The Language of Jesus and the Language of Today* (New York: The Seabury Press, 1980).

16. Ricoeur defines this "letting go" as "renouncing not only the empirical objects that are ordered by reason, but also those transcendental objects of metaphysics that might still provide support for thinking the unconditioned. . . . It is precisely this movement of letting go which bears reflection to the encounter with contingent signs of the absolute which the absolute in its generosity allows to appear" ("Toward a Hermeneutic of the Idea of Revelation," in *Essays on Biblical Interpretation*, 111).

17. Geoffrey Hill, "Redeeming the Time," *Agenda* 10, no. 4(1972–73): 94.

18. Ricoeur, "Specificity," 109. Ricoeur extends this discussion of theological and poetic language in his *Interpretation Theory: Discourse and the Surplus of Meaning* (Fort Worth: Texas Christian University Press, 1976) and two articles, "The Logic of Jesus, the Logic of God," *Anglican Theological Review* 62, no. 1(1980): 37–41; "The 'Kingdom' in the Parables of Jesus," *Anglican Theological Review* 63, no. 2(1981): 165–69.

19. Peter Milward, "Sacramental Symbolism in Hopkins and Eliot," *Renascence* 22, no. 2(1968): 107, offers a useful though perhaps too pat distinction between the Anglican poetry of Eliot and Herbert, and that of the Roman Catholic Hopkins and Crashaw. If we follow his definitions of Anglican versus Catholic spirituality, we see Donne and Thomas paradoxically edging toward Catholic, not Anglican, spirituality and Hill caught between the two:

. . . Anglican spirituality, as revealed in Herbert and Eliot, has a sober, refined quality. . . . Yet for this very reason, it is removed from the reality of common life, while, on the other hand, it tends to envisage God as remote. . . . It is not perhaps a spirituality for all men, but only for such as fit harmoniously within the English "establishment."
   The Catholic spirituality, on the other hand, as revealed in Crashaw and Hopkins has a more personal and intimate quality of tender devotion. It takes full account of the human need of imaginative and emotive aids to prayer; and at the same time it seems to penetrate that "cloud of unknowing" between the soul and God on which Eliot lays such emphasis.

20. *The Complete Poems and Plays: 1909–1950* (New York: Harcourt, Brace, 1952), 61, 11.38–39.

21. In a text with which Hill is clearly familiar, Newman states that notional (weaker) assent is conditional, based on inference, and that real assent is unconditional: "In its notional assents . . . the mind contemplates its own creations instead of things; in real, it is directed towards things, represented by the impressions which they have left on the imagination. These images, when assented-to, have an influence both on the individual and on society, which mere notions

cannot exert" (*An Essay in Aid of a Grammar of Assent* [1870; reprint, Notre Dame: University of Notre Dame Press, 1979], 76).

22. "Liturgy and Metaphor," *Notre Dame English Journal* 8(1981): 196.

23. Karsten Harries introduces "metaphors of collision" to explain the tension between discursive and poetic language: "no matter how radical the pursuit of presence, the work of art will always fall short of that purer art that is its telos. It points beyond itself and lacks the plenitude it demands" ("Metaphor and Transcendence," in *On Metaphor,* ed. Sheldon Sacks [Chicago: University of Chicago Press, 1978], 75). See also Max Black's "interaction view" of metaphor that grants presence to both parts of the metaphor and thereby produces a new meaning based on the interaction between the two parts (*Models and Metaphors* [Ithaca: Cornell University Press, 1962], 25–47).

24. *Modern Poetry and the Idea of Language* (New Haven: Yale University Press, 1974), 232.

25. See Ricoeur's distinction between metaphor and symbol in *Interpretation Theory:* "Metaphors are just the linguistic surface of symbols, and they owe their power to relate the semantic surface to the presemantic surface in the depth of human experience to the two-dimension structure of the symbol" (69).

26. Foucault, *The Order of Things* (New York: Pantheon, 1970), 298, explains that:

> In the sixteenth century, interpretation proceeded from the world [analogy] . . . towards the divine Word that could be deciphered in it; our interpretation . . . proceeds from men, from God, from knowledge or fantasies, towards the words that make them possible; and what it reveals is not the soveignty of a primal discourse, but the fact that we are already . . . governed and paralysed by language.

George Steiner dates this separation from the seventeenth century and blames it largely on Descartes and Spinoza for instituting an increasingly mathematical way of looking at the world (*Language and Silence: Essays on Language, Literature and the Inhuman* [New York: Atheneum, 1967], 14–20).

27. Nathan A. Scott, Jr., *The Wild Prayer of Longing: Poetry and the Sacred* (New Haven: Yale University Press, 1971), 25. Karlfried Froehlich, "'Always to Keep the Literal Sense in Holy Scripture Means to Kill One's Soul': The State of Biblical Hermeneutics at the Beginning of the Fifteenth Century," *Literary Uses of Typology from the late Middle Ages to the Present,* ed. Earl Miner (Princeton: Princeton University Press, 1977), 33. See also Malcolm Ross, *Poetry and Dogma: The Transfiguration of Eucharistic Symbols in Seventeenth-Century English Poetry* (New Brunswick: Rutgers University Press, 1954), who traces the descent of the eucharistic figural symbolism to dead metaphor and blames this process on the failure of the doctrine of analogy during the Reformation.

28. *The Wild Prayer of Longing,* 25.

29. "Final Soliloquy of the Interior Paramour," *The Collected Poems of Wallace Stevens* (New York: Knopf, 1981), 524, 1.18. Subsequent citations are noted parenthetically in text as *CP.*

30. Sister Bernetta Quinn, a friend of Wallace Stevens, argues persuasively for Stevens' religious mind as it is reflected in his poetry. Basing her argument on Stevens's late conversion to Roman Catholicism, she looks backward to the poetry to find glimmerings of this faith. My point is that Stevens's poetry does not, like that of Donne, Hopkins, Thomas, and Hill, reflect an incarnational belief in the

power of poetry ("Wallace Stevens: 'The Peace of the Last Intelligence,'" *Renascence* 41, no. 4 [Summer 1989]: 191–204).

31. "Shadows," *Selected Poems* (New York: New Directions, 1968), 159, ll.76–82. Subsequent citations are noted parenthetically in text as *SP*.

32. *The Order of Things*, 383.

33. *Collected Poems* (New York: Oxford University Press, 1986), 188.

34. "Poetry as 'Menace' and 'Atonement'," in *The Lords of Limit* (London: Andre Deutsch, 1984), 16.

35. "'Menace' and 'Atonement'," 16.

36. In his *Grammar of Assent* Newman argues that one can assent to a mystery if one realizes that mysteries represent the intersection of finite minds with something or someone greater than the finite mind:

A mystery is a proposition conveying incompatible notions, or is a statement of the inconceivable. Now we can assent to propositions . . . provided we can apprehend them; therefore we can assent to a mystery, for, unless we in some sense apprehended it, we should not recognize it to be a mystery . . . a statement uniting incompatible notions. (55).

Chapter 2. The Eschatology of Real Presence

1. On the long argument over Anglican views of Virtualism, Divine Receptionism, and Real Presence in the Eucharist, see Horton Davies, *Worship and Theology in England* (Princeton: Princeon University Press, 1970–75), vol. 1: 83; vol. 2:293–98. Briefly, the *Oxford Dictionary of Christianity* defines "Virtualism" as the Calvinistic belief that while bread and wine are unchanged after consecration, the communicant receives the virtue of Christ's Body and Blood after communion. Receptionism allowed for the communicant to receive together with the unchanged elements the "true Body and Blood of Christ" (1163).

2. John Donne, "Sermon No. 14," *The Sermons of John Donne*, ed. George R. Potter and Evelyn M. Simpson (Berkeley: University of California Press, 1953), 4:359. Subsequent citations are noted parenthetically in the text as *Sermons*.

3. For a discussion of the connection between poetry and meditation, both having colloquy as their final goal, see Louis Martz, *The Poetry of Meditation: A Study in English Religious Literature of the Seventeenth Century* (New Haven: Yale University Press, 1954).

4. "The Logic of Jesus, the Logic of God," *Anglican Theological Review* 62, no. 1(1980): 39.

5. "The 'Kingdom' in the Parables of Jesus," *Anglican Theological Review* 63, no. 2(1981): 167.

6. "The Specificity of Religious Language," *Semeia* 4(1975): 138.

7. "Specificity," 140–41.

8. Ibid., 141.

9. "'This Is My Body': Hermeneutics and Eucharistic Language," *Anglican Theological Review* 64, no. 3(1982): 305–6.

10. Ibid., 306.

11. Oliver O'Donovan, *On The Thirty Nine Articles: A Conversation with Tudor Christianity* (Exeter: Paternoster Press, 1986), 149. O'Donovan clarifies the import of this article: "The unreality of the wicked communicant's participation is not a matter of *his* failure to conjure up the memories and moral dispositions which the

believer has successfully conjured up; rather, it is the refusal of Christ to give himself to unbelief" (126).

12. "Metaphor and Transcendence," in *On Metaphor*, ed. Sheldon Sacks (Chicago: University of Chicago Press, 1978), 76. Harries speaks mainly of modern poets' attempts to reincarnate the spirit in words, yet his term applies equally well to Donne's paradoxes.

13. Barbara Kiefer Lewalski amends Louis Martz's Catholic application of the Ignatian meditative method to a "Protestant Meditative exercise of self-examination" with an "anguished Pauline speaker" (*Protestant Poetics and the Seventeenth-Century Religious Lyric* [Princeton: Princeton University Press] 265). Lewalski pushes too strongly for Donne's strictly Protestant belief in irresistible grace as a prerequisite for regeneration.

In *The Imagination of the Resurrection: The Poetic Continuity of a Religious Motif in Donne, Blake, and Yeats* (Lewisburg: Bucknell University Press, 1972), 92–93, Kathryn R. Kremen argues plausibly for the "cooperation of divine and human wills" in attaining grace. Although she treads a middle ground between Martz and Lewalski, she asserts less convincingly that the sexual experience of the secular lyrics prefigures the resurrection motifs of the divine poems: "The sexual union of man and woman on earth is the temporal and secular image which prefigures and commemorates the eternal and religious event which sanctions and fulfills it—the hypostatical union in body and soul of man and the Godhead in heaven." Neither Donne's sermons nor his poems corroborate this figural relation, although such secular lyrics as "The Canonization" and "The Relique" use the analogy to support secular, not spiritual, love.

14. Both Ernest B. Gilman and R. V. Young argue that Donne was caught between Roman Catholicism and Calvinist Protestantism, and that this position engenders the tension in his poems. Young sees the Holy Sonnets as epitomizing this tension as Donne was "neither still Catholic nor yet Protestant in a settled way that gave his conscience peace" ("Donne's Holy Sonnets and the Theology of Grace," in *"Bright Shootes of Everlastingnesse": The Seventeenth Century Religious Lyric*, ed. Claude J. Summers and Ted-Larry Pebworth [Columbia: University of Missouri Press, 1987], 38). Speaking of the emblematic tradition in metaphysical poetry, Gilman states, "Donne's spirituality stands isolated, spanning the poles of Crashaw's visual Catholicism and Herbert's aural Protestantism, unable to support his weight on either one, unable to let go" (*Iconoclasm and Poetry in the English Reformation* [Chicago: University of Chicago Press, 1986], 148). Both of these critics ignore the special position of Anglicanism as a religion midway between the two poles of Roman Catholicism and Calvinism.

In *The Anglican Tradition in Eighteenth-Century Verse* (The Hague: Mouton, 1971), 23, 30, Grant Sampson views Herbert rather than Donne as the Anglican poet par excellence and notes the Anglican proclivity for balances such as that between scripture and sacrament, private meditation and public hymn.

In *Poetry and Dogma: The Transfiguration of Eucharistic Symbols in Seventeenth-Century English Poetry* (New Brunswick: Rutgers University Press, 1954), Malcolm Ross chronicles the descent of the eucharistic symbol to metaphor after the Reformation where 'sacraments are retained as mere tokens of an economy of salvation which operates only in the deep interior of the individual belief" (47). Ross sees the Anglican poet caught between Catholic sacramentalism and Puritan asceticism where rhetoric and dogma no longer reinforce each other. He views Donne as a "Catholic-minded Anglican who hunts the Real Presence in the liturgical context of a Real Absence" (171).

15. Ernest Gilman addresses Donne's position in the "iconoclastic controversy" (121) between the Roman Catholics and the Protestants. Pursuing his thesis of Donne as a man caught between the two, he discusses Donne's "ambivalent regard for the image," his public disdain and private attraction for pictures of Christ (136).

16. *The Shape of the Liturgy* (1945; reprint, New York: Seabury Press, 1982), 256. Dix distinguishes between the Eucharist as mere metaphor as opposed to reality; Donne concurred with the latter: "the phrase 'the body of Christ' as applied however vivid, but as a reality, as the truth of things in God's sight. Both church and sacrament must *be* what they are called, if the church's act is to be truly Christ's act, her offering His offering, and the effects of His sacrifice are to be predicated on the present offering of the eucharist" (246).

17. Donne criticizes both Roman Catholic and Protestant extremes in his sonnet, "Show me deare Christ, thy Spouse, so bright and clear" as well: "What! is it She, which on the other shore / Goes richly painted? or which rob'd and tore / Laments and mournes in Germany and here?" (ll. 2–4).

18. A longer version of Article Twenty-eight in 1553 numbered Article Twenty-nine, reinforces Donne's discussion of the Roman Catholic tendency to locate Christ's body and blood in the Eucharist:

Forasmoche as the trueth of mannes nature requireth, that the bodie of one, and theself same manne cannot be at one time in diuerse places, but must nedes be in some one certaine place: Therefore the bodie of Christe cannot bee presente at one time in many, and diuerse places. And because (as holie Scripture doeth doeth teache) Christ was taken vp into heauen, and there shall continue vnto thende of the worlde, a faithful man ought not, either to belieue, or openlie to confesse the reall, and bodilie presence (as thei terme it) of Christes fleshe, and bloude, in the Sacramente of the Lordes supper. (*On the Thirty Nine Articles*, 148–49)

This clause was omitted from all later versions of the article.

19. *The Elegies and the Songs and Sonnets of John Donne*, ed. Helen Gardner (Oxford: Clarendon Press, 1965), 59, ll.17–18. Subsequent citations for secular poems from this edition are noted parenthetically in the text as *SS*.

20. Ibid., 261.

21. John E. Booty, ed., *The Book of Common Prayer 1559: The Elizabethan Prayer Book* (Charlottesville: University Press of Virginia, 1976), 264.

22. *Les Poètes Métaphysiques Anglais*, Tome 1: *John Donne et les Poètes de la Tradition Chretienne* (Paris: Libraire José Corti, 1960), 332–33.

23. Ibid., 333.

24. *Eucharistic Theology* (New York: Herder and Herder, 1967), 182.

25. In *Les Doctrines Médiévales Chez Donne* (London: Oxford University Press, 1916), Mary Ramsay compares the ecstatic union of the lovers in "The Exstasie" to the mystical union of St. Theresa with God. She outlines a three-part definition of the mystical experience that begins with a departure of soul from body and proceeds to an extinction of bodily limitations. Freed of the body, the soul may have contact with God (257). Ramsay's process corresponds to Ricoeur's final two stages of revelatory language: death of the substance and birth of the spirit. Ramsay asserts that this mystical union is more prevalent in Donne's love lyrics than in the more orthodox divine poems. Similarly, the moment of communion is more easily consummated in the love lyrics. The divine poems chronicle the struggle toward consummation, rarely the consummation itself.

In *The Metaphysical Poets: A Study in Religious Experience* (New York: Macmillan, 1936), Helen White qualifies Ramsay's identification of Donne with the mystical tradition, opposing the mystical impulse toward concentration to the poetic impulse toward diffusion: "The direction of poetry is first out from the center, then in, and of mystical expression, first in, then out" (20).

In *Self-Consuming Artifacts: The Experience of Seventeenth-Century Literature* (Berkeley: University of California Press, 1972), 3 & 51–52, Stanley Fish redefines this mystical tendency as a dialectic between secular word and mystical vision in which the word is silenced or killed in the vision. In approaching union with God, the religious poem destroys itself. More applicable to Donne is Fish's discussion of the subversion of a logic of reason by a logic of faith in the sermons.

26. *Poetry of Meditation,* 133.

27. *Poetry and Change: Donne, Milton, Wordsworth, and the Equilibrium of the Present* (Berkeley: University of California Press, 1974), 143.

28. "John Donne: The Despair of the 'Holy Sonnets,'" *ELH* 48, no. 4(1981): 13.

29. *The Poetry of Grace* (New Haven: Yale University Press, 1970), 28.

30. Ibid., 84.

31. As Helen Gardner notes, "Manna was a type or figure of the Host. Love performs the Eucharistic miracle in reverse by turning the sweetness of things to bitterness" (*Elegies and Songs and Sonnets,* 215).

32. Ellrodt, *Les Poètes,* 339.

33. Ibid., 341.

34. Ibid., 220.

35. David Jones discusses the analogy between poetry and sacrament in "Art and Sacrament," noting the conjunction between sign and form. Instead of being purely representational or hermetically self-referential, sacramental poetry re-unites word and object through the synthesizing agent of form. Form is analogous to the liturgical structure of the sacrament. Without the structure, the sacrament would be a private and wordless revelation (*Epoch and Artist,* ed. Harman Grisewood [New York: Chilmark Press, 1959], 157–70).

36. *The Divine Poems of John Donne,* 2d ed., ed. Helen Gardner (Oxford: Clarendon Press, 1978) 26, ll.9–18. (Subsequent citations for this edition are noted parenthetically in the text as *DP*).

37. Speaking of Donne's love of the crucifixion, Julia J. Smith notes a gradual movement from a desire to replace Christ on the cross to an identification with him. Of "The Crosse" Smith states, "We are exhorted to love the image of the Cross for the sake of Christ, who died on it; if we welcome our redemption we should not scorn its instrument" ("Donne and the Crucifixion," *Modern Language Review* 79, no. 3[1984]: 518).

38. Booty, *Book of Common Prayer,* 256–57.

39. Ibid., 257.

40. In "John Donne's Holy Sonnets and the Anglican Doctrine of Contrition," in *Essential Articles for the Study of John Donne's Poetry,* ed. John R. Roberts (Hampden, Conn.: The Shoe String Press, 1975), Peterson says that for Donne, grace is the "consummation of contrition" (319).

In "Augustinian Spirituality and the Holy Sonnets of John Donne," *ELH* 38, no. 4(1971): 542–61, Grant notes that Donne seems more concerned with the elimination of his own sin than with his union with Christ.

41. *Eucharist and Eschatology* (New York: Oxford University Press, 1981), 15.

42. Booty, *Book of Common Prayer,* 355.

43. In *Christ Revealed: The History of the Neotypological Lyric in the English Renaissance* (Gainesville: University of Florida Press, 1982), 75–79, Ira Clark

discusses Donne's tendency both to apply types to himself and himself to types, thus rupturing the traditional typological order.

44. Both John Stachniewski and William Halewood view the analogies in "Goodfriday" as faulty; the former argues that "analogies do not constitute arguments; they merely illustrate them" (692); the latter sees Donne merely creating the "appearance of argument" or a "dialectic illusion" that is finally undercut by faith (28).

45. Terry Sherwood discusses "Goodfriday" as an exercise in conversion in which *"aversio"* is opposed to *"conversio"* and where the logic of the uncorrected will battles against the corrected (faithful) will (*Fulfilling the Circle: A Study of John Donne's Thought* [Toronto: University of Toronto Press, 1984], 121).

46. Halewood, *Poetry of Grace,* sees the poem as presenting the "appearance of argument of balanced alternative possibilities" while being firmly rooted in the orthodox Anglican tradition. He parallels the thematic shift toward conversion with a grammatical "change from subjunctive to indicative, from conditional to actual" (30). This parallel grammatical shift occurs frequently in the divine poems, often ending in the future (eschatological) tense of the final couplet in the sonnets.

Helen Gardner states that the poem moves not toward colloquy, but from "discursive meditation" to "penitent prayer" and suggests that in "Goodfriday" there is no actual resolution, only a prayer for one (Introduction to the *Divine Poems,* xxxiii).

47. Gardner, *Divine Poems,* states, "The 'Hymn to God the Father' was written, according to Walton, during Donne's grave illness of 1623, and the 'Hymn to God my God, in my sickness,' whether it should be dated during the same illness or in 1631, was written when he thought himself at the point of death" (xxxiv).

48. John Donne to Sir Henry Goodyer, September 1608, *Selected Prose,* ed. Helen Gardner and Timothy Healy (Oxford: Clarendon Press, 1967), 129.

49. Donne to Mrs. Cokayne (1625–28), *Selected Prose,* 163.

50. Ibid., 390.

51. Ibid., 392.

52. Booty, *Book of Common Prayer,* 263.

53. Ibid., 259.

54. "The Logic of Jesus," 40.

55. Ibid., 40.

56. Robert Shaw notes the theological necessity for the final couplet: "Contrition for sins done appears not to alter a basically sinful disposition. What is needed is not only a purgation of past misdeeds, but an infusion of divine power which will turn the speaker to seek what is good. Thus Donne closes the sonnet with this petition" (48).

57. For a similar view, see Ira Clark: "Through this ambiguous syntax Donne is reinforcing the affirmation that faith leads to salvation by accenting a Christian paradox inherent in the neotypological structure of the poem. The poet is responsible for his acts; he must reform his own will. At the same time, he is incapable of his own salvation; he must be justified vicariously by Christ, an act symbolized in the sacrificial sacrament" (77–78).

58. *Devotions,* 94.

Chapter 3. Real Presence through Incarnation

1. W. H. Gardner, *Gerard Manley Hopkins: A Study of Poetic Idiosyncrasy in Relation to Poetic Tradition* (1944; reprint, London: Oxford University Press, 1961), 1:173.

2. Ibid., 374–75.

3. *The Sermons and Devotional Writings of Gerard Manley Hopkins,* ed. Christopher Devlin, S.J. (London: Oxford University Press, 1959), 154, 158. Subsequent citations are noted parenthetically in text as *Sermons.*

4. John Henry Cardinal Newman, *An Essay in Aid of a Grammar of Assent* (Notre Dame: University of Notre Dame Press, 1979), 86–92.

5. Gerard Manley Hopkins, Letter 90, 18 October 1882, *The Letters of Gerard Manley Hopkins to Robert Bridges,* ed. Claude Colleer Abbott (London: Oxford University Press, 1935; rev. ed. 1955), 155. Subsequent citations are noted parentically in text as *Letters to Bridges.*

6. David Morris, *The Poetry of Gerard Manley Hopkins in the Light of the Donne Tradition* (Bern: A Francke AG Verlag, 1951), 27.

7. Walter J. Ong, "Hopkins' Sprung Rhythm and the Life of English Poetry," in *Immortal Diamond: Studies in Gerard Manley Hopkins,* ed. Norman Weyand, S.J. (New York: Sheed and Ward, 1949), 162.

8. David Jasper notes that this attempt to find the one Word, Christ, is ultimately doomed to failure as it leads Hopkins into a fixed, solipsistic language: "The very fixing of language to the thing it represents robs the poet of that perfect image of Christ in which the essential element is not self-affirmation . . . but self-sacrifice" ("God's Better Beauty: Language and the Poetry of Gerard Manley Hopkins," *Christianity and Literature* 13, no. 3 [1985]: 19).

9. Gerard Manley Hopkins, Letter 5, 1 June 1864, *Further Letters of Gerard Manley Hopkins,* ed. Claude Colleer Abbott (London: Oxford University Press, 1956), 17. Subsequent citations are noted parenthetically in text as *Further Letters.*

10. Speaking of what she calls Hopkins's "fiduciary" use of language, Margaret Ellsberg states: "For an orthodox Catholic, the words spoken over a sacramental action are not simply the conveniently chosen signs of a philosophy: they embody truths. For a poet who wishes to reconcile linguistic art with his convictions, poetic words must somehow embody what is true about the reality they describe: (*Created to Praise: The Language of Gerard Manley Hopkins* [Oxford: Oxford University Press,1987], 47). Ellsberg frequently mentions the significance of eucharistic energy in Hopkins's sacramental poetry but does not posit a specific analogy between the performance of the Mass and the writing of a poem.

11. In a discussion of the Eucharist as the antithesis of the Victorian fear of entropy, James Leggio recognizes the significance of transubstantiation for Hopkins's poetry: "The language with which Hopkins describes the Incarnation and the Blessed Sacrament suggests that he sensed in them a theological counter to the predictions of the new astrophysics; the transformation of bread and wine into body and blood provided a model for change that served as an alternative to the physicist's model of thermodynamic decline. In transubstantiation there was change from a lower to a higher state of charge instead of the reverse; therein lay the action of grace" ("The Science of A Sacrament," *Hopkins Quarterly* 4, no. 2 [Summer 1977]: 63).

12. Thomas Altizer, *Total Presence: The Language of Jesus and the Language of Today* (New York: Seabury Press, 1980), 4.

13. Father John D. Boyd attributes this "driving" quality to Hopkins's "vital blend of imitation and imagination" transfused by the Incarnation. He sees the sacramental foundation of Hopkins's poetics "in his poetry's pervasive and intense Christian realism that was the root of its overall driving quality, the transformed expression of Hopkins's incarnational view of the world, especially of redeemed human life. The thoroughgoing realism of this view tends to make all creation sacramental in its revealing power" (" 'I Say More': Sacrament and Hopkins's Imaginative Realism," *Renascence* 42, no. 1–2 [Fall 1989-Winter 1990]: 56, 61).

14. Gerard Manley Hopkins, *The Journals and Papers of Gerard Manley Hopkins*, ed. Humphry House, completed by Graham Storey (1959; reprint, London: Oxford University Press, 1966), 261. Subsequent citations are noted parenthetically in text as *Journals*.

15. James Finn Cotter, *Inscape: The Christology and Poetry of Gerard Manley Hopkins* (Pittsburgh: University of Pittsburgh Press, 1972), 69, 98.

16. According to Father Devlin, after his ordination, Hopkins grew increasingly distrustful of the affective will, or the inclination, and increasingly committed to the dutiful elective will. Devlin suggests that this conflict was intensified by the Victorian preference for duty over inclination. This movement engendered a conflict between Hopkins's inherent love of natural beauty and his willed obedience toward God. Devlin suggests that Hopkins shifted away from "the presence of God's design or inscape (that is, Christ) in inanimate nature to the working-out of that design—by stress and instress—in the minds and wills of men" (*Sermons*, 109). Other critics, especially Peter Milward and Jeffrey Loomis, concur. The former points to Hopkins's conflict between the incarnational and eschatological poles of Christian faith and sees him moving in his later years toward the latter, a position Donne seems always to have espoused ("1888: The Heraclitean Fire of Nature and the Grace of the Resurrection," *Hopkins Quarterly* 14, no. 1–4 [April 1987–January 1988]: 81–83). Speaking primarily of the Terrible Sonnets, Loomis also perceives a conflict between affective physical and elective spiritual grace by the 1880s. Yet Loomis denies that this later stance moved Hopkins away from his early perception of Real Presence in nature (*Dayspring in Darkness: Sacrament in Hopkins* [Lewisburg: Bucknell University Press, 1988], 104, 115). James Cowles, writing primarily on the *Deutschland*, also alludes to the later poetry as epitomizing "the interior struggle of *arbitrium* with *voluntas* (affective will)." Cowles sees in this struggle evidence of Hopkins's apophatic theology where "the knowledge of God leads through periods of alternating light and darkness, for God Himself includes and yet transcends both" ("The Ethical Dilemma in *The Wreck of the Deutschland*" *Hopkins Quarterly* 13, no. 3–4 [October 1986–January 1987]: 72, 76).

17. Throughout both his journals and his spiritual writings, Hopkins speaks of "stress," "scape," "instress," and "inscape." Walter Ong has recently advanced a succinct definition: "Inscape refers to the utter individuality and distinctiveness that marks each individual existence, its 'thisness,' *haecceitas*. Instress refers to the fusion of the inscape of a given being with a given human consciousness in contact at a given moment with that being in all its uniqueness" (*Hopkins, the Self, and God* [Toronto: University of Toronto Press, 1986], 156). In eucharistic terms, instress occurs at the moment when Christ offers his body inscaped in the elements of bread and wine to the communicant.

18. Hopkins defines "Parnassian" as "the language and style of poetry mastered and at command but employed without any fresh inspiration" (*The Correspondence of Gerard Manley Hopkins and Richard Watson Dixon*, ed. Claude Colleer Abbott [London: Oxford University Press, 1935], 720. He opposes Parnassian to poetry of inspiration in a letter of 1864 to A. W. M. Baillie: "It [Parnassian] can only be spoken by poets, but it is not in the highest sense poetry. It does not require the mood of mind in which the poetry of inspiration is written. It is spoken *on and from the level* of a poet's mind, not as in the other case, when the inspiration which is the gift of genius, raises him above himself" (*Further Letters*, 216).

19. Gerard Manley Hopkins, *The Poems of Gerard Manley Hopkins*, ed. W. H.

Gardner, and N. H. MacKenzie, 4th ed. (London: Oxford University Press, 1967), Poem 6, 11.29–30. Subsequent citations are noted parenthetically in text as *Poems*.

20. Wendell Johnson sees these early poems as Protestant precursors of the later ones. He designates in Hopkins's poetry a move from Protestant typology to Catholic Real Presence and insists that the end of "The Half-way House" "is looking beyond typology to the Real Presence of Christ as a literal and daily feeding of faith" ("Halfway to a New Land: Herbert, Tennyson, and the Early Hopkins," *Hopkins Quarterly* 10, no. 3[Fall 1983]: 121). It seems unlikely, however, that Hopkins ever fully accepted the allegorical overtones of typology. For him, biblical types were not precursors of Christ; they were literally grounded in Christ. Instead of moving toward Real Presence in "Barnfloor and Winepress" and "The Half-way House," Hopkins is describing how acceptance of Real Presence alters one's perceptions of the natural world.

21. Geoffrey Hartman notes that for Hopkins hyphens act as "tension marks . . . they prevent words or syllables from collapsing into one another" ("Hopkins Revisited," in *Beyond Formalism* [New Haven: Yale University Press, 1970], 241).

22. Wendell Johnson thinks that this line refers to Hopkins's decision to abandon the Anglican Church and adds, "The speaker, then, still hungers for food divine that means the Real Presence, not only the type but the blood and flesh in a sacrament both sacrificial and eucharistic" (120).

23. John Henry Cardinal Newman, *Apologia Pro Vita Sua,* ed. David J. DeLaura (New York: Norton, 1968), 160.

24. Ibid., 185.

25. Robert Boyle, S.J., *Metaphor in Hopkins* (Chapel Hill: University of North Carolina Press, 1960), 198.

26. J. Hillis Miller, *The Disappearance of God: Five Nineteenth-Century Writers* (Cambridge: The Belknap Press of Harvard University, 1963), 285.

27. Ibid., 311.

28. Miller concedes that the inscapes of nature, man, and words all "flow from Christ the Word, and the inscapes of language flow from the same source" (317). He views poetry from Hopkins as "the medium through which man may best express the harmonious chiming of all three in Christ" (317).

29. By the time of his essay on Hopkins in *The Linguistic Moment: From Wordsworth to Stevens* (Princeton: Princeton University Press, 1985), 229–66, however, Miller has moved closer to a deconstructionist stance in which he argues that Hopkins's theology and poetic practice are at odds.

30. Jerome Bump, "Hopkins' Imagery and Medievalist Poetics," *Victorian Poetry* 15, no. 2(1977): 115.

31. James Milroy, *The Language of Gerard Manley Hopkins* (London: Andre Deutsch, 1977), 126.

32. Father Philip Endean argues that Hopkins's sacramentalism comes later in the Terrible Sonnets. He believes that the nature poems, including the *Deutschland,* "form a transition between the earlier ascetical spirituality and a sacramentalism that centres on the presence of Christ in each man, with nature in the background" ("The Spirituality of Gerard Manley Hopkins," *Hopkins Quarterly* 8, no. 3[Fall 1981]: 116).

33. Boyle, *Metaphor,* 6.

34. Cowles, "Ethical Dilemma," 86–87.

35. As Jerome Bump notes, "The reader's expectations of sequentiality are frustrated by Hopkins'[s] reversal of the narrative logic: the effect on the speaker

precedes the representation of the event that caused it" ("Reading Hopkins: Visual vs. Auditory Paradigms," *The Bucknell Review* 26, no. 2[1982]: 120).

36. See, for example, Alf Hardelin, *The Tractarian Understanding of the Eucharist* (Upsala: Almquist and Wiskells, 1965) and "Sacraments in the Tractarian Spiritual Universe" in *Tradition Renewed: The Oxford Movement Conference Papers*, ed. Geoffrey Rowell (Allison Park, Pa.: Pickwick Publications, 1986), 78–95. See also Pusey's sermon on Real Presence (1853) for which he was suspended, in *The Oxford Movement*, ed. Eugene R. Fairweather (New York: Oxford University Press, 1964), 368–76. Pusey takes pains to distinguish between real and natural, and to avoid precise definition of the nature of real presence: "We know not the manner of his presence, save that it is not according to the natural presence of our Lord's human flesh, which is at the right hand of God; and therefore it is called sacramental. But it is a presence without us, not within us only; a presence by virtue of our Lord's words, although to us it becomes a saving presence, received to our salvation, through our faith. It is not a presence simply in the soul of the receiver" (376). See also Newman's attempt to reconcile the Anglican Article Twenty-eight with the Roman Catholic doctrine of transubstantiation: "Christ's Body and Blood are *locally* at God's right hand, *yet* really *present* here,—present here, but not here in place,—because they are spirit" (*Tract Ninety or Remarks on Certain Passages in the Thirty-Nine Articles* [1841; reprint, London: Constable and Co., 1933], 70).

37. *Disappearance of God*, 323.

38. *The Traditional Latin Roman Catholic Mass*, trans. Father Gommar A. DePauw, J.C.D. (New York: C.T.M. Publications, 1977), 25–26.

39. F. L. Cross, ed. *The Oxford Dictionary of the Christian Church* (Oxford: Oxford University Press, 1958), 424.

40. Jacob Korg, "Hopkins' Linguistic Deviations," *PMLA* 92, no. 5(October 1977); 977–86. Michael Sprinkler notes, " 'The Wreck of the Deutschland' is 'about' Hopkins's will to master language and his realization of the degree to which he is necessarily mastered by it" (*"A Counterpoint of Dissonance": The Aesthetics and Poetry of Gerard Manley Hopkins* [Baltimore: Johns Hopkins University Press, 1980], 109). Korg and Sprinker argue that Hopkins is finally a victim of his language and that this autonomous language prevents him from approaching Real Presence.

41. For a corrective to this view see Philip Endean's comments on the difficulty of expressing the sacramental in empirical language: "the belief that a feature of the created world is in some radical sense one with the Creator resists clear linguistic expression. The claim that bread and wine, or the azurous hung hills, are, truly speaking, Christ, must involve a collapsing of categories of space and time and a suspension of normal criteria of identity. Even though we may refer to the world in which we live here and now, our belief undermines the empirical basis of linguistic reference" ("Spirituality," 108).

42. *Linguistic Moment*, 258.

43. Paul Mariani, " 'O Christ, Christ, Come Quickly!': Lexical Plenitude and Primal Cry at the Heart of *The Wreck*," in *Readings of The Wreck: Essays in Commemoration of the Centenary of G. M. Hopkins' The Wreck of the Deutschland*, ed. Peter Milward, S.J. (Chicago: Loyola University Press, 1976), 40.

44. *Linguistic Moment*, 257.

45. Closer to Hopkins's definition of overthought and underthought is Michael Ballin's thesis that the underthought of the *Deutschland* is the contemplation of the Feast of the Sacred Heart that runs throughout part 1. Ballin believes part 2

combines both this underthought with the narrative overthought ("Overthought and Underthought in Some Poems by Gerard Manley Hopkins," *Vital Candle: Victorian and Modern Bearings in Gerard Manley Hopkins*, ed. John S. North and Michael D. Moore [Waterloo, Ontario: University of Waterloo Press, 1984], 129, 132. Likewise Jeffrey Loomis, *Dayspring in Darkness*, argues that the " 'underthought' in all of Hopkins's poetry is always the availability of divine Real Presence" (159).

46. Miller, *Linguistic Moment*, 265. In a Derridian reading of *The Wreck*, Miller even denies the existence of a primal word, not just the futility of language to return to it. He thereby undercuts Hopkins's entire endeavor: "The center around which Hopkins's linguistic speculations revolve, the unsettling intuition that they approach and withdraw from, is the exact opposite of his theological insight. It is the notion that there is no primal word, that the divisions of language have always already occurred as soon as there is language at all. If so, there is no word for the Word, only displaced metaphors for it" (261).

47. Although he discusses *The Wreck* as a baptismal rather than a eucharistic poem, Jeffrey Loomis, *Dayspring in Darkness*, acknowledges the connection of Christ with language and reads Hopkins's inscape of the nun's cry oppositely from Miller: "The Word has . . . been now more fully revealed than before through the magical power (to Hopkins, the Really Present sacramental power) of human words" (75).

48. For interpretations of the nun's vision as a theophany, see Elizabeth Schneider's *The Dragon in the Gate: Studies in the Poetry of G. M. Hopkins* (Berkeley: University of California Press, 1968), 29; and Allison D. Sulloway's essay, " 'Strike You the Sight of It?': Intimations of Myth and Tragedy in *The Wreck*," in Milward, *Readings of "The Wreck*," 121–24. Ashton Nichols sees Hopkins's "epiphanies" crystalizing into theophanies when Hopkins interprets the significance of his personal experience. Nichols argues that "The mental manifestation, in Hopkins's case, always needs a theophanic buttress, lest it become only the flickering instability feared by Arnold and embraced by Hopkins's Oxford tutor, Walter Pater" (*The Poetics of Epiphany: Nineteenth-Century Origins of the Modern Literary Moment* [Tuscaloosa: University of Alabama Press, 1987], 173). Nichols does not, however, discuss Hopkins's incarnational view of language and nature in which a theophany—the visible experience of Christ—is actually the experience of the Real Presence of Christ.

49. In addition to the intimate connection of "fetch" with the body, it also has nautical connotations, namely as a noun meaning a bay and as a verb meaning to train a ship onto the correct course. Here the one word works to redeem both the nun and all the victims of the wreck. It also emphasizes the universality of Christ's presence—in each heart, in the storm, and in the bay.

50. See, for example, *Letters to Bridges* from May 1885 (216) and September 1885 (222).

51. Philip Endean briefly suggests that the Terrible Sonnets serve to teach the self its own insufficiency: "God shows that self-sufficiency leads not to fulfilment but only to damnation" ("Spirituality," 123).

52. Daniel Harris, *Inspirations Unbidden: The 'Terrible Sonnets' of Gerard Manley Hopkins* (Berkeley: University of California Press, 1982), 24. Harris argues for the loss of an "immanental vision" and the consequent disappearance of reciprocity on which both instress and inscape and, consequently, Real Presence depend. See also James Leggio's "The Science of a Sacrament" for a discussion of the opposite of eucharistic energy—entropy.

53. Ibid., 24, 52.

54. "Spiritual Mysteries in Hopkins's Dublin Years: 1885," *Hopkins Quarterly* 14, no. 1–4 (April 1987–January 1988): 50.

55. *Ibid.*, 51–52.

56. Milward, "Heruclitean Fire," 81; Loomis, *Dayspring in Darkness*, 104, 110.

57. *Dayspring in Darkness*, 137.

58. "Spiritual Mysteries," 47.

59. *Dayspring in Darkness*, 146.

60. "Spirituality," 123.

61. "God's Better Beauty," 19.

62. *Disappearance of God*, 347.

63. Walter Ong discusses the apparent conflict in Hopkins between the individual will and Christ but concludes that "The human person is not diminished in Christ, is not made into someone else or reduced to no one at all, but rather grows into a 'nobler me' " (*Hopkins, The Self, and God*, 87). Yet this belief seems to elude Hopkins in the Terrible Sonnets. Here he cannot realize Christ's presence but only his own unique self-taste.

64. *Language*, 190.

65. *Inspirations Unbidden*, 67–68.

Chapter 4. Wounding Presence

1. Aneirin Talfan Davies, *Dylan: Druid of the Broken Body* (J. M. Dent, 1964; reprint, Swansea: Christopher Davies, 1977), note 7, p. 34. Davies notes, however, that Thomas sometimes attended a local Anglican church and even borrowed Dom Gregory Dix's *The Shape of the Liturgy*, a history of Catholicism and Anglicanism. Thus he would have been familiar with the significance of the Eucharist in the Anglo-Catholic tradition.

2. *Dylan Thomas: The Collected Letters*, ed. Paul Ferris (New York: Macmillan, 1985), 12. Subsequent citations are noted parenthetically in text as *CL*.

3. Henry Treece was the first to argue for Thomas's indebtedness to Hopkins, a debt that Thomas denied. Treece says, "While Hopkins calls out to God, throwing the light of Heaven upon his anguish, Thomas again looks inwards, and as a God unto himself, analyzes and diagnoses for his own disorder" (*Dylan Thomas: "Dog Among the Fairies"* (London: Lindsay Drummond, 1949), 62. Comparing Thomas to Hopkins in a recent article, Jacob Korg denies that Thomas struggles with similar spiritual problems. He concludes, "For Hopkins the contradictions of a world that offers both anguish and joy were occasions for self-questioning and self-discipline; for Thomas they were, far more simply, and far less painfully, materials for poetry" ("Hopkins and Dylan Thomas," in *Hopkins Among the Poets: Studies in Modern Responses to Gerard Manley Hopkins*, ed. Richard F. Giles (International Hopkins Association Monograph Series 3, 1985), Hamilton, Ontario, 93. I argue throughout this chapter that Thomas did progress painfully toward a spiritual vision of self-sacrifice in nature, and that this progression was far from effortless.

4. Karl Shapiro denies the importance of God in Thomas's poetry as opposed to the role of God in Hopkins's poems: "Hopkins draws his symbology almost entirely from the God-symbol. God, in various attributes, is the chief process in Hopkins's view of the world. Sex is the chief process in Thomas's view of the world" ("Dylan Thomas," in *Dylan Thomas: A Collection of Critical Essays*, ed. C. B. Cox [Englewood Cliffs, N.J.: Prentice-Hall, 1966]), 174.

5. "Metaphor and Transcendence," in *On Metaphor,* ed. Sheldon Sacks (Chicago: University of Chicago Press, 1978), 86.

6. Ibid., 88.

7. In fact, Thomas takes pains to abjure Surrealism, especially in his own poetry. As he tells Richard Church who accused him of the taint of Surrealism, "I am not, never have been, never will be, or could be for that matter, a surrealist, and for a number of reasons: I have very little idea what surrealism is; until quite recently I had never heard of it; I have never . . . read even a paragraph of surrealist literature" (*CL,* 204–5). And to Henry Treece, he says, I haven't . . . ever read a proper surrealist poem" (*CL,* 282).

8. *The Poetry of Dylan Thomas* (Chicago: University of Chicago Press, 1954), 15.

9. *Druid,* 60.

10. *Dylan Thomas: A Literary Study* (New York: Citadel Press, 1965), 37. Stanford uses the term "sacramental" loosely; he does not equate sacramentalism with sacrifice nor with the spiritual implanted in the material.

11. Ibid., 203.

12. *Emergence From Chaos* (Boston: Houghton Mifflin, 1957), 81.

13. Ibid., 83.

14. "The Religious Poet," in *Dylan Thomas: The Legend and the Poet,* ed. W. E. Tedlock (London: Heinemann, 1960), 236.

15. *The Poems of Dylan Thomas,* ed. Daniel Jones (New York: New Directions, 1971), 54–55, ll.1–6. Subsequent citations for this edition are noted parenthetically in text.

16. *Criticism* 22(1980): 331.

17. *Poets of Reality: Six Twentieth-Century Writers* (Cambridge: Belknap Press of Harvard University Press, 1966), 214.

18. *Dylan Thomas: The Country of the Spirit* (Princeton: Princeton University Press, 1973), 115–19.

19. *Literary Study,* 49.

20. *Emergence from Chaos,* 15.

21. *The Making of a Poem* (1955, reprint; New York: Norton, 1962), 38.

22. *Literary Study,* 73.

23. *Country,* 129.

24. In *The Religious Sonnets of Dylan Thomas: A Study in Imagery and Meaning* (Berkeley: University of California Press, 1963), H. H. Kleinman notes, "The poem begins with a sonnet mocking the descent of the word; it concludes in a spiraling ascent of faith" (11). In an elaborate exposition in which he argues for the astrological influence on the sonnet sequence, Elder Olson, *Poetry of Dylan Thomas,* sees the poem moving in an eschatological fashion from pagan elements to Christian faith. This movement culminates with the Christian interpretation of sonnets 4 and 5 (64–86, *passim*).

25. "Dylan Thomas: The Christianity of the 'Altarwise by Owl-light' Sequence," *College English* 28, no. 8(1962): 627.

26. *Country,* 136.

27. Concurring with Kidder's verdict, Robert Adams compares Thomas with the metaphysical poet Crashaw and notes, "a poet may certainly enrich his poem by meaning two things at once, but he will certainly confuse it by meaning sixteen things at once, without making clear the relation between them" ("Crashaw and Dylan Thomas: Devotional Athletes," in C. B. Cox, *Dylan Thomas,* 137).

28. *Dylan Thomas* (New York: Twayne, 1965), 51.

29. Dylan Thomas, James Stephens, and Gerald Bullett, "On Poetry: A Discussion," *Encounter* 3, no. 5(1954): 25–26.

30. "Poetic Manifesto," *Texas Quarterly* 4(1961): 46.

31. *Religious Sonnets*, 13.

32. Ibid., 66.

33. Ibid., 94–95. Kleinman sees sonnet 8 as the initiation of New Testament time, which culminates in sonnet 10. Sonnets 1 to 7 have illustrated the seven days of creation. He views "gallow grave" as a fusion of Golgotha and Christ's tomb.

34. Knieger, "Dylan Thomas," views Thomas as speaker here: "the poet participates vicariously in the crucifixion of Christ, the world is his wound; also suggested is the wounding operation of time" (623).

35. *Religious Sonnets*, 99.

36. "The Logic of Jesus, the Logic of God," *Anglican Theological Review* 62, no. 1(1980): 39.

37. "Christian Love in Dylan Thomas," *Theology* 49, no. 548 (February 1966): 76.

38. Both "Fern Hill" and "In Country Sleep" exact personal sacrifice to realize sacramental presence also. In the former, Thomas depicts the prelapsarian world of his childhood and its inevitable ruin in adulthood. Yet here, the religious images are governed by human time. The persona's sacrifice fails to ensure a permanent presence.

39. " 'No Reason for Mourning': A Reading of the Later Poems of Dylan Thomas," *Approach* 42(1962): 6.

40. *Druid*, 68.

41. *Country*, 145.

42. Louise Baughan Murdy in *Sound and Sense in Dylan Thomas's Poetry* (The Hague: Mouton, 1960) discusses sound and sense in "Ceremony" and concludes that Thomas progresses "toward a phonetic 'symbolism' " in which sound truly echoes or symbolizes sense" (105).

43. *Dylan Thomas*, 114–15.

44. Davies, emphasizing Thomas's orthodox adherence to the Incarnation and Resurrection, sees part 1 as womblike, part 2 as crosslike, and Incarnation being completed by Crucifixion and promise of Resurrection (52). Nist agrees with Davies's interpretation of part 1 but sees part 2 as a chalice offering in communion the seal of the Resurrection (6).

45. *Country*, 164. Sister Roberta Jones sees part 2 as the intersection of the God-Man symbolized by the Greek *chi* or cross ("The Wellspring of Dylan," *English Journal* 55, no. 1[1966]: 81).

46. Shapiro in "Dylan Thomas," states, "Unlike Hopkins, he has no vision of nature and cannot break open the forms of nature; he cannot break open words. He focuses madly on the object, but it will not yield" (177).

47. Stanford in *Literacy Study*, sees in the final poems, particularly "In Country Sleep," a movement from expression to description and a resultant focus on surface as opposed to essence (136). In *Sound and Form in Modern Poetry* (Ann Arbor: University of Michigan Press, 1964), Harvey Gross sees the later poems moving toward "declamation" over presentation (271). Both critics blame this movement on a failure of vision and an angry reaction against this failure.

48. Asked by his editor to write a prose prologue to the *Collected Poems*, Thomas instead labored over an elaborate poem. As he tells Bozman, "I set myself, foolishly perhaps, a most difficult technical task: The Prologue is in two verses . . . of 51 lines each. And the second verse rhymes *backward* with the first.

The first and last lines of the poem rhyme; the second and the last but one, and so on and so on" (*CL*, 838).

49. "Christian Love," 58.

50. The first two stanzas stipulate the agony of not writing and the sacrifice involved in commencing:

> On no work of words now for three lean months in the bloody
> Belly of the rich year and the big purse of my body
> I bitterly take to task my poverty and craft:
>
> To take to give is all, return what is hungrily given
> Puffing the pounds of manna up through the dew to heaven,
> The lovely gift of the gab bangs back on a blind shaft.

(ll.1–6)

51. *Poets of Reality*, 7.
52. *Making of Poem*, 43.

Chapter 5. Signs of Presence and Absence

1. *The Lords of Limit: Essays on Literature and Ideas* (London: Andre Deutsch, 1984), 3. Subsequent citations are noted parenthetically in text as *LL*.

2. "Geoffrey Hill," in *Viewpoints: Poets in Conversation with John Haffenden* (London: Faber and Faber, 1981), 86.

3. Ibid., 87.

4. Christopher Ricks calls Hill "a religious man without, it must seem, a religion; a profoundly honest doubter" (*The Force of Poetry* [Oxford: Clarendon Press, 1984], 317. Although this assessment is plausible, I would argue that Anglo-Catholicism and increasingly Roman Catholicism is the dogmatic backdrop against which Hill erects many of his "doubting" poems. Were he to relinquish doubt for faith, it seems possible that he would espouse one of these two religions.

5. *The Uncommon Tongue: The Poetry and Criticism of Geoffrey Hill* (Ann Arbor: University of Michigan Press, 1987), 22. Sherry continues to elaborate Hill's conflict with religion as it surfaces in his poetry: "Despite this radical, apparently fanatical ideal of spiritual art, Geoffrey Hill is not speaking as a Christian fideist. A genuinely religious man, he is a true doubter, a believer who (22). In a review of Hill's *Collected Poems,* Peter Levi also addresses this conflict but sees it as actively aiding the poetry: "I cannot but believe this growth has been sees it as actively aiding the poetry: "I cannot but believe this growth has been nourished by the presence in his poetry of a religious element. The idea of a living God, like the prospect of being hanged, can sharpen one's wits and hone one's seriousness, whether one believes like Eliot or disbelieves like Empson and perhaps Milton" ("Geoffrey Hill," *Agenda* 23, no. 3–4[Autumn–Winter 1985–86]: 14).

6. Of the critics who detail Hill's obsession with martyrdom and sacrifice, W. S. Milne notes, "there is a compounding of self-seeking and self-sacrifice in the martyr's and writer's life which highlights the paradoxical nature of all human experience." Milne sees Hill's victory over this paradox in his "disciplined act of

attention," which counters the self-seeking absorption and achieves a balance between the two. Such an act requires a *kenotic* concentration. ("The 'Pitch of Attention': Geoffrey Hill's *Tenebrae*," *Agenda* 17, no. 1[1979]: 32–33). Thomas Getz echoes this conflict, citing Hill's "awareness of the difficulty of genuine self-abnegation of the contradictions involved in adopting a worshipful attitude toward human sacrifice ("Geoffrey Hill's *Mercian Hymns* and *Lachrimae:* The Languages of History and Faith," *Modern Poetry Studies* 10[1980]: 11). This dilemma recalls Donne's and Hopkins's discussions of human versus divine will and their anxiety to subordinate human to divine. Hill not only wrestles with this subordination; he is suspicious of those who seem to subordinate their wills to God.

7. *Agenda* 9, no. 4(1972): 16, 23.

8. Vincent Sherry speaks of Hill's shift from a transcendent ground to one of technique as the "sanctification of aesthetics" (177) where ambivalent language and strict form actually create a liberating presence: "The failure to incarnate the Logos . . . marks the creative opportunity for the poet-redeemer. Here . . . he might listen to its [the word's] layered recesses, tap the several meanings accumulated in its historical strata, and so liberate us from the bondage of a single fixed reference" (189). Although Hill would doubtless agree with Sherry's second statement, he would not assent to the first. He says in a 1980 interview with Blake Morrison: "The poet's true commitment must always be first to the vertical richness of language. The poet's gift is to make history and politics and religion speak for themselves through the strata of language" ("Under Judgment," *New Statesman,* 8 February 1980, 214). Hill does not regard himself as a potential redeemer, nor does he see his work in the romantic light of a failed prophet or priest. A more measured notion of Hill's project comes from John Bayley who believes that Hill's poetry is both "completely authoritative and implicitly renunciatory of the authority which its words totally establish" ("Somewhere is Such a Kingdom: Geoffrey Hill and Contemporary Poetry," in *Geoffrey Hill: Essays on his Work,* ed. Peter Robinson [Milton Keynes, England: Open University Press, 1985], 191). In other words, the self-conscious and historically guilty poet can never be the Shelleyean prophet or legislator. At best he can diagnose historical evils and point toward a presence forever postponed. Bayley astutely speaks of this delayed presence as the "peculiar air of perpetual expectancy, awaiting the unvouchsafed mystery, the miracle that can never take place" (192).

9. Hill uses Pound's problematic support of Fascism in his wartime broadcasts together with his retraction in the hearing for treason as the occasion for an inquiry into the statement "our word is our bond": "He is vulnerable to accusations that he naively or willfully regarded his wartime broadcasts as being in some way traditionally privileged and protected by his status as poet" (*LL*, 138).

10. *Viewpoints,* 88. Hill here is appropriating Father Christopher Devlin's description of Hopkins's sermons as " 'The lost kingdom of innocence and original justice.' " Peter Robinson views Hill as attempting to redeem a fallen language and so goes beyond Hill's idea of the poet as mere witness:

> Hill feels the shudder of fall in words, words that are *of* this world, and conceives of the acts of composition as a resistance to, and a seeking to ammend for, sin and shame. Employing the same old words, he attempts to restore to the world of usage, and to the world that usage may order, distinguishable senses and value embedded in them. (*Essays,* 205).

"Reading Geoffrey Hill" in *Geoffrey Hill: Essays on His Work,* ed. Peter Robinson (Milton Keynes, England: Open University Press, 1985), 205. In "Poetry as 'Menace' and 'Atonement' " Hill offers another dilemma the modern poet faces: "So there is a sense in which the modern artist is called upon to atone for his own illiberal pride and a sense in which he is engaged in vicarious expiation for the pride of the culture which itself rejects him" (*LL*, 4).

11. " 'Flesh of Abnegation': The Poems of Geoffrey Hill," *The Southern Review* 15(1979): 65.

12. "The Poetry of Geoffrey Hill," in *British Poetry Since 1960*, ed. Michael Schmidt and Grevel Lindop (Oxford: Carcanet Press, 1972), 146.

13. "Flesh and Blood," Review of *Somewhere is Such a Kingdom*, *The Sewanee Review* 84, no. 3(1976): xcvii.

Robert Richman echoes Hirsch's verdict: "the experience that brings the poem to life sets up a standard the poem cannot do justice to" (" 'The battle it was born to lose': the Poetry of Geoffrey Hill," *The New Criterion* 2, no. 8[1984]: 23).

14. Ibid., 28.

15. *Viewpoints*, 89.

16. *Viewpoints*, 98.

17. *Geoffrey Hill: Collected Poems* (New York: Oxford University Press, 1986), 207. Subsequent citations are noted parenthetically in text.

18. *The Oxford Dictionary of the Christian Church*, 2d ed., ed. F. L. Cross and E. A. Livingstone (New York: Oxford University Press, 1984), 490.

19. "Speaking of the Holocaust: The Poetry of Geoffrey Hill," *The Denver Quarterly* 12, no. 1(1977): 115.

20. Ibid., 118.

21. C. H. Sisson argues that Hill employs restrained forms to guard against his own passion: "There is in Hill a touch of the fastidiousness of Crashaw, which is that of a mind in search of artifices to protect itself against its own passions" (*The Avoidance of Literature: Collected Essays* [Manchester: Carcanet Press, 1978], 470). A. K. Weatherhead, "Geoffrey Hill," *Iowa Review* 8, no. 4(1977): 113. Merle Brown emphasizes Hill's divisiveness or doubleness between objective empiricism and subjectivity that manifests itself in the discrepancy between passionate message and ritualized style. Both content and form tend to deplete themselves, then return to a yearned-for fullness (*The Double Lyric: Divisiveness and Communal Creativity in Recent English Poetry* [New York: Columbia University Press, 1980], 28). At the level of punctuation, Christopher Ricks sees Hill's brackets as both containing and restraining feeling (293), whereas the hyphens are "forever both holding together and holding apart the elements which seek to constitute the non-word as a word" (326).

22. "On Geoffrey Hill," *Critical Quarterly* 23, no. 2(1981): 21.

23. "On Hill," 22.

24. "History and Faith," 11.

25. *Viewpoints*, 87.

26. *Force of Poetry*, 309.

27. Speaking of the use of parentheses in the poem, Christopher Ricks says of the last three words, "All creation against—and yet not *against* one woman. Those last three words incarnate a profound paradox, a crux and an aside, an admonition and a reassurance, such as allow Geoffrey Hill to share the studied reflex and the contained breath of George Herbert" (*Force of Poetry*, 318).

28. Both Merle Brown and A. K. Weatherhead have offered Bloomian readings of "Funeral Music," insisting on Hill's typological goals. Brown notes, "There is a momentous thrust forward between the first and second poems; the second bears the first with it and yet grows beyond it in the subtlety and delicacy of its oneness

and its divisiveness. And yet, though the individual poems do not move as son-nets—in which sestet follows octet and yet must be experienced as simultaneous with it—the sequence as a whole does work in just that way" (*Double Lyric,* 43). Brown sees Hill in a silent conflict with T. S. Eliot, the strong predecessor whom Hill must repudiate. Weatherhead suggests a task of resolution and redemption through language: "The poem's function is to cleanse the past, to liberate history from the stain occasioned by its association with putrescent flesh and sin. . . . The poem's act is one of love; as death frees the soul from its earthly bondage so the word may free history from the taint of the mire of human veins" ("Geoffrey Hill," 107). "Funeral Music" does not propose solutions, nor does it appear to be a disguised battle between Hill and Eliot. As in Hill's other poems, both earlier and later, it exposes the atrocities of history under the false guise of religion; it does not attempt a purgation.

29. Ricks notes of "Genesis" that Hill's clichés work literally to spawn new life from dead language ("Review of *Somewhere is Such a Kingdom*," *New York Times Book Review,* 11 January 1976, 6).

30. *On Christian Doctrine,* trans. D. W. Robertson, Jr. (Indianapolis: Bobbs-Merrill, 1958), 86.

31. "Promises, Promises," Review of *Tenebrae, New Statesman,* 5 January 1979, 19.

32. *Viewpoints,* 89.

33. Calvin Bedient argues that *Tenebrae* represents "a failure of nerve" in which "conscience is sent to church, if only to other people's churches. If *Mercian Hymns* is the crime, *Tenebrae* is the penitence" ("On Hill," 22–23). Likewise, although he concedes that *Tenebrae* "contains, probably, Hill's most masterfully crafted verse," Vincent Sherry states that Hill has "relaxed to a degree in the authority of traditional form" and that this relaxation makes the poems less interesting than those of his first two books (*Uncommon Tongue,* 157). Conversely, W. S. Milne and Brian Oxley see the book as a victory over the "inertia" of matter. Milne notes, "It is Hill's intention in *Tenebrae* to reveal the triumphs of the spirit over the inertia of matter in each of the poems . . . by the disciplined act of attention." He goes on to state that the act of attention counters the "act of 'absorption' which concentrates on another realm of reality, whether it be the spiritual one of the saint or the truly 'fictional' one of the artist" (" 'The Pitch of Attention,' " 32). Oxley is more specific and more orthodox, indicating that *Tenebrae* is a "poetic way of the cross": "The book gathers-in and sharpens-up contradictions as if to make a sum of human disunity, revealing in such purposive concentration its formal design as a *poetic* way of the cross. It suffers the cross of disunity in order to become the integral substance that redeems and unifies" ("Geoffrey Hill's 'Christian Year,' " *Essays in Criticism* 29[1979]: 286).

34. Christopher Ricks remarks that for Hill punctuation serves as a metaphor of constraint or containment that calls attention to the limits of speech (*Force of Poetry,* 293). Accordingly, "Pentecost Castle" is freedom from such constraint. It mixes speech with meditation and operates on several levels simultaneously. Conversely, Donald Hall says of the poem, "The lines move down the page erasing themselves" (*The Weather of Poetry* [Ann Arbor: University of Michigan Press, 1980], 90). Hall argues for absence, not presence.

35. Henry Hart sees "Pentecost Castle" as a mystical poem that initiates an *Imitatio Christi* theme that runs throughout *Tenebrae.* In fact, he views section 9 as achieving "Eucharistic 'at-one-ment.' " He argues that "The poet converts . . . his sexual losses into spiritual gains" (*The Poetry of Geoffrey Hill* [Carbondale:

Southern Illinois University Press, 1986], 210–11). By section 12, however, this " 'at-one-ment' " is revealed as illusory: "each of us dispossessed / so richly in my sleep / I rise out of my sleep / crying like one possessed" (*CP*, 143). In response to a question about the mysticism in the poem, Hill states, "Paradox, and the closely related oxymoron, belong both to the tradition of mystical poetry and to the tradition of Petrarchan poetry, which are the main models for 'The Pentecost Castle' and 'Lachrimae' " ("Under Judgment," 212).

36. *Double Lyric*, 68.

37. "Languages of History and Faith," 21.

38. "Under Judgment," 212.

39. Ibid., 213.

40. Hart regards "Lachrimae" as a reversal of the final purpose in Christian meditation—colloquy—and states that Hill "imagines Christ on the cross so he can heckle and interrogate him" (*Geoffrey Hill*, 213).

41. Hart optimistically states that the "Lachrimae" sonnets "suggest that creation is crucifixion, the redemptive word nailed and twisted into significant shape" (*Geoffrey Hill*, 222), but Vincent Sherry convincingly contradicts such resolution between word and deed and instead sees the artistry of the form taking priority over the search for belief: "A poem . . . may express a desire for union with God, while its achieved perfection and technical self-sufficiency preclude the needed humility" (*Uncommon Tongue*, 197). It seems that both of these interpretations are too definitive. Hill is acutely aware of the dangers of aesthetic perfection at the expense of meaning or ethics. Likewise he is suspicious of the power of words to effect a reconciliation between willed faith and actual faith.

42. In "The Absolute Reasonableness of Robert Southwell," a tribute to the sixteenth-century Roman Catholic martyr, Hill continues his concern with the connection between word and deed, word and faith. He sees in Southwell's "reasonable" style a restraint, a choosing not to say (*LL*, 27), as opposed to "Donne's words [which] relish their own seductive strength" (*LL*, 34). In a phrase that well might apply to his own poetry, Hill admires the element of sacrifice in Southwell's style: "The correlative of equity is sacrifice and Southwell sacrifices a great deal, even the poet's delight in self-sustaining, self-supporting wit" (*LL*, 34).

43. *Viewpoints*, 81.

44. Thomas Getz and Merle Brown interpret this last line differently. Getz sees it in a more personal light: "Through communion one dominates Christ, takes him into one's own body and blood, and also convinces oneself that one gains dominion over life" ("Languages of History and Faith," 20). Brown offers a more imperialistic interpretation: "to take part in communion is to turn the truth into a saleable object, to swallow his Lord's blood is to swallow dominion, lordship entailing ownership, a sliding from the Lord to his 'lords of revenue' " (*Double Lyric*, 70).

45. *On Christian Doctrine*, 9.

46. Ibid., 32.

47. "The Thick and the Thin of It: Contemporary British and Irish Poetry," *Kenyon Review* 3, no. 3(1981): 44.

48. "The Language of Poetry: Materiality and Meaning," *Essays in Criticism* 31, no. 3(1981): 243.

49. W. S. Milne discusses the theme of "committed suffering" throughout the poem and argues for a religious interpretation: "There is a feeling here of passion (if not The Passion) being reenacted, of some presence continually re-asserting itself" (" 'Images of Earth and Grace': Geoffrey Hill's *The Mystery of the Charity*

of Charles Peguy, Agenda 21, 3[1983]: 15–16). That presence seems to be Hill's ambivalent relationship to and envy of Peguy reduced, as Robert Richman notes, to a "portrait without a face" ("The Battle," 31). Discussing Peguy in light of Hill's essay, "Our Word is Our Bond," John Lucas notes that "Peguy behaved towards his time as the poet should behave toward language." Yet Lucas regards the poem as failing to live up to this standard: "It is demanding to be taken as important, but ends up seeming merely self-important" ("Accidents of Language: *The Mystery of the Charity of Charles Peguy,*" *London Review of Books* 5, no. 20[3 December 1983]: 16). Vincent Sherry sees the poem as subverting an incarnational theory of language: "His poetics of ambiguity challenge the authority of the Church in a radical sense, strike at the Church's sustaining root, and defy the legend that would license it to embody, inviolably, a single divine Logos in one utterance: the incarnational myth of language, the doctrine of essential linkage between a word's abstract meaning and its physical substance" (*Uncommon Tongue,* 231).

50. "Thick and Thin of It," 47–48.

Chapter 6. The Word Dispersed

1. *Mythical Intentions in Modern Literature* (Princeton: Princeton University Press, 1981), 201.

2. "White Mythology: Metaphor in the Text of Philosophy," *New Literary History* 6, no. 1(Autumn 1974): 48.

3. Ibid., 48.

4. Ibid., 70.

5. Ibid., 71.

6. *Essays on Biblical Interpretation,* trans. David Stewart and Charles E. Reagan, ed. Lewis S. Mudge (Philadelphia: Fortress Press, 1980), 104.

7. Ibid., 101.

8. "White Mythology," 72.

9. *Linguistic Moment,* xvii.

10. *Mythical Intentions,* 243.

11. *Poetics of Epiphany,* 31.

12. *The Christian Image: Studies in Religious Art and Poetry* (Pittsburgh: Duquesne University Press, 1966), 31.

13. Ibid., 81.

14. *Towards a Christian Poetics* (Grand Rapids, Mich.: William B. Eerdmans, 1984), 10.

15. *Poetic Presence and Illusion,* 12.

16. Ibid., 23.

17. Ibid., 143.

18. *Language and Silence: Essays on Language, Literature and the Inhuman* (New York: Atheneum, 1967), 37.

19. Ibid., 39.

20. Ibid., 41.

21. Steiner complains of Thomas that "He realized, with the flair of a showman, that a wide, largely unqualified audience could be flattered by being given access to a poetry of seeming depth. He combined a froth of Swinburnean rhetoric with cabalistic devices of syntax and imagery. He showed that one could have one's Orphic cake and eat it too. But barring certain eloquent exceptions, there is in his poems less than meets the dazzled eye" (Ibid., 28).

22. *Real Presences,* The Leslie Stephen Memorial Lecture, 1 November 1985 (Cambridge: Press Syndicate of the University of Cambridge, 1986), 6.

23. Ibid., 12.

24. Ibid., 15.

25. Ibid., 16.

26. Ibid., 23.

27. Ibid., 18.

28. Ibid., 19.

29. Ibid., 19.

30. Ibid., 23.

31. *Grammar of Assent,* 96.

32. *The Force of Poetry* (Oxford: Clarendon Press, 1984) 304.

Bibliography

Primary Sources

Donne, John. *Devotions Upon Emergent Occasions.* 1624. Reprint. Ann Arbor: University of Michigan Press, 1959.

———. *The Divine Poems.* Ed. Helen Gardner. Oxford: Clarendon Press, 1978.

———. *The Elegies and the Songs and Sonnets.* Ed. Helen Gardner. Oxford: Clarendon Press, 1965.

———. *Selected Prose.* Chosen by Evelyn Simpson. Ed. Helen Gardner and Timothy Healy. Oxford: Clarendon Press, 1967.

———. *The Sermons of John Donne.* 10 vols. Ed. George R. Potter and Evelyn M. Simpson. Berkeley: University of California Press, 1953.

Hill, Geoffrey. *Collected Poems.* New York: Oxford University Press, 1986.

———. " 'The Conscious Mind's Intelligible Structure': A Debate." *Agenda* 9, no. 4 (1972): 14–23.

———. "Geoffrey Hill." In *Viewpoints: Poets in Conversation with John Haffenden,* ed. John Haffenden. London: Faber and Faber, 1981.

———. *The Lords of Limit: Essays on Literature and Ideas.* London: Andre Deutsch, 1984.

———. "Under Judgment: An Interview with Blake Morrison." *New Statesman* (8 February 1980): 212–14.

Hopkins, Gerard Manley. *Correspondence of Gerard Manley Hopkins and R. W. Dixon.* Ed. Claude Colleer Abbott. London: Oxford University Press, 1955.

———. *Further Letters of Gerard Manley Hopkins.* Ed. Claude Colleer Abbott. London: Oxford University Press, 1956.

———. *The Journals and Papers of Gerard Manley Hopkins.* Ed. Humphry House. Completed by Graham Storey. London: Oxford University Press, 1959.

———. *The Letters of Gerard Manley Hopkins to Robert Bridges.* Ed. Claude Colleer Abbott. London: Oxford University Press, 1935. Rev. ed. 1955.

———. *The Poems of Gerard Manley Hopkins.* 4th ed. Ed. W. H. Gardner and N. H. MacKenzie. London: Oxford UP, 1967.

———. *The Sermons and Devotional Writings of Gerard Manley Hopkins.* Ed. Christopher Devlin. S. J. London: Oxford University Press, 1959.

Thomas, Dylan. *The Collected Letters.* Ed. Paul Ferris. New York: Macmillan, 1985.

———, James Stephens, and Gerald Bullett. "On Poetry: A Discussion." *Encounter* 3, no. 5(1954): 23–26.

———. *The Poems of Dylan Thomas.* Ed. Daniel Jones. New York: New Directions, 1971.

———. "Poetic Manifesto." *Texas Quarterly* 4(1961): 45–53.

Critical Works

Addis, William E., and Thomas Arnold. *A Catholic Dictionary.* New York: The Catholic Publication Society, 1884.

Altizer, Thomas J. *Total Presence: The Language of Jesus and the Language of Today.* New York: Seabury Press, 1980.

Attridge, Derek. "The Language of Poetry: Materiality and Meaning." *Essays in Criticism* 31, no. 3(1981): 228–45.

Auerbach, Erich. *Scenes from the Drama of European Literature.* New York: Meridian Books, 1959.

Augustine, Saint. *On Christian Doctrine.* Trans. D. W. Robertson, Jr. Indianapolis: Bobbs-Merrill, 1958.

Bayley, John. "A Retreat or Seclusion: Tenebrae of Geoffrey Hill." *Agenda* 17, no. 1(1979): 38–42.

Bedient, Calvin, "On Geoffrey Hill." *Critical Quarterly* 23, no. 2(1981): 17–26.

———. "The Thick and the Thin of It: Contemporary British and Irish Poetry." *Kenyon Review* 3, no. 3(1981): 32–48.

Bennett, Joan. *Four Metaphysical Poets.* 1934. New York: Vintage, 1953.

Bicknell, E. J. *A Theological Introduction to the Thirty-nine Articles of the Church of England.* 3rd ed. Rev. H. J. Carpenter. London: Longman, 1955.

Bond, Ronald. "John Donne and the Problem of 'Knowing Faith.' " *Mosaic* 14, no. 1(1981): 25–35.

Booty, John E., ed. *The Book of Common Prayer 1559: The Elizabethan Prayer Book.* Charlottesville: University Press of Virginia, 1976.

Boyd, John D., S.J. " 'I Say More': Sacrament and Hopkins's Imaginative Realism." *Renascence* 42, no. 1–2 (Fall 1989–Winter 1990): 51–64.

Boyle, Robert, S.J. *Metaphor in Hopkins.* Chapel Hill: University of North Carolina Press, 1960.

Breslin, Paul. "Wary and Ironic." *New York Times Book Review* 1 April 1979: 19–20.

Brown, Merle E. *Double Lyric: Divisiveness and Communal Creativity in Recent English Poetry.* New York: Columbia University Press, 1980.

Brownjohn, Alan. "Fascination of What's Difficult." *Encounter* 52, no. 3(1979): 61–65.

Bruns, Gerald L. *Inventions: Writing, Textuality, and Understanding in Literary History.* New Haven: Yale University Press, 1982.

———. *Modern Poetry and the Idea of Language.* New Haven: Yale University Press, 1974.

Buckley, Vincent. *Poetry and the Sacred.* London: Chatto and Windus, 1968.

Bump, Jerome. "Hopkins' Imagery and Medievalist Poetics." *Victorian Poetry* 15, no. 2(1977): 99–119.

———. "Reading Hopkins: Visual vs. Auditory Paradigms." *The Bucknell Review* 26, no. 2(1982): 119–149.

Burdette, Robert K. *The Saga of Prayer: The Poetry of Dylan Thomas.* The Hague: Mouton, 1972.

Cannons and Decrees of the Council of Trent. Trans. Rev. H. J. Schroeder, O.P. Rockford, Ill.: Tan Books, 1978.

Clark, Ira. *Christ Revealed: The History of the Neotypological Lyric in the English Renaissance.* Gainsville: University of Florida Press, 1982.

Cotter, James Finn. " 'Hornlight Wound to the West': The Inscape of the Passion in Hopkins' Poetry." *Victorian Poetry* 16, no. 4(1978): 297–313.

———. *Inscape: The Christology and Poetry of Gerard Manley Hopkins.* Pittsburgh: University of Pittsburgh Press, 1972.

Cowles, James. "The Ethical Dilemma in *The Wreck of the Deutschland.*" *Hopkins Quarterly* 13, no. 3–4 (October 1986–January 1987): 67–98.

Cox, C. B., ed. *Dylan Thomas: A Collection of Critical Essays.* Englewood Cliffs, N.J.: Prentice-Hall, 1966.

Cross, F. L., and E. A. Livingstone, eds. *The Oxford Dictionary of the Christian Church.* 2d ed. New York: Oxford University Press, 1974.

Davies, Aneirin Talfan. *Dylan: Druid of the Broken Body.* 1964. Reprint. Swansea: Christopher Davies, 1977.

Davies, Horton. *Worship and Theology in England.* 2 vols. Princeton: Princeton University Press, 1970–75.

Derrida, Jacques. "White Mythology: Metaphor in the Text of Philosophy." *New Literary History* 6, no. 1(1974): 5–74.

Deutsch, Babette. *Poetry in Our Time.* New York: Henry Holt, 1952.

Dix, Dom Gregory. *The Shape of the Liturgy.* 1945. Reprint. New York: Seabury Press, 1982.

Downes, David A. "Spiritual Mysteries in Hopkins's Dublin Years: 1885." *Hopkins Quarterly* 14, no. 1–4 (April 1987–January 1988): 37–53.

Edwards, Michael. *Towards a Christian Poetics.* Grand Rapids: William B. Eerdmans, 1984.

Eliot, T. S. *The Complete Poems and Plays: 1909–1950.* New York: Harcourt Brace, 1952.

———. *To Criticize the Critic.* New York: Farrar, Straus and Giroux, 1965.

Ellrodt, Robert. *Les Poètes Métaphysiques Anglais. Tome 1: John Donne et les Poètes de la Tradition Chrétienne.* Paris: Libraire José Corti, 1960.

Ellsberg, Margaret. *Created to Praise: The Language of Gerard Manley Hopkins.* Oxford: Oxford University Press, 1987.

Endean, Philip, S.J. "The Spirituality of Gerard Manley Hopkins." *Hopkins Quarterly* 8, no. 3(1981): 107–29.

Fairweather, Eugene R., ed. *The Oxford Movement.* New York: Oxford University Press, 1964.

Fish, Stanley E. *Self-Consuming Artifacts: The Experience of Seventeenth-Century Literature.* Berkeley: University of California Press, 1972.

Foucault, Michel. *The Order of Things.* New York: Pantheon, 1970.

Frye, Northrop. *The Great Code: The Bible and Literature.* New York: Harcourt, Brace, 1982.

Galdon, Joseph A., S.J. *Typology and Seventeenth-Century Literature.* The Hague: Mouton, 1975.

Gardner, W. H. *Gerard Manley Hopkins: A Study of Poetic Idiosyncrasy in Relation to Poetic Tradition.* Vol. 1. 1944. Reprint. London: Oxford University Press, 1961.

Getz, Thomas H. "Geoffrey Hill's 'Mercian Hymns' and 'Lachrimae': The Languages of History and Faith." *Modern Poetry Studies* 10(1980): 2–21.

Giles, Richard F., ed. *Hopkins Among the Poets: Studies in Modern Responses to Gerard Manley Hopkins.* Hamilton, Ontario: International Hopkins Association Monograph 3, 1985.

Gilman, Ernest B. *Iconoclasm and Poetry in the English Reformation.* Chicago: University of Chicago Press, 1986.

Gould, Eric. *Mythical Intentions in Modern Literature.* Princeton: Princeton University Press, 1981.

Grant, Patrick. "Augustinian Spirituality and the Holy Sonnets of John Donne." *ELH* 38, no. 4(1971): 542–61.

Grisewood, Harman, ed. *Epoch and Artist.* New York: Chilmark Press, 1959.

Gross, Harvey. *Sound and Form in Modern Poetry.* Ann Arbor: University of Michigan Press, 1964.

Halewood, William H. *The Poetry of Grace.* New Haven: Yale University Press, 1970.

Hall, Donald. "Naming the Devils." *Poetry* 86, no. 2(1980): 102–110.

———. *The Weather of Poetry.* Ann Arbor: University of Michigan Press, 1980.

Hammerton, M. J. "Christian Love in Dylan Thomas." *Theology,* 49, no. 548 (February 1966): 72–77.

Hans, James S. "Presence and Absence in Modern Poetry." *Criticism* 22(1980): 320–40.

Hardelin, Alf. *The Tractarian Understanding of the Eucharist.* Upsala: Almquist and Wiskells, 1965.

Hart, Henry. *The Poetry of Geoffrey Hill.* Carbondale: Southern Illinois University Press, 1985.

Hartman, Geoffrey H. *Beyond Formalism.* New Haven: Yale University Press, 1970.

———, ed. *Hopkins: A Collection of Critical Essays.* Englewood Cliffs, N.J.: Prentice-Hall, 1966.

———. *The Unmediated Vision.* 1954. Reprint. New York: Harcourt, Brace, 1966.

Harris, Daniel A. *Inspirations Unbidden: The 'Terrible Sonnets' of Gerard Manley Hopkins.* Berkeley: University of California Press, 1982.

Hester, Marcus B. *The Meaning of Poetic Metaphor.* The Hague: Mouton, 1967.

Hirsch, Edward. "Flesh and Blood." *The Sewanee Review* 84, no. 3(1976): xcvi–xcviii.

Holroyd, Stuart. *Emergence from Chaos.* Boston: Houghton Mifflin, 1957.

Ignatius, Loyola. *The Spiritual Exercises of St. Ignatius Loyola.* Trans. Thomas Corbishley. Weathampstead: Anthony Clarke, 1973.

Jacobson, Roman. "Poetry of Grammar and Grammar of Poetry." *Lingua* 21(1968): 597–607.

Jasper, David. "God's Better Beauty: Language and the Poetry of Gerard Manley Hopkins." *Christianity and Literature* 13, no. 3(1985): 7–22.

Jones, Sister M. Roberta. "The Wellspring of Dylan." *English Journal* 55, no. 1(1966): 78–82.

Kelly, Bernard. *The Metaphysical Background of Analogy.* London: Aquinas Press, 1958.

Kidder, Rushworth. *Dylan Thomas: The Coutnry of the Spirit.* Princeton: Princeton University Press, 1973.

Kleinman, H. H. *The Religious Sonnets of Dylan Thomas: A Study in Imagery and Meaning.* Berkeley: University of California Press, 1963.

Klemm, David E. " 'This Is My Body': Hermeneutics and Eucharistic Language." *Anglican Theological Review* 64, no. 3(1982): 293–310.

Knieger, Bernard. "Dylan Thomas: The Christianity of the 'Altarwise by Owllight' Sequence." *College English* 23, no. 8(1962): 623–28.

Knoepflmacher, U. C., and G. B. Tennyson, eds. *Nature and the Victorian Imagination.* Berkeley: University of California Press, 1977.

Korg, Jacob. *Dylan Thomas.* New York: Twayne Publishers, 1965.

———. "Hopkins' Linguistic Deviations." *PMLA* 92, no. 5(1977): 977–86.

———. *Language in Modern Literature: Innovation and Experiment.* New York: Barnes and Noble, 1979.

Kremen, Kathryn R. *The Imagination of the Resurrection: The Poetic Continuity of a Religious Motif in Donne, Blake, and Yeats.* Lewisburg: Bucknell University Press, 1972.

Krieger, Murray. *Poetic Presence and Illusion: Essays in Critical History and Theory.* Baltimore: Johns Hopkins University Press, 1979.

Lawler, Justus George. *The Christian Image: Studies in Religious Art and Poetry.* Pittsburgh: Duquesne University Press, 1966.

Leamon, Warren. "Prayer in an Age of Criticism: The Hopkins Problem." *South Carolina Review* 12, no. 1(1979): 36–43.

Leggio, James. "The Science of a Sacrament." *Hopkins Quarterly* 4, no. 2(1977): 55–68.

Levi, Peter. "Geoffrey Hill." *Agenda* 23, no. 3–4 (1985-1986): 13–14.

Lewalski, Barbara Kiefer. *Protestant Poetics and the Seventeenth-Century Religious Lyric.* Princeton: Princeton University Press, 1979.

Loomis, Jeffrey B. *Dayspring in Darkness: Sacrament in Hopkins.* Lewisburg: Bucknell University Press, 1988.

Low, Anthony. *Love's Architecture: Devotional Modes in Seventeenth-Century English Poetry.* New York: New York, University Press, 1978.

Lucas, James L. *The Religious Dimension of Twentieth-Century British and American Literature.* Washington: University Press of America, 1982.

———. "Accidents of Language: 'The Mystery of the Charity of Charles Peguy.' " *London Review of Books* 3–16 November 1983: 16.

McInerny, Ralph. *Studies in Analogy.* The Hague: Martinus Nijhoff, 1968.

MacKenzie, Norman H. "Resources of Language and Imagery in 'The Wreck of the Deutschland.'" *Seventh Annual Hopkins Lecture*. London: University of London, 1976.

Mariani, Paul L. *A Commentary on the Complete Poems of Gerard Manley Hopkins*. Ithaca: Cornell University Press, 1970.

Martz, Louis L. *The Poetry of Meditation: A Study in English Religious Literature of the Seventeenth Century*. New Haven: Yale University Press, 1954.

Maud, Ralph. *Entrances to Dylan Thomas's Poetry*. Pittsburgh: University of Pittsburgh Press, 1963.

Mazzeo, Joseph Anthony. *Renaissance and Seventeenth-Century Studies*. New York: Columbia University Press, 1964.

Middleton, David E. "The Ultimate Kingdom: Dylan Thomas's 'Author's Prologue' to 'Collected Poems.'" *The Anglo-Welsh Review* 63(1978): 111–23.

Miles, Josephine. *Poetry and Change: Donne, Milton, Wordsworth and the Equilibrium of the Present*. Berkeley: University of California Press, 1974.

Miller, J. Hillis. *The Disappearance of God: Five Nineteenth-Century Writers*. Cambridge: Belknap Press, 1975.

———. *The Linguistic Moment: From Wordsworth to Stevens*. Princeton: Princeton University Press, 1985.

———. *Poets of Reality: Six Twentieth-Century Writers*. Cambridge: Belknap Press, 1966.

Milne, William S. "'Creative Tact': Geoffrey Hill's 'King Log.'" *Critical Quarterly* 20, no. 4(1978): 39–45.

———. "'Images of Earth and Grace': Geoffrey Hill's 'The Mystery of the Charity of Charles Peguy.'" *Agenda* 21, no. 3(1983): 12–23.

———. "'The Pitch of Attention': Geoffrey Hill's 'Tenebrae.'" *Agenda* 17, no. 1(1979): 25–37.

Milroy, James. *The Language of Gerard Manley Hopkins*. London: Andre Deutsch, 1977.

Milward, Peter, S.J. "1888: The Heraclitean Fire of Nature and the Grace of the Resurrection." *Hopkins Quarterly* 14, no. 1–4(April 1987-January 1988): 77–83.

———., ed. *Readings of "The Wreck": Essays in Commemoration of the Centenary of G. M. Hopkins' "The Wreck of the Deutschland."* Chicago: Loyola University Press, 1976.

———. "Sacramental Symbolism in Hopkins and Eliot." *Renascence* 22, no. 2(1968): 104–111.

Miner, Earl. *Literary Uses of Typology from the Late Middle Ages to the Present*. Princeton: Princeton University Press, 1977.

———. *The Metaphysical Mode from Donne to Cowley*. Princeton: Princeton University Press, 1969.

Morris, David. *The Poetry of Gerard Manley Hopkins and T. S. Eliot in Light of the Donne Tradition*. Bern: A. Franke, 1951.

Mudge, Lewis S., ed. *Essays on Biblical Interpretation*. Philadelphia: Fortress Press, 1980.

Murdy, Louise Baughan. *Sound and Sense in Dylan Thomas's Poetry*. The Hague: Mouton, 1960.

Needham, John. "The Idiom of Geoffrey Hill's 'Mercian Hymns.'" *English* 28, no. 131(1979): 139–49.

Newman, John Henry. *Apologia Pro Vita Sua.* 1864. Ed. David J. DeLaura. New York: Norton, 1968.

———. *An Essay in Aid of A Grammar of Assent.* 1870. Notre Dame: University of Notre Dame Press, 1979.

———. *Tract Ninety or Remarks on Certain Passages in the Thirty-nine Articles.* 1841. Reprint. London: Constable, 1933.

Nichols, Ashton. *The Poetics of Epiphany: Nineteenth-Century Origins of the Modern Literary Movement.* Tuscaloosa: University of Alabama Press, 1987.

Nicholson, Marjorie Hope. *The Breaking of the Circle.* New York: Columbia University Press, 1960.

———. *Science and Imagination.* Ithaca: Great Seal Books, 1956.

Nist, John. "'No Reason for Mourning': A Reading of the Later Poems of Dylan Thomas." *Approach* 42(1962): 3–7.

North, John S., and Michael D. Moore, eds. *Vital Candle: Victorian and Modern Bearings in Gerard Manley Hopkins.* Ontario: University of Waterloo Press, 1984.

O'Donovan, Oliver. *On the Thirty Nine Articles: A Conversation with Tudor Christianity.* Exeter: Paternoster Press, 1986.

Olson, Elder. *The Poetry of Dylan Thomas.* Chicago: University of Chicago Press, 1954.

Ong, Walter J., S.J. *Hopkins, The Self and God.* Toronto: University of Toronto Press, 1986.

———. *The Presence of the Word.* New Haven: Yale University Press, 1967.

Oxley, Brian. "Geoffrey Hill's 'Christian Year.'" *Essays in Criticism* 29, no. 3(1979): 285–292.

Patridge, A. C. *John Donne: Language and Style.* London: Andre Deutsch, 1978.

Peters, Robert L. "The Uneasy Faith of Dylan Thomas: A Study of the Last Poems." *Fresco* 9, no. 1(1958): 25–29.

Pick, *Gerard Manley Hopkins: Priest and Poet.* New York: Oxford University Press, 1966.

Powers, Joseph M. *Eucharistic Theology.* New York: Herder and Herder, 1967.

Prickett, Stephen. *Words and the Word: Language, Poetics and Biblical Interpretation.* Cambridge: Cambridge University Press, 1986.

Quinn, Sister Bernetta. "Wallace Stevens: 'The Peace of the Last Intelligence.'" *Renascence* 41, no. 4(Summer 1989): 191–204.

Raine, Craig. "Promises, Promises." *New Statesman* (5 January 1979): 19–20.

Ramsay, M. P. *Les Doctrines Médievales Chez Donne, Le Poète Métaphysicien d'Angleterre.* London: Oxford University Press, 1916.

Raschke, Carl A. *The Alchemy of the Word: Language and the End of Theology.* Ann Arbor: American Academy of Religion, 1979.

Richman, Robert. "'The Battle It Was Born to Lose': The Poetry of Geoffrey Hill." *The New Criterion* 2, no. 8(1984): 22–34.

Ricks, Christopher. *The Force of Poetry.* Oxford: Clarendon Press, 1984.

Ricks, Christopher. Rev. of *Somewhere is Such a Kingdom*, by Geoffrey Hill. *New York Times Book Review,* 11 January 1976: 6.

Ricoeur, Paul. *Essays on Biblical Interpretation.* Ed. Lewis S. Mudge. Trans. David Stewart and Charles E. Reagan. Philadelphia: Fortress Press, 1980.

————. *Interpretation Theory: Discourse and the Surplus of Meaning.* Fort Worth: Texas Christian University Press, 1976.

————. "The 'Kingdom' in the Parables of Jesus." Trans. Robert F. Scuca. *Anglican Theological Review* 63, no. 2(1981): 165–69.

————. "The Logic of Jesus, the Logic of God." *Anglican Theological Review* 62, no. 1(1980): 37–41.

————. "The Specificity of Religious Language." *Semeia* 4(1975): 107–45.

Roberts, John R., ed. *Essential Articles for the Study of John Donne's Poetry.* Hamden, Conn.: Shoe String Press, 1975.

Robinson, John. *In Extremity: A Study of Gerard Manley Hopkins.* Cambridge, Mass.: Cambridge University Press, 1978.

Robinson, Peter, ed. *Geoffrey Hill: Essays on his Work.* Milton Keynes: Open University Press, 1985.

Rose, Alan M. "Hopkins' 'Carrion Comfort': The Artful Disorder of Prayer." *Victorian Poetry* 15, no. 3(1977): 207–18.

Ross, Malcolm. *Poetry and Dogma: The Transfiguration of Eucharistic Symbols in Seventeenth-Century English Poetry.* New Brunswick, N.J.: Rutgers University Press, 1954.

Roston, Murray. *The Soul of Wit: A Study of John Donne.* Oxford: Clarendon Press, 1974.

Rowell, Geoffrey, ed. *Tradition Renewed: The Oxford Movement Conference Papers.* Allison Park, Pa.: Pickwick, 1986.

Sacks, Sheldon, ed. *On Metaphor.* Chicago: University of Chicago Press, 1978.

Sampson, H. Grant. *The Anglican Tradition in Eighteenth-Century Verse.* The Hague: Mouton, 1971.

Saunders, Thomas. "Religious Elements in the Poetry of Dylan Thomas." *Dalhousie Review* 45(1965-66): 492–97.

Schmidt, Michael, and Grevel Lindop, eds. *British Poetry Since 1960.* Oxford: Carcanet Press, 1972.

Schillebeeckx, E. *The Eucharist.* Trans. N. D. Smith. New York: Sheed and Ward, 1968.

Schneider, Elizabeth W. *The Dragon in the Gate: Studies in the Poeetry of G. M. Hopkins.* Berkeley: University of California Press, 1968.

Scott, Nathan, Jr. *The Broken Center: Studies in the Theological Horizon of Modern Literature.* New Haven: Yale University Press, 1966.

————. *The Wild Prayer of Longing: Poetry and the Sacred.* New Haven: Yale University Press, 1971.

Scotus, Duns. *Philosophical Writings.* Ed. and trans. Allan Wolter, O.F.M. New York: Nelson, 1962.

Searle, Mark. "Liturgy and Metaphor." *Notre Dame English Journal* 8(1981): 185–206.

Sebeok, Thomas A., ed. *Style and Language.* Cambridge: MIT Press, 1960.

Sergeant, Howard. "The Religious Development of Dylan Thomas." *A Review of English Literature* 3, no. 2(1962): 59–67.

Shaw, David. "Mimesis as Invention: Four Interpretative Models in Victorian Poetry." *New Literary History* 12, no. 2(1981): 303–28.

Sherry, Vincent. *The Uncommon Tongue: The Poetry and Criticism of Geoffrey Hill.* Ann Arbor: University of Michigan Press, 1987.

Sherwood, Terry. "Conversion Psychology in John Donne's Good Friday Poem." *Harvard Theological Review* 72, no. 1–2(1979): 101–22.

Sisson, C. H. *The Avoidance of Literature: Collected Essays.* Manchester: Carcanet Press, 1978.

Smith, Julia J. "Donne and the Crucifixion." *Modern Language Review* 79, no. 3(1984): 513–25.

Spender, Stephen. *The Making of a Poem.* 1955. Reprint. New York: Norton, 1962.

Sprinker, Michael. *'A Counterpoint of Dissonance': The Aesthetics and Poetry of Gerard Manley Hopkins.* Baltimore: Johns Hopkins University Press, 1980.

Stachniewski, John. "John Donne: The Despair of the 'Holy Sonnets.'" *ELH* 48, no. 4(1981): 677–705.

Stanford, Derek. "Dylan Thomas' Animal Faith." *Southwest Review* 42(1957): 205–12.

———. *Dylan Thomas: A Literary Study.* New York: Citadel Press, 1965.

Stanwood, P. G. "Seventeenth-Century English Literature and Contemporary Criticism." *Anglican Theological Review* 62, no. 4(1980): 395–410.

———. "Time and Liturgy in Donne, Crashaw and T. S. Eliot." *Mosaic* 12, no. 2(1979): 91–105.

Steiner, George. *Language and Silence: Essays on Language, Literature and the Inhuman.* New York: Atheneum, 1967.

———. *Real Presences.* The Leslie Stephen Memorial Lecture. 1 November 1985. Cambridge: Press Syndicate of the University of Cambridge, 1986.

Stevens, Wallace. *The Collected Poems of Wallace Stevens.* New York: Knopf, 1981.

Summers, Claude J., and Ted-Larry Pebworth, eds. *"Bright Shootes of Everlastingnesse": The Seventeenth-Century Religious Lyric.* Columbia: University of Missouri Press, 1987.

Tennyson, G. B., and Edward E. Ericson, Jr., eds. *Religion and Modern Literature.* Grand Rapids: William B. Eerdmans, 1975.

Traditional Latin Roman Catholic Mass. Trans. Father Gommar A. DePauw. New York: C.T.M. Publications, 1977.

Treece, Henry. *Dylan Thomas: "Dog Among the Fairies."* 1949. Folcroft, Pa.: Lindsay Drummond, 1974.

Turnell, Martin. *Modern Literature and Christian Faith.* Westminster, Md.: Newman Press, 1961.

Utz, Stephen. "The Realism of Geoffrey Hill." *Southern Review* 12, no. 2(1976): 426–33.

Verghese, C. Paul. "Religion in Dylan Thomas's Poetry." *The Literary Criterion* (Winter 1968): 35–41.

Wainwright, Geoffrey. *Eucharist and Eschatology.* New York: Oxford University Press, 1981.

Weatherby, Harold L. *The Keen Delight: The Christian Poet in the Modern World.* Athens: University of Georgia Press, 1975.

Weatherhead, A. K. "Geoffrey Hill." *Iowa Review* 8, no. 4(1977): 104–16.

Webb, Igor. "Speaking of the Holocaust: The Poetry of Geoffrey Hill." *The Denver Quarterly* 12, no. 1(1977): 114–25.

Weyand, Norman, S.J., ed. *Immortal Diamond: Studies in Gerard Manley Hopkins.* New York: Sheed and Ward, 1959.

White, Helen. *The Metaphysical Poets: A Study in Religious Experience.* New York: Macmillan, 1936.

Wiley, Margaret L. *The Subtle Knot: Creative Skepticism in Seventeenth-Century England.* New York: Greenwood Press, 1968.

Williams, W. C. *Selected Poems.* New York: New Directions, 1968.

Wimsatt, William. "In Search of Verbal Mimesis." *Yale French Studies* 52(1976): 229–48.

Index